SAGGISTICA 14

THEATER OF THE MIND, STAGE OF HISTORY

THEATER OF THE MIND, STAGE OF HISTORY
Italian Legacies between Europe, the Mediterranean, and North America on the 150th Anniversary of Unification

A *Festschrift* in Honor of Mario Mignone on his 70th birthday

Edited by
Peter Carravetta

BORDIGHERA PRESS

Library of Congress Control Number: 2014948817

Sponsored by
The Alfonse M. D'Amato Chair in Italian and Italian American Studies at
State University of New York at Stony Brook
Stony Brook, NY, 11794 USA

© 2014 by Peter Carravetta & authors

All rights reserved. Parts of this book may be reprinted only by written permission from the respective authors, and may not be reproduced for publication in book, magazine, or electronic media of any kind, except for purposes of literary reviews by critics.

Printed in the United States.

Published by
BORDIGHERA PRESS
John D. Calandra Italian American Institute
25 West 43rd Street, 17th Floor
New York, NY 10036

SAGGISTICA 14
ISBN 978-1-59954-083-2

TABLE OF CONTENTS

Introduction
    Peter Carravetta ix

Arturo Giovannitti and the American Literary Establishment
    Luigi Bonaffini 1

The Unfortunate Pilgrim: You Can't Get There From Here
    Jerome Krase 17

Lingua Esule: The Risorgimento Exiles and the Teaching of Italian in the United States
    Stefano Luconi 49

What Italy Got for Her Twenty-First Birthday
    Sante Matteo 76

Remittances and Purchases of Emigrants: Resource for the Development of the Unitary State
    Mario Mignone 114

Intellectuals and Expatriates: Bridging the Gap
    Vincenzo Pascale 146

Stories that Shaped Italian Unification: Ugo Foscolo's *Le ultime lettere di Jacopo Ortis*
    Joseph Perricone 157

Tommaso Bordonaro's *La spartenza*: Between Tradition and Singularity
    Anita Pinzi 178

An Allegorist in America: Cultural Identity in Calvino's Travelogues from the United States
    Alessandro Raveggi 193

Il Mutualismo dei Siciliani d'America
Marcello Saija 215

You are an Italian American Writer, Like it or Not
Richard Vetere 276

Contributors 283

Index of Names 287

Conference Program 292

Introduction

The year 2011 marked the 150th anniversary of the founding of the modern nation-state of Italy. Innumerable conferences and celebrations were held in Italy and abroad in which scholars, critics, intellectuals of all stripes and of course students and teachers reflected upon, and expressed their views on, the meaning of this socio-historical event. In Italy political authorities went all out to sponsor marches, exhibits, publications, and media programs. The number of flags visible even in stores, cafes, stadiums, and of course around monuments was impressive. A spirit of reconnaissance, pride, and positive reassessment of the country's heritage was paraded everywhere. As with all such national-popular celebrations, there were many contrarian and dissident voices that managed to grab attention. The national allegory was not a thorough success story, it was argued. There were, and there still are, some complex, unresolved, often dark aspects to the (Hi)story. Starting with the disturbing overarching possibility that the present configuration, born on throws of widespread nationalistic uprisings in the XIX century, may be approaching the end of a historical cycle, and at least theoretically the nation-state is in dire straits, as its "historical necessity" or "moment" may have outlived its reason for being. Not that people – patriots to presidents – ever let go of their cherished myths of the motherland easily, without putting up a fight. Whatever the variety of interpretations, certain facts are obvious: the European Union and the growing trans-nationality of capitalism have weakened sovereignty, exacting new compromises and inaugurating processes of bi- and multi-lateral exchanges and organization for which the tenets of the previous century seem inadequate; social and political configurations that consolidated during the half-century of the Cold War frayed and a substantial number of ideological and institutional frameworks started rattling perilously; the welfare state entered a now perennial state of crises and is in danger. The economic miracle of the Sixties and the Seventies that catapulted Italy among the top seven richest countries in the world is fast becoming a memory. Unprecedented immigrations, endemic corruption, and undecisive policies have weakened the sense of an alleged homogeneity that was cobbled over ten-twelve decades, surviving the wreckage of two world wars and a dictatorship. 2011 was indeed an appropriate juncture to look back and reckon with what has actually been happening, or at least to attempt to reframe the narrative. In particular, it was a time to expand the historical memory and consider issues, problems, and the lives of people who have *not* made it into the schoolbooks. If some citizens in Italy could not understand why anyone could be critical of the country's success, perhaps it was in part due to the fact that so much had been forgotten, suppressed, or conveniently ignored.

With these ideas in the background, the D'Amato Chair organized a two-day conference to attempt some inroads into this complex network. Under the aegis of the Forum in Italian American Criticism (FIAC), which I launched in 2008, and which to date has organized seven major annual gatherings, the conference aimed at charting various itineraries through little explored clusters of what we can rightly call "Italies," in the plural, and which have existed within and outside of the nation-state called Italy. These Italies are not to be understood solely in terms of circumscribed socio-geographical sites – as colonies, professional settlements, or ethnic enclaves, – though these of course have been and continue to be the source of powerful and intriguing discourses. The Italies we wished to explore are those marked by a more subterranean genealogy, the rhizomes that inform symbolic presences in art, architecture, jurisprudence, and streams of cultural products which by their very nature are – and actually have been – trans-national, often created without anyone realizing that they were somehow "Italian" and yet manifest unmistakable signs associated with the historical palimpsest called Italy.

The conference wished to be an open forum which, starting from the peninsula, engaged larger constellations – the Europe, Mediterranean, and North America indicated by the subtitle -- and perhaps propose some new ideas on how Italian culture may develop in the near and far future. No better metaphor to serve this broad objective than by looking at how Italians themselves have performed as if it were a mental proscenium where irony and tragedy, comedy and melodrama stood at crossroads interrogating themselves on the sense of these 150 years, and looked at the history of a people in a world-historical framework, however one wishes to understand the notion of history.

The conference, which featured sixteen speakers (see Program at end of book), was dedicated to Mario Mignone, Distinguished Service Professor of Italian, and Founder and Director of the Center for Italian Studies at Stony Brook University, as well as editor for a quarter of a century of the journal *Forum Italicum*. In a period of over thirty years Mignone has brought well over 3000 students to study Italian language and culture at the Stony Brook Rome Center, which he also started. A committed intellectual and author of critical works on fiction and theatre, as well as on Italian migration, editor of several anthologies and author of the most accessible general Introduction to Modern Italy, it is fitting that on his 70th birthday the community of friends, colleagues, and scholars dedicate this gathering to him as a token of appreciation for his lifetime achievement in bridging cultures across time and space

Peter Carravetta
Stony Brook, August 2014

Arturo Giovannitti and the American Literary Establishment

Luigi Bonaffini
CUNY Brooklyn College

Arturo Giovannitti knew three languages well: Italian, English, and French, but French was certainly much less important than the other two, and according to his son Len he could also read Spanish and German. In a short time he was able to reach an extraordinarily high level of linguistic competence in English, both spoken and written, and the accounts that have come down to us in that respect, even from Americans, speak of an exceptional ability. Eric Amfitheatrof, for instance, says that "Giovannitti was a fascinating and imposing figure ... his language rich and fabulous."[1]

In dealing with Giovannitti's relationship with the American literary establishment, I will focus on two periods: the first beginning with the year of the Lawrence trial of 1912 until 1919, the year in which Giovannitti appears in Untermeyer's important anthology; and then the second very recent period, that covers the last fifteen years and unexpectedly shows a renewed interest for the socially engaged literature of the first decades of the twentieth century and for Giovannitti as one of the leading figures of that literature.

---

[1] Joseph Harrington, *Poetry and the Public: The Social Form of Modern U.S. Poetics* (Middletown, CT: Wesleyan University Press, 2003) 117.

From: *Theater of the Mind, Stage of History*. Bordighera Press, 2015

"Arturo Giovannitti"

Period 1912-1919

For the first part, the main source for most of my observations are the two fundamental studies by Hester Furey, indispensable for anyone who wants to delve deeper into Giovannitti's relationship with the literary circles of his time.[2]

Giovannitti began publishing regularly in the *Proletario*, in the May 1908 issue, with his poem "Il vecchio del mare," and would occasionally use as pseudonym the anagram "Nino Gavitti" or "Il Corsaro." For several years he published exclusively in the *Proletario* and *La plebe*, producing a dozen poems reflecting his radical vision, including "Morte di fame" and "Nenia sannita," later translated into "Samnite Cradle Song" in his 1914 English collection *Arrows in the Gale*. Giovannitti's poetry was relatively unknown until the Lawrence strike of 1912.

On January 1, 1912, in accordance with a new state law, the textile mills of Lawrence, Massachusetts, posted new rules limiting the hours of workers to 54 a week, down from a standard of 56 previously in effect. It soon became clear that the employers had no intention of adjusting wage rates upwards to compensate for the lost work time, and a strike ensued.

Giovannitti had been called by union organizer Joseph Ettor, even though he was not officially a member of the Industrial Workers of the World, because he spoke three languages fluently and two thirds of the workers were Italian.

---

[2] Hester L. Furey, "The Reception of Arturo Giovannitti's Poetry and the Trial of a New Society," *Left History*, 2, Spring (1994): 27-50; *Dictionary of Literary Biography*, V. 303: *American Radical and Reform Writers, First Series*, A Bruccoli Clark Layman Book, Edited by Steven Rosendale (Northern Arizona University, Gale, 2004) 158-167.

For this reason it was important to deal directly with the problem of the widespread stereotype of Italians as being ignorant and prone to crime, and the IWW shrewdly exploited Giovannitti's poetry to influence public opinion. Giovannitti's public image had to express the humanitarian intentions of the IWW, show the sensitivity of its members and their ability to appreciate high culture, and thus give an idea of how unjustly they had been portrayed in the press. Soon there was a lively discussion among East Coast journalists who competed to meet this pale and well-mannered young man who read Shakespeare and Immanuel Kant. They were not surprised by the fact that an Italian revolutionary union member worked with the IWW, but that he came from a good family, that he was educated, that he had thought of becoming a preacher, and that he wrote a kind of poetry they could not ignore. In other words, it was difficult to understand how someone who could have easily joined the mainstream of American society had decided to support the class struggle and fight for the working class, and this apparent contradiction would become one of the distinctive features of Giovannitti's relationship with the literary establishment.

The debate among journalists aroused interest in Giovannitti's poetry and became a stimulus for the various publications of that period. The *International Poetry Review* published the poems "The Walker" and "The Republic." *The Masses* and *Mother Earth* published "The Burn." Progressive journals like *Survey*, *Outlook*, and *Harper's Weekly* spoke favorably of his case before the trial. The literary journals *Literary Digest Current Literature*, and *Current Opinion* published biographical pieces based on interviews to prisoners. *Literary*

"Arturo Giovannitti"

Digest reprinted an article from the *Boston Herald* on the prison life of Ettor and Giovannitti that gave an intellectual profile of the Molisano, including a list of his readings as well – Taine's *English literature*, Shakespeare, Shelley, Byron, Carlyle, Balzac, and Kant – and this contributed to the validation of Giovannitti's image as a cultured person unjustly accused. While he was in jail, the journal *Survey* published one of the most favorable reviews of his poetry:

> We in America today are quick to respond to the poet of a Russian dungeon who sings of the wrongs of Russian peasants, but what of a lyric singer in a New England jail, whose arraignment of American democracy would put it on a par with Russian despotism? Surely we are not so rich in lyric poets that we can afford to send this one to the chair.[3]

After the trial, the question of Giovannitti's character became part of what Lawrence could mean for the future. The journal *Current Opinion* published a few segments of the poem "The Walker" in an article titled "The Social Significance of Arturo Giovannitti."[4] This piece is important because it shows why even a conservative journal could show so much interest in Giovannitti, who seemed to embody the perceived contradiction between poetry and public role, literature and social activism. Giovannitti is a great poet, but unfortunately he has let himself be brainwashed by the rhetoric of the revolutionary movement, and this does not bode well for the future of society:

---

[3] Mary Brown Summer, *Survey*, 2 November (1912): 163-6.
[4] *Current Opinion*, January (1913): 24-6.

> He has the soul of a great poet, the fervor of a prophet, and, added to these, the courage and power of initiative that mark the man of action and the organizer of great crusades. This jail experience of Giovannitti's has given the world *one of the greatest poems ever produced in the English language* [italics mine]...'The Walker' is more than a poem. It is a great human document."

But immediately after it concludes:

> For it is surely an ominous thing that a young man of good family, well educated, markedly religious by nature, coming to this land in search of freedom and opportunity, actively associated with the church in its missionary work among the poor, should in a few years be transformed by his experiences into an extreme revolutionary, bitter against authority of all kinds, flouting the Constitution and denying God.

The first comments about his poetry were generally very positive, even outside the radical left. *Current Literature*, for example, presenting The Walker" in November 1912, noted that Whitmanesque poems are usually slavish imitations, but this one is sincere, vivid, and memorable.[5] Giovannitti's work never received a bad review. It was compared to Whitman, Shelley, Wilde, and James Oppenheimer.

Giovannitti's self-defense before the jury at his trial in Salem was a call to arms for the progressive reform movement. It echoed many of his poems and speeches to the strikers, in

---

[5] *Current Literature*, November (1912): 593.

particular "The sermon on the Common," in the way it offered a moral justification for the IWW struggle:

> It may be that we are fanatics.... And so was ... Jesus Christ.... And so were all the philosophers and all the dreamers.... We have been working in something that is dearer to us than our lives and our liberty. We have been working in what are our ideas, our ideals, our aspirations, our hopes – you may say our religion, gentlemen of the jury ... we have come here to proclaim a new truth; we are the apostles of a new evangel, of a new gospel.

No doubt the jurors were very impressed by the biblical and religious tones of this speech and many of the journalists left the room in tears. After Ettor and Giovannitti were acquitted in December, 1912, the debate over the importance of the trial continued in the press, and it came as a surprise when the conservative editor of the important review *Atlantic Monthly* in June 1913, before the first edition of Giovannitti's book of poetry *Arrows in the Gale*, published the poem "The Cage," written in jail, in which Giovannitti describe the experience of the accused during the trial. Says the editor: "if there is a poetry of anarchy, this is it ... whether the poem repels or attracts the reader, he will find in it ... more of the heart and soul of the Syndicalist movement than all the papers of all the economists can teach him."[6]

In July 1913, the journal *Outlook* described "The Cage" as "the voice of a man at war with history," noting that "curiously enough, in condemning our civilization he adopts bodily one of civilization's most time-honored delusions ...

---

[6] "The Poetry of Syndicalism," *Atlantic Monthly*, June (1913): 853-4.

the 'Golden Age' of labor." It then concludes that Giovannitti was a genius in writing verse, but as a social critic he was not only a fool but an ingrate, since he attacked the court that had acquitted him.[7]

The notoriety stemming from the Lawrence strike encouraged Giovannitti to identify himself mainly as a literary artist, and for a few years he strengthened his ties with the group of Greenwich Village radicals, especially Max Eastman, John Reed, Floyd Dell, Helen Keller, Art Young, and Mike Gold. He also grew closer with the circle of anarchist feminist Emma Goldman and the anarchists of the Ferrer Colony.

Giovannitti's first book of poetry, *Arrows in the Gale*, came out in 1914 with an introduction by Helen Keller, who had just joined the Socialist party and had gone to Lawrence during the strike. She begins by saying that:

> [T]he poet has tried to render his ideas of the world he lives in. As a poet he is to be judged by his success in rendering these ideas in verse, and not by his relations to Syndicalism or Socialism or any other movement in which he happens to be active. The laws of poetic beauty and power, not one's beliefs about the economic world, determine the excellence of his work.

But then she goes on to discuss Giovannitti's poetry only in terms of his political ties and his resistance against unjust laws, without saying a single word about the transcendental beauty of the poems. Hester Furey interprets this apparent contradiction as resulting on the one hand from the combination of an obligatory gesture towards the poetry estab-

---

[7] "A Poet of the IWW," *Outlook*, 5 July (1913): 504-505.

lishment of the time and on the other from the American left's own untheorized practices with regard to poetry.

The first review of *Arrows in the Gale* was penned by Florence Converse in the journal *Survey* in June 1914. She notes that the title is fitting because:

> [T]hese verses are indeed winged things, and barbed.... Despite the adverse winds of indifference and hostility, some of them will lodge and rankle in the human heart.

More significant, however, was the review written by Harriet Monroe in April 1915 in the literary journal *Poetry* which she founded in 1912 and which still remains one of the most important literary journals in the United States. As editor of *Poetry*, Monroe played a crucial role in the development of modern American poetry, first as editor and then as promoter of poets like Ezra Pound, T.S. Eliot, William Carlos Williams, and others. Thanks to her bold leadership, the journal *Poetry* became the most important poetry journal of the time. In her very positive review Monroe speculates on the possible effects of this kind of poetry for the future of American letters:

> It may be that the future of the arts in America is in the hands of these immigrants and their variously intermarrying children; that they will endow us with that quick expressiveness, that enthusiasm for beauty, that warmth of passion, which have been chilled out of Angle-Saxon [sic] blood by ten centuries or more of British fog.[8]

---

[8] Harriet Monroe, *Poetry*, April (1915): 36-38.

Yet, even more far-reaching was the inclusion of Giovannitti in the all-important anthology by Louis Untermeyer, *Modern American Poetry*, 1919, and the same year in his other anthology *The New Era of American Poetry*. Untermeyer was a poet and critic who became famous for his numerous poetry anthologies, which would be adopted as textbooks in American schools and universities until the fifties, setting down an indispensable list of modernist poets: first of all Robert Frost, with Ezra Pound, T.S. Eliot, Wallace Stevens, William Carlos Williams, Harte Crane, and many more. In his vision of America, poetry had to come from every side, not just one or two privileged centers of culture: a kind of poetry whose most notable effect was its refusal to follow the models of official poetic history and the idea that social change could be reflected in poetry and even be directed by it.

This is why Untermeyer devoted an entire chapter to Giovannitti. If one could measure quantitatively the importance that Untermeyer attributed to the Italian American author, it would suffice to compare the number of pages devoted to Giovannitti with those devoted in *The New Era of American Poetry* to other famous poets of the time. Giovannitti is not only one of the thirteen poets to whom a whole chapter is devoted, but Untermeyer assigned 18 pages to him, 15 to Carl Sandburg, 13 to Ezra Pound, while Robert Frost, the most important at the time, got 25. Other poets like T.S. Eliot and William Carlos Williams do not even merit a separate chapter.

The essay on Giovannitti begins:

NOTHING is a clearer proof of the rich variety and polyphonic character of contemporary American poetry than the work of Arturo Giovannitti. He echoes the hopes and hatreds of the workers as authentically as Masters dealt with the despairs of his villagers and Amy Lowell voiced the experimental desires of those who were "above the conflict." In his stark and barbaric hymns of labor we hear a note that is, for all its international significance, definitely national. And yet it is a note that has been little heard in American poetry. It is strange that this theme should have been expressed with such force and authority by one who was almost a stranger to the English language.[9]

For Untermeyer "'The Walker' is clearly Giovannitti's masterpiece: it is epical; epochal. As an art-work, it is one of the most remarkable things our literature can boast."

Finally, in 1929 Alfred Kreymborg devoted several pages to Emaneule Carnevali and Giovannitti in *Our Singing Strength*. He says of Giovannitti: "The Walker" has been compared to Oscar Wilde's "Ballad of Gaol," but "The Walker" is simpler, more realistic, more powerful.[10]

Period 1996-2006

Aaron Kramer, in his book *Neglected Aspects of American Poetry*, 1997, devotes 33 pages to Giovannitti and intentionally avoids discussing his most famous poems, "The Walker" "The Cage" and "When the Cock Crows" — also to show that it was not true at all, as Olga Peragallo had maintained in

---

[9] Louis Untermeyer, *The New Era in American Poetry* (New York: H. Holt, 1919) 183-199.
[10] Alfred Kreymborg, *Our Singing Strength: An Outline of American Poetry (1620-1930)* (New York: Coward-McCann, Inc., 1929) 475.

1949,[11] that Giovannitti had not written anything after *Arrows in the Gale*. Says Kramer:

> There are many ways to approach Arturo Giovannitti: as an immigrant poet, an Italo-American poet, a socialist-syndicalist labor poet, an evangelical poet, a war poet, a city poet, a love poet, a prophetic poet.[12]

After a long analysis of his poetry, at the end Kramer concludes:

> Although the focus here has not been on Giovannitti the Prophet, one cannot but feel sweeping through most of these excerpts the great wind of prophecy – that brand of song which, anathematized by the high priests of 20th century American criticism, may yet be rediscovered with delight by a generation weary of sterile formalism and cerebral gymnastics, when the pendulum swings again.[13]

The book also contains an interview with Giovannitti's son, Len Giovannitti, who among other things reveals that his father was an avid reader of the bible, that he had been influenced by Walt Whitman more than by anyone else, and that he always spoke with contempt of D'Annunzio for having embraced fascism.

---

[11] Olga Peragallo, *Italian American Authors and their Contributions* (New York: Nanni, 1949).

[12] Aaron Kramer, *Neglected Aspects of American Poetry* (Oakdale, NY: Dowling College Press, 1997) 275.

[13] Ibid., 285.

"Arturo Giovannitti"

In *The American Prose Poem: Poetic Form and the Boundaries of Genre*, by Michel Deville, 1998[14] one finds some interesting observations on Giovannitti, particularly with regard to his originality as a poet. For example, speaking about Carl Sandburg, considered one of the greatest poets of the early twentieth century, one reads:

> "Personality," one of Carl Sandburg's famous *Chicago Poems* (1916), signals an interesting move away from the Whitmanesque long line resulting in a mixed form halfway between free verse and the prose poem... Sandburg's transformation of the Whitmanian line into a hybrid sentence-paragraph ... was not an altogether unprecedented phenomenon. Two years before the appearance of *Chicago Poems*, Italian American poet and social activist Arturo Giovannitti (1884-1959) had already used the sentence-paragraph to convert a similar mixture of lyric fervor and prosaic sobriety into a poetic expression of his socialist convictions... "The Walker," one of Giovannitti's *Arrows in the Gale* (1914), is a remarkable example of such a synthesis of personal feeling and political commitment.[15]

But besides the link between Giovannitti and Sandburg, one reads further that by reading the political consciousness of the lyric self through the lens of its social and historical environment, Giovannitti had already anticipated the major methodological determinants of Sherwood Anderson's early experiments with the prose poem form (15). Anderson, as is

---

[14] Michel Deville, *The American Prose Poem: Poetic Form and the Boundaries of Genre* (Gainesville: University Press of Florida, 1998).
[15] Ibid., 64.

well known, was one of the major proponents of the prose poem in the United States.

In *Revolutionary Memory: Recovering the Poetry of the American Left* (Routledge, 2001), another attempt to recover the poems "we wanted to forget," the author Cary Nelson publishes Giovannitti's poem "Te Deum Labore" and devotes several pages to him: "For the twelve years between 1912 and 1924, however, no other poet, save perhaps the legendary songwriter Joe Hill (1879-1915), was so full identified at once with the abstract ideals of the labor movement and with the history of suppression by the American legal system. Hester Furey calls him "the poet of the legal system." And he cites Hester Furey when he says:

> Giovannitti's poems foreground the contradiction between his society's supposed value of individual fulfillment and inner life and that society's investments in capitalism—he insists that workers have souls. Once in circulation, the poems came to be read not only as emblems of Ettor and Giovannitti in the Essex County jail, but of the plight of unskilled workers subject to the whims of capitalism, in Lawrence and all over the world.[16]

He then concludes that Giovannitti and the other historically engaged poets on the left wrote from an unpopular political perspective and dealt with topics still considered "unpoetic." This was enough to sweep them up and cover them over in the same wave of conformist values dominating English departments for several decades.

---

[16] Cary Nelson, *Revolutionary Memory: Recovering the Poetry of the American Left* (New York: Routledge, 2001) 44.

"Arturo Giovannitti"

In his book *Poetry and the Public: The Social Form of Modern U.S. Poetics*, 2003, Joseph Harrington historicizes the triumph of High Modernism (Eliot, Stevens, Pound) and New Criticism (Tate, Ransom, Brooks) indicating valid alternatives for poetry, both as a literary genre and as a form of public discourse, in the first decades of the twentieth century. And he shows how important poets of this period have been badly interpreted and underestimated precisely because it had become impossible to observe this period outside the standards set by Modernism and the New Criticism. The whole first part of the book in effect focuses on two proto-proletarian poets of the time, Arturo Giovannitti and Anna Strong. Using numerous examples, Harrington attempts to show how these poets blended the new techniques of Modernism with radical populism in order to create sharply original public voices. And instead of speaking of a vague recognition of these poets thanks to their popular appeal, Harrington explains how they combined a rigorous aesthetics with very sophisticated ideas about what poetry was or could be. Harrington's conclusive argument is that the work and ideas of poets like Giovannitti, which remained submerged for decades during the course of literary history, have resurfaced in America in the nineties in the form of poetry slams and then in the ubiquitous poetry workshops:

> For readers of the 1910s (as in the mid- and late-nineteenth century) poetry was efficacious. Poetry worked on a personal level and a social level at the same time. It was the vehicle for a soul to speak to another soul, and, by the same token, it could work spiritual change in the reader/recipient. This personal change, many believed, issued forth in social change.[17]

---

[17] Joseph Harrington, op. cit., 124.

At the beginning of the twentieth century, poetry had a social and public function as well, a very different thing from the sharp separation of poetry from the public sphere that took place around the middle of the century through the canons of New Criticism. This is why Giovannitti and the historical moment he represented were forgotten by everybody, but for many of Giovannitti's contemporaries his poetry existed simultaneously in both the private and public sphere, as an artistic expression and a political manifesto. He also points out how Untermeyer, in his 1923 anthology *American Poetry since 1900*, after the publication of T.S. Eliot's *The Wasteland* and the growing rise of the poetics of Modernism, modified what he had said about Giovannitti in 1919:

> The poetry of Giovannitti rouses [sic] the problem of the relations of art and propaganda. Is Art, as many have claimed, cramped and distorted by the message? Or is the message weakened by Art? The propagandist in Giovannitti sometimes plays traitor to Giovannitti, the poet, but in his longer poems the balance is nicely adjusted.[18]

A few years prior, poetry seemed indistinguishable from propaganda, and the difference for Untermeyer had been irrelevant.

For John Timberman Newcomb, author of *The Footprint of the Twentieth Century: American Skyscrapers and Modernist Poems* (2003), American poets became modernist not only by adopting new formal techniques, but by immersing themselves in the metropolitan surroundings of the age of the machine. The subject matter of poetry has always been neglected because it goes

---

[18] Ibid., 125.

against the predominant perspective of Modernism as defined by its refusal of urban industrial modernity.[19] Newcomb includes Giovannitti among the poets of the time willing to deal with urban reality and he does a long analysis of the poem "The Day of War: Madison Square, June 1920," coming to the conclusion that by associating the skyscraper with the young radicals beneath it Giovannitti proposes a Marxist reading of capitalist modernity as an epoch that has generated on the one hand higher levels of inhuman exploitation, and on the other the class conscience necessary for a radical change, whose time is inexorably approaching. For Giovannitti and other contemporary poets on the left, the skyscraper stands not only for alienating an inhuman modernity, but also for the human race's capacity to create and build.

In conclusion, in light of the recent interest in Giovannitti one can venture to say that there is an ongoing reassessment of his poetry, especially with respect to the historical context of the time. And if further studies should confirm that his poetry preceded and maybe even influenced important authors like Sandburg and Anderson, then Giovannitti's stature as a link between nineteenth century Whitmanian poetry and the new American poetry would not be a minor one.

---

[19] John Timberman Newcomb, *The Footprint of the Twentieth Century: American Skyscrapers and Modernist Poems* (Baltimore: John Hopkins University Press, 2003) 97.

The Unfortunate Pilgrim
You Can't Get There From Here

Jerome Krase
CUNY Brooklyn College

When I was invited to present a paper at the Third FIAC Forum on Italian American Criticism, I was caught a bit off guard as I am hardly a "critic" of anything Italian American. Then I realized that its run-on title was an excuse to honor my older friend, Professor Mario Mignone, on his 70th birthday. I was greatly honored by the request, but not at all surprised, as he was one of the few who has consistently included me among his "Italian" (as opposed to "Italian American") friends. He has always understood that despite my ignorance of much of that which makes one Italian in his esteemed estimation, he understood that I treasured my marvelously mysterious patrimony that includes, among other poignant cultural insights, the fact that all Italians are anarchists, that is, until they are in charge. He also has faithfully shared my observation that being Italian, or even Italian-American, is not merely a matter of having an "appropriate" surname. It is in these ways that Mario is partially culpable for my Columbus-like search for, and non-discovery of, my Sicilian roots and so I have cryptically subtitled this paper "You can't get there from here." This Columbus-like search and discovery will be presented as an allegorical journey through the mountains of Campania and a real trip to find half of my roots in Sicily.

From: *Theater of the Mind, Stage of History*. Bordighera Press, 2015

In one way or another, most of my fellow presenters at the "Theatre of the Mind, Stage of History: Italian Legacies Between Europe, the Mediterranean, and North America on the 150th Anniversary of Unification" conference have been directly involved in the "creation" or "production" of Italian American history. Some have done it by exemplification. For example, Luigi Bonaffini, spoke about the radical cultural icon "Arturo Giovannitti and the American Literary Establishment." Others such as Marcello Saija, have more of an institutional focus, as he examined "Sicilian Mutualism in USA During the Great Migration." Others, such as Luigi Fontanella, Paolo Valesio, and Robert Viscusi literally (excuse the pun) *are* Italian American history. As individual, often self-absorbed, self-reflections have, in my experience, been the major mode of presentation by and about Italian Americans, I shall re-mimic that approach in this autoethnographic account of how I came to be, or perhaps better — not to be, an Italian American scholar. Although I often use autoethnographic approaches in my visual sociological work, I seldom make myself the central object, so here I will add autobiography as well to the visually enhanced narrative concoction.

Autoethnography is today a popular genre in qualitative research, but it is often criticized as less rigorous than other methods. In this regard, Leon Anderson noted that most of it is evocative or emotional, and its advocates draw "...upon postmodern sensibilities" and "...distance themselves from realist and analytic ethnographic traditions." For more solid grounding in social science methods, he proposed an "analytic" version of the research practice in which the researcher, among less important things, is "committed to developing theoretical understandings of broader social phenomena." This practice, that I also follow, "...is consistent with qualitative inquiry rooted in traditional symbolic interactionism." To which I am also an adherent.[1] An interesting application of this approach was done by John Joe Schlictman and Jason Patch who, quoting Burnier[2] combined their personal and scholarly stories to create an account that "is not strictly scholarly because it contains the personal, and ... not strictly personal because it contains the scholarly."[3]

I think of the history of, let us say, Italian immigrants as having at least three levels. The first of these is the actual "History Making" by the real people who actually do remarkable things such as those who have made their way to the United States of America from Italy. The second level I prefer to call "History Gathering" which is done by variously defined researchers collecting the histories manifested by immigrants and their more numerous descendants. The final, third, level, "History Mass Production," is the assembly and codification by, in "our" case, Italian and Italian American scholars, of these collections: e.g., Italians and Italian Americans writing multiple Italian American histories (the "canon") and producing from them the contestable metanarratives of Italian America.

---

[1] Leon Anderson, "Analytic Autoethnography," *Journal of Contemporary Ethnography* 35 (4) (2006): 373-395.
[2] DyLysa Burnier, "Encounters with Self in Social Science Research: A Political Scientist Looks at Autoethnography," *Journal of Contemporary Ethnography* 35 (4) (2006): 412.
[3] John Joe Schlichtman and Jason Patch, "Gentrifier? Who, Me? Interrogating the Gentrifier in the Mirror," *International Journal of Urban and Regional Research*, 2013, doi: 10.1111/1468-2427.12067.

"The Unfortunate Pilgrim"

My First person narrative of when and I how I learned that "you can't get there from here."

After you, the reader, have finished this essay it will be clear why I have never in my life applied for anything that had "Italian or Italian American" in the title. This rather "unethnic" attitude is a family tradition that can be traced to my mother Martha (Cangelosi) Krase who told all of her seven half-Sicilian children that she got no help from any of the New York City Civil Service Columbian Associations because her married name was "Krase." The only person of Italian descent who ever suggested that I should apply for anything Italianate was in fact the object of this Festschrift — Mario Mignone. I of course demurred at the unique offer and explained that as to "only real Italians need apply," I already had had too many bad experiences. A few of which should suffice for explanation.

As might Max Weber[4] and Frederik Barth,[5] I think of Italian Americanness (*Italo-Americanità*) as an ethnicity that is a socially and culturally constructed. Whereas most people, including most Italian Americans, are primordialists and think of Italian Americans as an ethnic group with different, mostly biological, membership requirements. Clifford Geertz offered that blood ties, language, territory, and cultural differences are important because they are part of the way that ordinary people symbolically experience the world.[6]

---

[4] Max Weber, *Economy and Society: An Outline of Interpretive Sociology*, ed. G. Roth and C. Wittich (Berkeley: University of California Press, 1978).
[5] Frederik Barth, ed., *Ethnic Groups and Boundaries: The Social Organization of Cultural Difference* (Boston: Little, Brown, 1969).
[6] Clifford Geertz, ed., *Old Societies and New States: The Quest for Modernity*

For Weber ethnic groups were not "natural (racial)" but were social constructs based on a subjective belief in shared *Gemeinschaft* (community). He used the term "putative" to characterize their common pasts and common destinies. Furthermore, the beliefs they shared did not create the ethnic group; rather, it was the group that created their beliefs. Frederik Barth's "Ethnic Groups and Boundaries" went further than Weber in stressing the constructed nature of ethnicity. To Barth, ethnicity was constantly being negotiated by both external ascription and internal self-identification. Therefore boundaries were critical as they "entail(ed) social processes of exclusion and incorporation whereby discrete categories are maintained despite changing participation and membership in the course of individual life histories."[7]

Primordialism and Me

Those who maintain the boundaries of Italian Americanness are primordialists. I held the post of Director of the Center for Italian American Studies at Brooklyn College for nine years (1975-1984) and for which there was no compensation. In appreciation for my service, I was informed that several Italian American faculty members both at Brooklyn College and elsewhere in the City University of New York were upset that a "non-Italian" was holding the post. Few people know that during that time I conducted pioneering research[8] that contributed to establishment of the Institute to

---

in Asia and Africa (New York: Free Press, 1967); Clifford Geertz, *The Interpretation of Cultures: Selected Essays* (New York: Basic Books, 1973).
[7] Barth, *Ethnic Groups and Boundaries*.
[8] Jerome Krase and Vincent J. Fuccillo, *Italian Americans and College Life: A Survey of Student Experiences at Brooklyn College*.

"The Unfortunate Pilgrim"

Foster Higher Education that was the precursor of the John Calandra Italian American Institute. Other outcomes toward which my work modestly contributed were an "Italian Affirmative Action Program" and the Distinguished Professorship of Italian American Studies at the City University of New York. While serving on the 1996 search committee, CUNY Distinguished Professor Henry Wasser nominated me for the post. Rather than embarrassing him and myself by asking him to withdraw my name, I thanked him for the honor and at the next search committee meeting I asked that my name be excluded from consideration. Despite my withdrawal, a short time later I received an angry telephone call from a prominent Italian American leader and "friend" in the frame of "how dare you...."

The tradition at the American Italian Historical Association (AIHA, now the IASA) was that AIHA officers automatically moved up the ladder to become the President. Following this normative formula, I served two terms each as Secretary, Treasurer, and Vice President and although I ran for and won the presidency of the American Italian Historical Association I was the only candidate ever chosen by the Nominations Committee who was ever graced by balloted election opponents. As one might guess, they, with Italian surnames but often with scant service to the group, almost won. Finally, during a long conversation with an old friend and AIHA stalwart, Frank Femminella, he discovered I was "half-Italian" and that my whole-Italian American wife lived in the old Pig Town neighborhood where his uncle shepherded goats to keep down the grass at a local Brooklyn Union Gas plant. Embarrassed, he admitted to me that since he did not know I was "Italian" he had not invited me, AIHA

Jerome Krase

Vice President, to travel with other AIHA officers on a subsidized trip to Campobasso, Italy that seemed to be exclusively for "Italian American" scholars, as opposed to scholars of Italian America.

Of course, primordial ethnic exclusivity, as an affliction, is not only an Italian American disease. I discovered in my so-called career that ethnicity mattered, even when they said it did not. I was the Program Director of the Eastern European Section of the European Studies Institute at the CUNY Graduate and University Center from 1975-77. While delivering a yet unpublished paper with the title "An American of Unknown Ethnicity"[9] I explained that one of the many languages that my (not very well-educated) father understood was "Serbo-Croatian," at which point an elderly gentleman jumped up in the audience and shouted angrily at me: "There is no Serbo-Croatian language!" Twenty years later that point was made even clearer in places like Srebrenica as "Serbo-Croation" had been the official language of Tito's multicultural Yugoslavia. Then, after about a decade as Deputy Chairman of the Sociology Department at Brooklyn College, I overheard the secretary, who was a friend, talking to a professor, who was also a friend, caution him in Yiddish as I walked in the door "Shh, *fremd yn shtetl*" (stranger in town).

Even outside of CUNY, language is a major marker of authentic ethnicity. Another concept that can help understand my ethnic biography is "Situational Ethnicity," ethnic identity that is created for the moment based on the social setting or situation. To be is to speak, so to speak. My daughter Karen's husband Carlos is from Puerto Rico and both are fluent

---

[9] Jerome Krase, "An American of Unknown Ethnicity," MS.

in Spanish. They are raising my granddaughters (*mis nietas*), Isabella and Amelia, to be bilingual. She once asked me to wait at her house and open the door for her contractor, who was of Puerto Rican origin, when he showed up to do some work. When we met, I used up all of my Spanish in a few sentences and when he continued *en Español*, I quickly lost track of the conversation; at which point he turned to one of his workers and said, *"No entiendo. Su hija es puertorriqueña pero él no habla español."* (I don't understand. His daughter is Puerto Rican but he can't speak Spanish.)

Even though I am not even half-Polish, I was accepted as a member of the Polish Institute of Arts and Sciences in American in 1974, having been sponsored by a prominent member whose offer could not be refused. While at the 2002 PIASA annual conference at Georgetown University to present a paper, I shared the elevator with another member. During the short ride up to the meeting rooms, he spoke to me in Polish and when it became obvious to him that my Polish was limited, he audibly shared with his fellow actually Polish members: *Nie rozumiem. Jest członkiem Polskiego Instytutu, ale nie mówi sie po polsku.* (I don't understand. He is a member of the Polish Institute but he doesn't speak Polish.)

Discovering my Italian Roots: Metaphorically That Is

As to historical memory, we think that two centuries is a very long time but it really is not. In our lifetimes we have been close to people who span those ages. I was born in 1943, my grandparents were born in the 1880s, my parents in the 1910s, my children in the 1960s, and my grandchildren between 1999 and 2007. They will live until the end of this, the 21st century. If I am lucky, as did my own parents, I will be alive to see my great grandchildren near the middle of this century (2030). I know my wife will, as her parents died in their mid-90s while my parents were just about the age of 80 (79 mother, 82 father). Unfortunately, little of this is likely to be included in the "Mass Production" phase of Italian American History.

Because of the hyper-multi-ethnic environments in which I grew up, I was confused as to the putative groups to which I might belong. When as I started dating my current wife Suzanne Nicoletti, in 1958, she said her parents wanted to know my "nationality." I think that was the word people used then. I replied, honestly, "I didn't know," but would investigate. When I looked through some family papers I discovered that my mother's maiden name was "Cangelosi" and subsequently confronted her: "Mom how come you never told us we were Italian." She said, "We're not" and calmly explained that her mother said they were "Sicilian." Since I knew my girlfriend's parents were Italian, I thought this was a positive romantic development, so I told Suzanne the "good news," which she said some days later was for her quasi-Neapolitan parents rather bad news. As we will see later, her parents' actual roots were not in Naples (Napoli) at all, but they descended from parents from the town of Laurino and perhaps the city of Salerno. Note: I was told they had walked from Laurino to Salerno to get the boat to Naples and beyond.

In the summer of 1985, I was awarded a grant from the PSC/CUNY Faculty Research Award to do "Photographic Research in Southern Italy." When we shared this information with some of Suzanne's relatives in New York City we were encouraged to visit the hometown of one side of her family in Laurino in the Province of Salerno. In preparation I had borrowed a detailed Italian Auto Club road map. For a more direct route from Potenza to Laurino, it showed a road of odd color (*Stada Provinciale* 11e and 11f). My fluency did not allow me to decipher the meaning in the legend, so we took, what turned out not to be, the short cut. My Italian was sufficient that I could stop and ask along the way "*È questa la strada per Laurino?*" However the responses, whether in Italian or dialect was incomprehensible: *Si, ma bla, bla, bla, bla.*" Is this the road to Laurino? Yes, but blah, blah, blah, blah. As we drove along the road it changed from a two-lane paved, to two-lane unpaved, to one-lane totally unimproved upon which we encountered goats and herders and one equally lost car going in the opposite direction at a point at which we barely were able to allow it past (See Figure 1). After unanticipated several hours of breath-taking views and back breaking bumps the devolution of the road reversed and we entered Laurino much worse for the wear (See Figure 2).

In town we asked for the residence of the *la famiglia De Gregorio* and were energetically pointed the way. We entered the three story stuccoed structure situated on a steep incline and knocked on the door. The small three-generation extended family was just finishing dinner and when we explained who were they treated us like lost, royal, relatives. The table was quickly re-set and after we finished eating and drinking a wonderful repast we were invited to stay longer (even a few days). Although my Italian was limited we were able to converse in German, French, and a bit in English because we shared the table with Italians who had found it necessary to spend years working abroad. We thanked them for their kind invitation to stay but (truthfully) explained that we were on our way to meet people in Sorrento and needed to make up for the time lost on the road through the mountains (See Figure 3). After we left the house and waved goodbye, we were taken to a local bar and introduced to neighbors and friends over *un caffè*. When we finally departed, there were some tears, and we felt as though we were leaving "home" for the first time, but then again only symbolically.

When I got back to "The States," I decided to explore the one-way communication I had with people along the side of the road (*Strada Statale 11*) on the way to Laurino. Therefore I sent the message, which follows below, about the experience to some of my academic Italian friends by e-mail. Their responses, that I have arranged below for conversational analysis, reveal a great deal about authentic Italian *bontà*:

> *Amici,* I need help with a translation of phrase from English into Italian for a paper I am writing about my own, and my wife Suzanne's, search for our roots in Italy. It regards traveling to a remote village in (Campania) Italy and asking people along the way whether this was the road to the town. The question I asked, perhaps incorrectly, was: "*È questa la strada per laurino?*" The answer in Italian was (*credo che*): "Yes, but you can't get there from here."; "Yes, but you can't get there this way."; or "Yes, but the road turns into a goat path (which it did)." *Grazie tante, Mino Cangelosi* Krase

These were the replies:

> 1. "*Sì, ma non ci arriva da qui - Sì, ma non è questa la strada - Sì, ma la strada diventa una strada da capre.* Hope to see you soon. All the best *Mino Vianello*"

"The Unfortunate Pilgrim"

> 2. *Traduzione: "è questa la strada per Laurino?" Sì, ma non ci si arriva da qui. La strada diventa una mulattiera (mule trail). Saluti, Maddalena Tirabassi*
> 3. *"Sì, ma non ci si arriva da qui." / "Sì, ma la strada va a finire in un sentiero"* (but I would not know how to translate "goat path)." Best, *Cristina Allemann-Ghionda*
> 4. Dear Jerry: My translation: *"sì, ma non ci si arriva da qui"; "sì, ma non ci si arriva da questa parte"; "sì, ma la strada diventa una mulattiera"*. Best, *Stefano Luconi*
> 5. Jerry, I am on my way to Venice for a MA thesis discussion where I acted as co-supervisor. *"Si, ma non puoi/può andarci da qui..."* Will get back to you soon again, best!
> 6. The most Italianate response, which I gratefully received from my Italian colleagues was as follows:

> > Jerry: the question *"È questa la strada per Laurino?"* is perfect, in Italian. The problem is that, encountering a "native" in Italy, the native — only to be kind — tends to reply to the question as if it were: "Is this one the best way to Laurino?"; so that the reply is: "Ok, this way is good, inasmuch as it goes to Laurino; the best way, however, is ......". In fact, replying: "No, it's wrong, the good way is another one" the native could have felt uneasy, since the reply would be a bit rude. Anyway: your question was classical; I also would have used the same linguistic form; and I would have had the same reaction. Bye. Leonardo Cannavo

I replied to Leonard, thusly: *grazie tante, ma come si dice in italiano la frase?* How would you say it in Italian? And can I quote you in my paper? I think your understanding of the situation is perfect: *la tua comprensione della situazione è perfetta!*

To which he wrote:

Ok, sorry, I didn't get the point. The easiest translations for the three phrases is as follows:

"yes, but you can't get there from here" = "*Sì, ma da qui non ci può arrivare*".

"yes, but you can't get there this way" = "*Sì, ma da questa strada non ci può arrivare*".

"yes, but the road turns into a goat path" = "*Sì, ma la strada diventa un sentiero per capre.*"

If you quote me in a paper of yours, it will be an honor; you need not ask for permission. Most unfortunately, few methodologists (and consider that I feel uneasy wearing the hat of a methodologist) refuse to consider the cultural and psychosocial frames of their job. Speech interaction is both amusing and revealing. Bye. L.

Some Bio-Historical Facts

Simple facts do not say much about ethnic history. My mother's family name was "Cangelosi" and it is spelled a number of different ways by extensions of the family in the Untied States, many of whom I met once at a Cangelosi family reunion in a public park in Garfield, New Jersey. All the members of her immediate family were consistent in their particular version. I researched the family name on The Statue of Liberty-Ellis Island Foundation's website for the Passenger Arrivals at the American Family Immigration Center. It was relatively easy to find my grandfather Girolamo Cangelosi. Ethnicity: Italian. Date of Arrival: February 12, 1895. Age at Arrival: 11. Ship of Travel: Bolivia. Port of Departure: Naples & Gibraltar (See Figure 4).

"The Unfortunate Pilgrim"

My cousin, Jerry (Jerome J. Libasi), the son of my Godfather Gus, has researched his mother's, my Aunt Josie's, family, and even made contact with a few Cangelosis in Sicily. From him, I learned that all the Cangelosis are from Marineo, a small hill town in the Plain of the Albanians (*Piana degli Albanesi*) that was once referred to as the Plain of the Greeks (*Piana dei Greci*). It is not far from Corleone, and Palermo, Sicily. My maternal grandfather Girolamo's parents were Salvatore Cangelosi (1833-?) and Maria V. Licastri (1833-1902). Girolamo's grandparents were Gaetano Cangelosi (1805-?), who was a baker, and Ninfa Trentecoste (1810-?). Both the Cangelosis and Trentecostes settled in Manhattan's Little Italy on Elizabeth Street. Donna Gabaccia noted that in 1905 the largest chain of families, more than 200, on Elizabeth Street were from Marineo.[10] Matthew Trentecoste (1818-?) and his wife Josephine arrived in 1893 with my Grandmother Maria Antonina, while my grandfather Girolamo arrived with his parents in 1895, also from Marineo. The 1920 US Census for Brooklyn notes that Girolamo Cangelosi was a "fruit and vegetable market" owner and Maria was a "bench worker." Both had "no" education, and were listed as having at the time five children; three, including my mother Martha, came later and one died at the age of two. Girolamo died in 1928 at the age of 51 and my maternal grandmother, Maria Antonina died in 1962 at the age of 78.

Census data do not say much about life. My mother seldom talked about her parents or her childhood, at least to

---

[10] Donna R. Gabaccia, *From Sicily to Elizabeth Street: Housing and Social Change Among Italian Immigrants, 1880-1930* (Albany: State University of New York Press, 1984), 61.

me. Perhaps it was because I was the next to last of seven children. I also had very little contact with my mother's family. Looking back, I think it was because her marriage was such a disappointment to her parents on both ethnic as well as economic terms. Her family was Sicilian and successful, his family was Slavic and not. As my mother essentially hid our ethnicity from us, I have only a few stories with an ethnic tint to them. The discovery of my Sicilian roots when I was fourteen immediately raised the question of the *mafia* because it was the only thing I had ever heard about Sicilians. She said the word "*mafia*" meant "strong," and did not think of it as a group of people. People were *mafia* or not *mafia*. Nobody was a member of it. On the other hand, she told me about the Black Hand in Greenpoint who had once threatened to kidnap my godfather's (Gus Libasi the barber) daughter. I asked if they went to the police to report the threat, and she said that the local Irish cops could not care less. The Black Hand was the Italians' problem not theirs.

She also said rather casually that her father worked for a time on the building of the Panama Canal, and then later for Standard Oil in New York City before going into his own business. He used to drive his horse and cart over to what were called "truck farms" in New Jersey to pick up produce and bring it back to his store in Brooklyn. Girolamo also owned a number of apartment buildings. My mother told me that the Polish tenants they rented to would spit on the ground when she went to their apartments every month to collect the rent. This is a fact I have never spoken about at Polish and Polish-American academic conferences. Her best friend was a Jewish girl whose father owned a local beer garden. She told me only one story about her father's life in Sicily. He used to joke that he grew up in a palace, and then say he lived there as a stable boy (See Figure 5).

Marineo

In the summer of 2009 my wife and I travelled with another mixed Sicilian-Italian couple, partially in search of our Sicilian roots. We made a circle to and from Catania by way of Sciacca and Palermo. Prior to the journey, I decided not to make contact with any of my putative Sicilian kin in Marineo but instead to travel there to search out my grandfather's "palace," photograph around the town, and pay a visit to the cemetery to find the graves of my great and great-great grandparents (See Figure 6).

On one morning, toward the end of the trip we drove twenty-one kilometers from our hotel in Palermo southwest to the town of Marineo, which had, according to Wikipedia, about 7,000 inhabitants. My first stop was at my grandfather Girolamo's palace which turned out to be a 16th century castle built by the Marchesi Beccadelli-Bolognese that was now serving as an archeological museum (See Figure 7). Architecturally and culturally the village, founded in the 7th-8th century, reflects the influences of the Phoenicians, Greeks, Romans, Byzantines, Normans, and Arabs. While I walked around the center of the hillside town street I met an older gentleman to whom I explained my connection to Marineo and asked (as we did about my wife's family in Laurino), where I might find the Cangelosis and Trentacostes. He just laughed and said here those names are like "Smith" and "Jones" in America (See Figure 8). The cemetery was located a short distance from the town at the top of a steep hill. When I got there, however, I failed in my attempt to pay direct homage to my great-great-grandparents (See Figure 9). I could not, even with the help of the caretaker, find their graves because I did not know how to say *bis-bis-nonno*. He persisted in showing me the burial records and plaques for all the potential *bisnonni* (See Figure 10). I would estimate that at least a quarter of the names inscribed in various ways in the cemetery were variations of "Trentecoste" and "Cangelosi." On the way back down the steep hill, by accident, I did find San Ciro's, the church where my great-grandparents were wed but did not pause to go inside.

Summary

Although I always feel quite at home during my frequent trips to Italy, the only place where I felt somehow "connected" was at that cemetery, but my roots were not deep enough to keep me from only staying a few hours, and I already planned the visit in such a way that I could not stay longer even if I had wanted. It is difficult, even for me, to understand why I followed a path to nowhere in search of my roots in Sicily. Perhaps it was a perversion of the "Thomas effect;" "If men define situations as real, they are real in their consequences."[11] After all, my fellow social scientists have declared that any claim by people like me, an assimilated American of European extraction, is at most "symbolic" and certainly not "authentic." Herb Gans[12] would include me among those whose ethnic fascination is more nostalgia than socially con-

---

[11] William I. Thomas and Dorothy S. Thomas, *The Child in America: Behavior Problems and Programs* (New York: Knopf, 1928), 571-72.
[12] Herbert Gans, "Symbolic Ethnicity: The Future of Ethnic Groups and Cultures in America," *Ethnic and Racial Studies* 2 (1) (1979): 1-21.

sequential, to which Mary Waters would add the adjective "voluntary."[13]

> For all of the ways in which ethnicity does not matter for White Americans, it does matter for non-Whites. Who your ancestors are does affect your choice of spouse, where you live, what job you have, who your friends are, and what your chances are for success in American society, if those ancestors happen not to be from Europe. The reality is that White ethnics have a lot more choice and room to maneuver than they themselves think they do. The situation is very different for members of racial minorities, whose lives are strongly influenced by their race or national origin regardless of how much they choose to identify themselves in terms of their ancestries."[14]

Even my fellow co-ethnic Richard D. Alba would say that my attachment is more about the symbols of *Sicilianità* than with *Sicilianità* itself and even the commitment I may have to that identity is most likely attached to "… a few symbolic commitments (such as St. Patrick's Day among the Irish)."[15] Having never marched in honor of the despoiler of the New World, perhaps my friend Richard is right. As I have written about Little Italies, or as I call them "Ethnic Theme Parks":

---

[13] Mary Waters, *Ethnic Options: Choosing Identities in America* (Berkeley: University of California Press, 1990).

[14] Mary Waters, "Symbolic and Involuntary Ethnicity," in *Race, Ethnicity, and Gender: Selected Readings*, eds. Joseph F. Healey and Eileen O'Brien (Thousand Oaks: Pine Forge Press, 2007), 408.

[15] Richard D. Alba, *Ethnic Identity: The Transformation of White America* (New Haven: Yale University Press, 1992), 306.

In the post-modern society, neighborhoods are less important to individuals, but new functions for them evolve such as people returning from the suburbs to their own and other's old neighborhoods to visit, shop, and recharge their "soul," attend celebrations, buy things unavailable in deracinated settlements, visit old relatives, occasionally demonstrate ethnic pride, and increasingly to re-discover one's roots. Finally, in the post-modern world which allows for voluntary ethnicity, those who wish to be ethnic can choose to live in an ethnic enclave among co-ethnics.[16]

I have often thought of making contact with my now, very distant, Sicilian relatives, as well as those in what is now Slovakia. After watching so many "roots" and family reunion films, and hearing stories told by friends I can visualize what it would look like. As a child, I had attended a few Italian "football" weddings, and I did go to a rather unsatisfying Cangelosi reunion, more like a picnic, in Garfield, New Jersey. My hope is that such a grand gathering of the Cangelosi clan would be more like the Sicilian wedding scene from the *Godfather, Part II*, that took place in Savoca rather than in Corleone. Or perhaps it would be like musical scenes from, the albeit Greek-themed, *Mamma Mia!* For essentially deracinated hyphenated ethnics like myself, our expectations, or better or "demands," for authentic experiences (Italian ones in this case) can never be fulfilled because they have no actual referents. People like us move through the scenes but have never been, and will never be, part of them.

---

[16] Jerome Krase, "Little Italies in New York City: A Semiotic Approach" *Italian American Review* 5 (1) (1996): 18-19.

"The Unfortunate Pilgrim"

Despite my late friend Rudy Vecoli's frequent and often loud protestations,[17] Oscar Handlin[18] was more right than wrong. To be American is to be uprooted, if not rootless, in the sense of having roots elsewhere, and my journey to my imaginary Sicilian home made that clear to me. I certainly can still imagine being Italian and/or Italian American, but making a claim to that status evokes incredulity from friends, colleagues, and even most of my relatives and in-laws. Searching for my roots has been as unsatisfactory as trying to match my personal narrative to the meta-narrative of my "putative" ethnic group. As I am a social scientist rather than a novelist, however, the quest has nevertheless been enlightening. An apt title for my autobiography, or this autoethnography for that matter, might be *The Unfortunate Pilgrim*.

---

[17] Robert J. Vecoli, "Contadini in Chicago: a Critique of *The Uprooted*," *Journal of American History* 51 (1964): 404-17; Robert J. Vecoli, "Are Italian Americans just White Folks?" *Italian Americana* 13 (2) (1995): 149–61.

[18] Oscar Handlin, *The Uprooted: The Epic Story of the Great Migration that Made the American People* (New York: Grosset & Dunlop, 1951).

Appendix

Figure 1: Road to Laurino. Jerry Krase 1985.

"The Unfortunate Pilgrim"

Figure 2: Laurino. Jerry Krase 1985.

Figure 3: Family in Laurino. Jerry Krase 1985.

"The Unfortunate Pilgrim"

Figure 4: My Great-grandfather and Grandfather, Circa 1892. Courtesy of Jerome J. Libasi.

Figure 5: My Grandfather, Circa 1905. Courtesy of Jerome J. Libasi.

"The Unfortunate Pilgrim"

Figure 6: Marineo. Jerry Krase 2009.

Figure 7: "Palace," Marineo. Jerry Krase 2009.

"The Unfortunate Pilgrim"

Figure 8: Man in Marineo. Jerry Krase 2009.

Figure 9: Cemetery, Marineo. Jerry Krase 2009.

"The Unfortunate Pilgrim"

Figure 10: Cemetery Caretaker, Marineo. Jerry Krase 2009.

Works Cited

Alba, Richard D. *Ethnic Identity: The Transformation of White America*. New Haven: Yale University Press, 1992.

Anderson, Leon. "Analytic Autoethnography." *Journal of Contemporary Ethnography* 35 (4) (2006): 373-395.

Barth, Frederik, ed. *Ethnic Groups and Boundaries: The Social Organization of Cultural Difference*. Boston: Little, Brown, 1969.

Burnier, DyLysa. "Encounters with Self in Social Science Research: A Political Scientist Looks at Autoethnography." *Journal of Contemporary Ethnography* 35 (4) (2006): 410–18.

Gabaccia, Donna R. *From Sicily to Elizabeth Street: Housing and Social Change Among Italian Immigrants, 1880-1930*. Albany: State University of New York Press, 1984.

Gans, Herbert. "Symbolic Ethnicity: The Future of Ethnic Groups and Cultures in America." *Ethnic and Racial Studies* 2 (1) (1979): 1-21.

Geertz, Clifford, ed. *Old Societies and New States: The Quest for Modernity in Asia and Africa*. New York: Free Press, 1967.

———. *The Interpretation of Cultures: Selected Essays*. New York: Basic Books, 1973.

Handlin, Oscar. *The Uprooted: The Epic Story of the Great Migration that Made the American People*. New York: Grosset & Dunlop, 1951.

Krase, Jerome. "An American of Unknown Ethnicity." Paper presented at the European Institute, Eastern European Section, CUNY Graduate and University Center conference in New York, New York, March 16, 1976.

———. "Educational Attainment and Educational Values of Italian American over the Generations." In *The Italian Americans through the Generations*, edited by Rocco Caporale. Staten Island, New York: American Italian Historical Association, 1986.

———. "Educational Attainment and Educational Values of Italian American over the Generations." Reprinted in *Italian-*

American Students in New York City, 1975-2000: A Research Anthology, edited by Nancy L. Ziehler. New York: John D. Calandra Italian American Institute, 2011.

———. "Little Italies in New York City: A Semiotic Approach." *Italian American Review* 5 (1) (1996): 103-116.

Krase, Jerome and Fuccillo, Vincent J. *Italian Americans and College Life: A Survey of Student Experiences at Brooklyn College.* 1975. Reprinted in *Italian-American Students in New York City, 1975-2000: A Research Anthology*, edited by Nancy L. Ziehler. New York: John D. Calandra Italian American Institute, 2011.

Schlichtman, John Joe and Patch, Jason. "Gentrifier? Who, Me? Interrogating the Gentrifier in the Mirror." *International Journal of Urban and Regional Research.* 2013. doi: 10.1111/1468-2427.12067.

Thomas, William I. and Thomas, Dorothy. S. *The Child in America: Behavior Problems and Programs.* New York: Knopf, 1928.

Vecoli, Rudolph J. "Contadini in Chicago: a Critique of *The Uprooted*." *Journal of American History* 51 (1964): 404-17.

———. "Are Italian Americans just White Folks?" *Italian Americana* 13 (2) (1995): 149–61.

Waters, Mary. *Ethnic Options: Choosing Identities in America.* Berkeley: University of California Press, 1990.

———. "Symbolic and Involuntary Ethnicity." In *Race, Ethnicity, and Gender: Selected Readings*, edited by Joseph F. Healey and Eileen O'Brien. Thousand Oaks: Pine Forge Press, 2007.

Weber, Max. *Economy and Society: An Outline of Interpretive Sociology*, edited by Guenther Roth and Claus Wittich. Berkeley and Los Angeles: University of California Press, 1978.

LINGUA ESULE: THE RISORGIMENTO EXILES AND THE TEACHING OF ITALIAN IN THE UNITED STATES

Stefano Luconi
University of Padua

This essay offers a case study of the transnational role of language in the Italian Risorgimento. Specifically, it examines how what Donna R. Gabaccia has called – albeit improperly – "the diaspora of elite supporters of the Risorgimento" endeavored to exploit the teaching of Italian in the United States to make a contribution to the cause of Italy's political unification and independence in the mid-nineteenth century.[1] In other words, this chapter focuses on the expatri-

---

[1] Donna R. Gabaccia, *Italy's Many Diasporas* (London: UCL Press, 2000) 12. The concept of diaspora implies the awareness of a definitive separation from the motherland [see, e.g., David Dowling, "Languages of exile," *Canadian Literature* 115 (1987): 216]. Yet the Risorgimento exiles often moved back and forth between Italy and their temporary destinations abroad and, in any case, looked forward to repatriation [Maurizio Isabella, *Risorgimento in Exile: Italian Émigrés and the Liberal International in the Post-Napoleonic Era* (New York: Oxford University Press, 2009)]. A case in point for the expatriates' circulation across the Atlantic is the experience of Felice Argenti, who sought sanctuary three times in the United States following his participation in the failed 1821, 1831, and 1848 insurrections in northern Italy and after serving a prison sentence from 1832 to 1836. See Francesco Caravatti, *Un martire viggiutese dello Spielberg: Felice Argenti nel centenario del suo processo* (Varese: La Tipografica, 1932); Mario Barsali, "Argenti, Felice," in *Dizionario biografico*

ates who sought sanctuary in America in the first half of the nineteenth century and became instructors of Italian not only to make a living, but also to make the U.S. public opinion sensitive to the struggle of the Italian national movement.

Lorenzo Da Ponte, Wolfgang Amadeus Mozart's well-know former librettist, who landed in Philadelphia in 1805 and moved straight to New York City, is usually credited with being the initiator of the teaching of the Italian language in the United States in the mid 1820s.[2] He even proclaimed himself the "creator of the Italian language in America."[3] However, other-than-Italian instructors had operated schools in foreign languages, including Italian, in colonial America since the late 1740s.[4] Moreover, an Italian immigrant by the name of Anthony Fiva, the first of his nationality, gave private lessons of his mother tongue in New York City in 1773.[5] Another newcomer – Carlo Bellini, who taught Italian at William and Mary College in Williamsburg, Virginia, from 1779 to 1803 – was the first instructor of this lan-

---

degli italiani, vol. 4 (Rome: Istituto della Enciclopedia Italiana, 1962) 117-19.

[2] Workers of the Federal Writers' Project, *The Italians of New York* (New York: Random House, 1938) 9; Joseph G. Fucilla, *The Teaching of Italian in the United States* (New Brunswick, N.J.: American Association of Teachers of Italian, 1967) 26-29; Hermann W. Haller, "Italian in New York," *Multilingual Apple: Languages in New York City*, ed. Ofelia García and Joshua A. Fishman (Berlin: Mouton de Gruyter, 2002) 134.

[3] Emelise Aleandri, *The Italian-American Immigrant Theatre of New York City, 1746-1899* (Lewiston, N.Y.: Edwin Mellen Press, 2006) 21.

[4] Robert Francis Seybolt, "Notes on the Curriculum of Colonial America," *Journal of Educational Research* 12 (1925): 277.

[5] Howard R. Marraro, *Relazioni fra l'Italia e gli Stati Uniti* (Rome: Edizioni dell'Ateneo, 1954) 80.

guage at college level in North America. He was also one of the early political expatriates from Italy, as he had to leave the Grand Duchy of Tuscany because of his liberal ideas.⁶

The Italian language was indeed en vogue in the upper echelon of American society in the late eighteenth and early nineteenth centuries. Even the Founding Fathers, including Benjamin Franklin, learnt and practiced it.⁷ A letter by John Adams to Thomas Jefferson offers enough evidence of how fashionable Italian was in the early Republic: "tell [Filippo] Mazzei, he cannot conceive what an Italian I am become. I read nothing else, and if he writes to me it must be in that language. [...] You, too, write Italian."⁸ Adams even encouraged young Americans "to make yourself master of the Italian language."⁹

Notwithstanding this late eighteenth-century fascination, it was Da Ponte who actually lifted the Italian literature and language into the realm of respectable academic disciplines in 1824 when, after giving private lessons for almost twenty years, he was appointed as the first professor of Italian at Columbia College (now Columbia University) through the influence of Clement Clarke Moore, one of the trustees and a

---

⁶ "Charles Bellini, First Professor of Modern Languages in an American College," *William and Mary Quarterly* 2 (1925): 1-29; Angelina La Piana, *La cultura americana e l'Italia* (Turin: Einaudi, 1938) 62-63.

⁷ Benjamin Franklin, *Memoirs of the Life and Writings of Benjamin Franklin*, vol. 1 (London: Colburn, 1818) 80-81.

⁸ John Adams to Thomas Jefferson, Grosvenor Square, July 10, 1787, in *The Adams-Jefferson Letters*, ed. Lester J. Cappon, vol. 1 (Chapel Hill: University of North Carolina Press, 1959) 187-88.

⁹ John Adams, *A Defence of the Constitutions of Government of the United States of America*, vol. 2 (London: Dilly and Stockdale, 1797) 445.

former student of his at the beginning of his stay in New York City. Such a standing of Italian, however, resulted less from Da Ponte's idiosyncratic teaching than from his own tireless self-promotion as an instructor.[10]

Da Ponte retained his chair until he died in 1838 and, the following year, Columbia replaced him with Eleuterio Felice Foresti, who also taught Italian at the University of the City of New York (now New York University) from 1841 to 1856.[11] Foresti was a former member of the *Federati*, a secret society operating in Lombardy, an Italian region under Austrian domination in the early Restoration years. In 1820, the *Federati* vainly endeavored to persuade the King of Sardinia to make war on Austria in order to liberate their homeland from foreign rule. When the Austrian police discovered Foresti's conspiratorial activities, he was convicted for high treason and began to serve a twenty-year prison sentence in the dungeons of the notorious Spielberg fortress until he was deported to the United States in 1836. There he became Giuseppe Mazzini's spokesperson and chief coordinator for North America as the chairperson of the Congrega Centrale of the Giovine Italia, the organization grouping the Republican refugees in the United States, which Foresti helped found in 1841.[12]

---

[10] Fucilla, *The Teaching of Italian in the United States*, 104-6; Sheila Hodges, *Lorenzo Da Ponte: The Life and Times of Mozart's Librettist* (Madison: University of Wisconsin Press, 2002) 198; La Piana, *La cultura americana e l'Italia*, 89-96.

[11] Howard R. Marraro, "Da Ponte and Foresti: The Introduction of Italian at Columbia," *Columbia University Quarterly* 29 (1937): 23-32.

[12] Salvatore Candido, "L'azione mazziniana delle Americhe e la congrega di New York della Giovine Italia (1842-1852) attraverso lettere inedite di

Like Foresti, a few other Risorgimento exiles ended up teaching Italian in the United States. For instance, no sooner did Orazio De Attellis, Marquis of Sant'Angelo, land at New York City in May 1824, fleeing a death sentence for his participation in the 1820 liberal revolution in the Kingdom of the Two Sicilies, than he opened a private school to teach young American ladies his own mother tongue. Overall, he eventually operated three schools in New York City and another in New Orleans during his stay in the United States from 1824 to 1836.[13] Similarly, Pietro Borsieri, another participant in the conspiracy of the *Federati* and a former prisoner in the Spielberg castle, gave classes in his apartment and at his students' homes in both Princeton and Philadelphia between 1836 and 1837.[14] Giovanni Francesco Secchi De Casali, an expatriate who had conspired against Duchess of Parma and Piacenza Marie-Louise in 1836, also taught Italian upon settling in Philadelphia in 1844. When he moved to New York in 1846, before he devoted himself to journalism, the time he spent for his lessons could take as many as seventeen hours of his day.[15] Likewise, Ignazio Batolo, alias Pietro

---

E.F. Foresti e G. Albinola a G. Garibaldi e G.B. Cuneo," *Bollettino della Domus Mazziniana* 18 (1972): 123-75; Giuseppe Monsagrati, "Foresti, Felice Eleuterio," *Dizionario biografico degli italiani*, vol. 48 (Rome: Istituto della Enciclopedia Italiana, 1997) 797-801.

[13] Luciano G. Rusich, *Un carbonaro molisano nei due mondi* (Naples: Glaux, 1982) 33. For De Attellis, see also Cinzia Cassani, "De Attellis, Orazio," in *Dizionario biografico degli italiani*, vol. 33 (Rome: Istituto della Enciclopedia Italiana, 1987) 329-32.

[14] Fucilla, *The Teaching of Italian in the United States*, 41. For Borsieri, see Michele Lupo Gentile, "Pietro Borsieri, un martire dello Spielberg," *Rassegna Nazionale* 32 (1910): 430-42.

[15] Giovanni Francesco Secchi De Casali, "Trent'otto anni d'America –

Bachi, who had been involved in a 1820 uprising in Palermo and eventually sought sanctuary from the Bourbon police in Boston, started to teach Italian at Harvard University in 1826.[16] Two other conspirators, Giuseppe Attinelli and Carlo Serretta, similarly sailed to Massachusetts and made a living by giving Italian lessons in Salem following the execution of the leader of the 1820 plot, Salvatore Meccio.[17] A few years after Harvard University had dismissed Bachi in 1846, another exile, Luigi Monti, took his place in 1851.[18] Monti belonged to a later generation of the Italian patriots because he had been implicated in Palermo's 1848 anti-Bourbon riots and fled Sicily in January 1850. Yet his devotion to the cause of the Risorgimento was indisputable.[19]

The mid nineteenth century marked perhaps the climax of U.S. intellectuals' attention to Italian culture as the cradle of the Renaissance and, in part, Romanticism. For instance, Henry Wadsworth Longfellow, Monti's main sponsor for an academic position, James Russell Lowell, Charles Eliot Norton, and Thomas William Parsons, a prominent translator of Dante Alighieri's *Divine Comedy* into English, were at the

---

XVI," *L'Eco d'Italia*, January 28-29, 1883, 1. For Secchi De Casali's career in journalism, see Bénédicte Deschamps, "Dal fiele al miele: La stampa esule italiana di New York e il Regno di Sardegna (1849-1861)," *Annali della Fondazione Luigi Einaudi* 42 (2008): 81-98.

[16] S. Eugene Scalia, "Figures of the Risorgimento in America: Ignazio Batolo, Alias Pietro Bachi and Pietro D'Alessandro," *Italica* 42 (1965): 311-24.

[17] Valentino Labate, *Un decennio di carboneria in Sicilia, 1821-1831*, vol. 1 (Rome: Società Editrice Dante Alighieri, 1904) 205.

[18] Fucilla, *The Teaching of Italian in the United States*, 94-95.

[19] Francesco Durante, *Italoamericana: Storia e letteratura degli italiani negli Stati Uniti, 1776-1880* (Milan: Mondadori, 2001) 447.

core of a circle of Italophiles at Harvard University.[20] The choice of the peninsula as a favorite destination in the European grand tour offered further evidence of such an appreciation for Italy.[21] This climate of opinion contributed to enhancing the interest in Italian and, consequently, created employment opportunities for teachers of the language in the United States.

The Italian political exiles usually did not let this chance pass by regardless of their lack of previous experience in this field. This was, for instance, the case of Piero Maroncelli, a fellow conspirator of Borsieri and Foresti. Although he had specialized in music in Italy, after landing in the United States in 1837 Maroncelli briefly taught Italian before realizing that lessons of his initial expertise would grant him a larger income to make a living in his adoptive land.[22]

The American hatred of European monarchic regimes and the awareness of the mistreatment of political prisoners by the Austrian police turned the survivors of detention at the Spielberg fortress almost instantly into heroes in the eyes of the U.S. public opinion. Large crowds welcomed them as they disembarked in New York City. In particular, the

---

[20] John Paul Russo, "The Harvard Italophiles: Longfellow, Lowell, and Norton," in *L'esilio romantico: Forme di un conflitto*, ed. Joseph Cheyne and Lilla Maria Crisafulli Jones (Bari: Adriatica Editrice, 1990) 303-24; Austin Warren, "T.W. Parson, Poet and Translator of Dante," *More Books* 13 (1938): 287-303.

[21] Van Wyck Brooks, *Dream of Arcadia: American Writers and Artists in Italy, 1760-1915* (New York: Dutton, 1958) 13-109; Paul R. Baker, *The Fortunate Pilgrims: Americans in Italy, 1800-1860* (Cambridge, Mass.: Harvard University Press, 1964).

[22] Pietro Borsieri, *Avventure letterarie di un giorno e altri scritti editi ed inediti*, ed. Giorgio Alessandrini (Rome: Edizioni dell'Ateneo, 1967) 267.

American press hailed them as either "the champions of human rights and national independence" or "the illustrious martyrs of freedom."[23] Foresti remarked that U.S. newspapers continued to publish articles about them as late as two months after their arrival.[24]

After all, Italophilia had political implications, too. For example, the reports that Margaret Fuller wrote for the *New York Tribune* on the struggle of Mazzini and Giuseppe Garibaldi to save the Roman Republic from the restoration of papal rule in 1849 contributed to winning many friends to the cause of the Risorgimento in the United States because her articles seemed to give evidence that the nationalistic fight of the Italian people had turned away from monarchy and the Catholic Church, the main European institutions that were anathema to the American primarily Protestant and almost exclusively republican public opinion.[25] Against

---

[23] Marraro, *Relazioni fra l'Italia e gli Stati Uniti*, 136-37; Ginevra Battistini, "La città commerciale: Luigi Tinelli tra Manhattan e Weehawken," *Storia Urbana* 105 (2003): 57.

[24] Felice Foresti, "Ricordi di Felice Foresti," in Atto Vannucci, *I martiri della libertà italiana: Dal 1794 al 1848* (Milan: Bortolotti, 1878) 365.

[25] Margaret Fuller, *"These Sad but Glorious Days": Dispatches from Rome, 1846-1850*, ed. Larry J. Reynolds and Susan Belasco Smith (New Haven, Conn.: Yale University Press, 1991); Howard R. Marraro, *American Opinion on the Unification of Italy, 1846-1861* (New York: Columbia University Press, 1932) 48-100; Francesca Bisutti, "The Sad Nymph of Margaret Fuller: A Description for a Besieged City," *Rivista di Studi Anglo-Americani* 3 (1984-1985): 557-64; Giuseppe Monsagrati, "Gli intellettuali americani e il processo di unificazione italiana," *Gli Stati Uniti e l'Unità italiana*, ed. Daniele Fiorentino and Matteo Sanfilippo (Rome: Gangemi, 2004) 17-44; Peter R. D'Agostino, *Rome in America: Transnational Catholic Ideology from the Risorgimento to Fascism* (Chapel Hill: University of North Carolina Press, 2004) 26-31; Paola Gemme,

this backdrop, Norton came to admire Garibaldi and raised more than 1,300 dollars for his Thousand Redshirts' expedition to conquer the Kingdom of the Two Sicilies in 1860.[26] With reference to this military campaign, which paved the way for Italy's political unification and took place while Abraham Lincoln was running for the White House, Norton also wrote that "the progress of Garibaldi is just now even of greater interest to us than that of our own presidential campaign. [...] The new birth of Italy is already the grandest event of the modern period."[27]

Among the former inmates of the Spielberg fortress who made their way across the Atlantic upon their release to seek sanctuary in America, Maroncelli was the best known because of his own personal plight, as he had had a leg amputated during his detention.[28] At the beginning of his stay in the United States, Maroncelli tried to exploit his renown and political reputation in the fruitless effort to be appointed as Da Ponte's successor to the chair of Italian at Columbia. After the college selected Foresti, he made a similarly vain attempt at securing a teaching position at the University of Virginia before resorting to give private lessons.[29]

Domesticating Foreign Struggles: The Italian Risorgimento and Antebellum American Identity (Athens: Georgia University Press, 2005) 89-106.
[26] Aida Audeh and Nick Havely, *Dante in the Long Nineteenth Century* (New York: Oxford University Press, 2012) 256-57.
[27] Charles Eliot Norton to Arthur Hugh Clough, Newport, September 24, 1860, in Sara Norton and M.A. DeWolfe Howe, *Letters of Charles Eliot Norton with Biographical Comment*, vol. 1 (Boston: Houghton Mifflin, 1913) 210
[28] Angeline H. Lograsso, *Piero Maroncelli* (Rome: Edizioni dell'Ateneo, 1958) 186-89.
[29] Fucilla, *The Teaching of Italian in the United States*, 32-33, 129: Howard R.

Maroncelli's efforts to get a stable job as a professor of Italian at a U.S. academic institution can be reasonably explained. Scholarship has long emphasized how thin the line between political exile and economic emigration is, on the grounds that refugees and banished people, too, have to make ends meet and cannot live on ideals alone.[30] With their properties in Italy usually seized or unavailable to them, many of the Risorgimento expatriates looked for sources of income upon settling in the United States. A few of these exiles were literally scared by the high cost of living in America, as opposed to the European prices they had been used to. Luigi Tinelli, for instance, complained in a 1836 letter to his brother that he and fellow political refugee Alessandro Bargnani had spent as much as twenty dollars each for food and lodging during their first four days in New York City.[31]

Marraro, "Pioneer Italian Teachers of Italian in the United States," *Modern Language Journal* 28 (1944): 563-64.

[30] Émile Témine, "Émigration 'politique' et émigration 'économique,'" in École Française de Rome, *L'émigration politique en Europe aux XIXe et XXe siècles* (Rome: École Française de Rome, 1991) 57-72. Studies have acknowledged such fuzziness not only in contemporary but in modern history as well. See, e.g., James H. Jackson and Leslie Page Moch, "Migration and the Social History of Modern Europe," *Historical Methods* 22 (1989): 27-36. For the specific case of Italian emigration, see Maurizio Degl'Innocenti, "L'esilio nella storia contemporanea," in *L'esilio nella storia del movimento operaio e l'emigrazione economica*, ed. Maurizio Degl'Innocenti (Manduria: Lacaita, 1992) 16-17; Matteo Sanfilippo, *Problemi di storiografia dell'emigrazione italiana* (Viterbo: Sette Città, 2002) 111-20.

[31] Luigi Tinelli to Carlo Tinelli, New York, October 22, 1836, in Giancarlo Peregalli, "L'emigrazione politica forzata: Luigi Tinelli attraverso una sua lettera," in *Emigrazione e territorio: Tra bisogno e ideale*, ed. Carlo Brusa and Robertino Ghiringhelli (Varese: Lativa, 1995) 312.

He subsequently concluded, not without sarcasm, that the United States was a "magnificent Republic" where "without money one was likely to die like a dog."[32] Furthermore, many refugees, such as Tinelli and Foresti, sailed to North America on the eve of the 1837 financial crisis that pushed the U.S. economy into recession until 1844, causing a significant rise in unemployment that in some locales reached as much as a quarter of the workforce.[33]

With reference to the Risorgimento émigrés, Da Ponte himself pointed out, not without contempt, that "a swarm of exiles arrived at New York, without means or profession, and unfortunately for themselves, without abilities. They exchanged their rifles and bayonets for dictionaries and grammars and set about teaching languages."[34] In Da Ponte's view, among all these refugees, only De Attellis had enough expertise to become an effective instructor of Italian, but he, too, chose this job to make a living.[35] Indeed, the search for "a decent and useful occupation" was De Attellis main concern upon landing in New York City.[36] Even Foresti

---

[32] Luigi Tinelli to Carlo Tinelli, New York, February 2, 1872, as quoted in Marco Sioli, "*Se non c'è il conquibus si muore come cani*: Luigi Tinelli a New York (1851-1873)," in *Gli Stati Uniti e l'Unità d'Italia*, 149.

[33] Alasdair Roberts, *America's First Great Depression: Economic Crisis and Political Disorder after the Panic of 1837* (Ithaca, N.Y.: Cornell University Press, 2012).

[34] Lorenzo Da Ponte, *Memoirs of Lorenzo Da Ponte: Mozart's Librettist*, ed. Leslie Alfred Sheppard (London: Routledge, 1929) 355.

[35] Rusich, *Un carbonaro molisano nei due mondi*, 32.

[36] Oreste De Attellis, "I miei casi di Roma sotto il triumvirato Mazzini, Armellini, Saffi: Preceduti da una sinopsi biografica di tutta la mia vita militare e politica da ottobre 1774 a oggi," 1849, 20, unpublished manuscript no. V A 47/3, Biblioteca Nazionale Vittorio Emanuele III, Naples, Italy.

"Lingua Esule"

was glad that he had found a student, the wife of a Senator who paid for his Italian lessons in advance, a very short time after arriving in the United States because "everything" was "quite expensive" in the country of his destination.[37] When Federico Confalonieri – another martyr of Spielberg who spent a few months time in the United States in 1837 – endeavored to persuade Borsieri to move from Princeton to Philadelphia, he made a point of stressing that the city of brotherly love was home to many people eager to study the Italian language.[38]

Following on Da Ponte's footsteps, Giovanni Ermenegildo Schiavo – perhaps the initiator of Italian-American studies – remarked that "most of the Italian teachers of languages in the United States during the nineteenth century were 'improvised teachers,' that is men who found in the teaching of their native language [...] the only honest way of eking out a living. Most of them were political refugees [...], in a good many cases men without a trade, technical knowledge, or business activity, possessing only a university degree in jurisprudence or 'belles letters.'"[39] The latter, for instance, was the case of Pietro D'Alessandro, who held a degree in humanities and gave private lessons of Italian in Boston, where he settled in 1833 after leaving Sicily for political reasons.[40]

---

[37] Felice Foresti to Bettina Brenta Masuelli, New York, October 26, 1836, in Durante, *Italoamericana*, 376-77 (quote 376).
[38] Richard N. Juliani, *Building Little Italy: Philadelphia's Italians Before Mass Migration* (University Park, Pa.: Pennsylvania State University Press, 1998) 129.
[39] Giovanni Ermenegildo Schiavo, *Four Centuries of Italian-American History* (New York: Vigo Press, 1952) 264.
[40] Antonio Gallenga, *Episodes of My Second Life: American Experiences*, vol.

Yet teaching Italian was not only a source of income. It was also a means by which the exiles could enhance the cause of the Risorgimento in the United States because this extemporary occupation had political implications and aims as well.

On the one hand, sharing a common language and culture is one of the foundations of a nation, especially from the standpoint of Romanticism.[41] Therefore, teaching Italian and Italian literature helped make American public opinion aware of the existence of a stateless Italian people longing for the political unification of their territory and independence from foreign powers. In other words, Italian classes became a sort of political statement by itself. Against the backdrop of Italy's long division into a multiplicity of States and regions under foreign rule, emphasizing Italian against the numerous dialects that were spoken in the peninsula as a result of its historical partition equaled an implicit call for political unification. In addition, although Lombardy and Veneto enjoyed a special status that allowed Italian to be spoken and written in the civil service and public administration, German had been designated as the official language of the Italian regions of the Habsburg Empire since Joseph II's 1790 imperial decree and was used especially in communications with the central authorities in Vienna.[42]

---

1 (London: Chapman and Hall, 1884) 68; Durante, *Italoamericana*, 301.

[41] For a brief but insightful overview of the relationship between language and nation in Italian history, see Nancy C. Carnevale, *A New Language, A New World: Italian Immigrants in the United States, 1890-1945* (Urbana: University of Illinois Press, 2009) 22-27.

[42] Gualtiero Boaglio, "Language and Power in an Italian Crownland of the Habsburg Empire: The Ideological Dimension of Diglossia in

"Lingua Esule"

Moreover, as for the northwestern section of the peninsula, the king of Sardinia spoke either the Piedmontese dialect or French even at the meetings of his own cabinet.[43] Therefore, the stress on Italian by the Risorgimento exiles in the United States was a symbolic claim for Italy's self-rule and independence from foreign influence.

On the other hand, the exiles' selection of the readings for the Italian classes contributed to building up consensus and sympathy for the Risorgimento among their students and, consequently, helped the support for Italy's political unification make inroads into U.S. public opinion.

In 1838, Antonio Gallenga published a survey on Italian Romantic literature in the influential *North American Review*.[44] He was another refugee who had fled Italy after his involvement in an ill-devised plot to assassinate King Charles Albert of Sardinia for the latter's alleged betrayal of the ideals of the Risorgimento.[45] After seeking temporary

---

Lombardy," in *Diglossia and Power: Language and Policies and Practices in the 19th Century Habsburg Empire*, ed. Rosita Rindler Schjerve (Berlin: Walter de Gruyter, 2003) 202-5.

[43] Christopher Duggan, *A Concise History of Italy* (New York: Cambridge University Press, 2006) 28.

[44] Antonio Gallenga, "Romantic Poetry in Italy," *North American Review* 47 (1838): 206-36. The article was published anonymously, but Gallenga later received the credit for its authorship. See William Cushing, *Index to the North American Review* (Cambridge, Mass.: Press of John Wilson and Son, 1878) 56. See also Antonio Gallenga, *Episodes of My Second Life: English Experiences*, vol. 2 (London: Chapman and Hall, 1884) 25.

[45] Pietro Orsi, "Antonio Gallenga (con documenti inediti)," *Nuova Antologia* 1439 (1932): 31-35; Aldo Garosci, *Antonio Gallenga: Vita avventurosa di un emigrato dell'Ottocento*, vol. 1 (Turin: Centro Studi Piemontesi, 1979) 29-67.

haven in Malta and Morocco, Gallenga settled in the United States in 1836. Here, he, too, ran into financial distress. "The education which had made me an Italian patriot and driven me out as a political exile – he subsequently recalled – had done nothing to prepare me for the lot of an ordinary emigrant." So, like many of his fellow refugees, Gallenga ended up teaching Italian, in his case at Harvard Young Ladies' Academy thanks to his friendship with Longfellow.[46]

Besides discussing coeval Italian literary works, in his article Gallenga also elaborated on the prospects for the spread of Italian language and literature in the United States. He concluded that a major difficulty in encouraging the study and practice of Italian had been theretofore a widespread misconception of the American public according to which Italian was a classical language, like Latin and ancient Greek, whose Augustan age and literary masterpieces hardly went beyond Dante's *Divine Comedy* (presumably written between 1308 and 1321), Niccolò Machiavelli's *The Prince* (1513), and Torquato Tasso's *Jerusalem Delivered* (1581). As Gallenga specifically pointed out, "it is a general persuasion, received and accredited among sensible persons, that the literature of that country is dead and that Italy, exhausted with the production of five centuries [...] is resting now under the shades of her laurels."[47]

In order to encourage the spread of Italian, some of the Risorgimento refugees – such as De Attellis – stressed the

---

[46] Gallenga, *Episodes of My Second Life: American Experiences*, vol. 1, 65-67, 146-48, 167, 360 (quote 360).
[47] Antonio Gallenga, "Romantic Poetry in Italy," *North American Review* 47 (1838): 208.

importance of the knowledge of this language for commercial purposes at a time the United States strengthened its economic relations with the Italian pre-unification states. Actually, in the late eighteenth century, the United States had established consulates at Leghorn (Grand Duchy of Tuscany) in 1793, Naples (Kingdom of the Two Sicilies) in 1796, Rome (Papal States) in 1797, and Genoa (Kingdom of Sardinia) in 1798.[48] The total volume of U.S. exports to the peninsula almost doubled in the third decade of the nineteenth century, rising from 1,139,000 dollars in 1811-1820 to 2,281,000 in 1821-1830. It reached 3,073,000 dollars in 1831-1840 and even 11,785,000 in 1841-1850.[49] In 1838 the Kingdom of Sardinia even signed a commercial treaty with Washington that granted the United States "most favored nation" status and trade between the two countries via the port of Genoa increased by 146 percent between 1845 and 1852.[50] Italy, therefore, had become a profitable market for American merchants and speaking the native language represented a valuable means to access it.

Other exiles and pioneers of the teaching of Italian in America, however, intended to demonstrate that the lan-

---

[48] Giorgio Spini, "Le relazioni politiche fra Italia e gli Stati Uniti durante il Risorgimento e la guerra civile," in *Italia e Stati Uniti nell'età del Risorgimento e della guerra civile: Atti del II Symposium di Studi Americani, Firenze, 27-29 maggio 1966* (Florence: La Nuova Italia, 1969) 122.

[49] Charles Evans, *Exports, Domestic and Foreign, from the United States to all Countries from 1789 to 1882* (Washington, D.C.: U.S. Government Printing Office, 1884) 84.

[50] Marco Mariano, "Da Genova a New York? Il Regno di Sardegna e gli Stati Uniti tra Restaurazione e integrazione nel mondo atlantico," *Annali della Fondazione Luigi Einaudi* 42 (2008): 31, 36.

guage was alive in the literary field as well. To this end, they extended the canon of the Italian literature in their own syllabi and supplemented such traditional authors as Dante, Machiavelli, and Tasso with present-day writers.

These additions usually included the protagonists and the advocates of the Risorgimento. For instance, almost all the refugees-instructors placed Silvio Pellico's *Le mie prigioni* (my prisons) among the required readings for their students of Italian language and literature. Pellico was so central to the canon that the *Literary World* maintained in 1848 that *Le mie prigioni* had been "for many years the first book put into the hands of the student of Italian."[51]

Pellico was another patriot who had been detained in the Spielberg fortress for about ten years. He offered an emotional account of his sufferings in *Le mie prigioni*, a recollection of his experience in jail that was published in 1832, two years after his release.[52] Although the narrative was quite self-centered, the volume turned Pellico into the symbol of all the patriots in the Austrian-dominated regions of northern Italy and the case study of an individual plight easily offered a harsh exposure of the mistreatment of the Risorgimento conspirators by the government in Vienna. Charles Klopp has aptly emphasized that, by denouncing the tyranny of the foreign rulers in the northeastern regions of the peninsula, "*Le mie prigioni* became such a powerful weapon in the struggle for independence that its effect on the Austri-

---

[51] Dennis Berthold, *American Risorgimento: Herman Melville and the Cultural Politics of Italy* (Columbus: Ohio State University Press, 2009) 40.
[52] Aldo A. Mola, *Silvio Pellico: Carbonaro, cristiano e profeta della nuova Europa* (Milan: Bompiani, 2005).

ans has been described as the equivalent of a battle lost to the Italian forces."[53]

Of course, the inclusion of Pellico's work in the canon of Italian literature was motivated on the grounds of literary and aesthetic reasons. For instance, in *A Reader of the Italian Language*, an anthology of Italian literature published in 1855, Luigi Monti argued that Pellico's prose was the best contemporary example of a style that was "calm and chaste, subdued to mildness by the gentle and blessed spirit of Christianity."[54] Monti's assessment was not without precedents. Few years earlier, in an article about the pleasures of literature, the *Democratic Review* had praised the beauty of Pellico's prose.[55] One, however, may reasonably suggest that Pellico's patriotism was definitely not unrelated to the use of *Le mie prigioni* in Monti's Italian classes. Indeed, subsequent studies have not credited Pellico's book with significant artistic value. Sufficient is to quote Giulio Natali, who has argued that Pellico was "a poor thinker and a shabby writer."[56] On the other hand, among his contemporaries, Longfellow himself criticized Pellico's sentimentality.[57]

---

[53] Charles Klopp, *Sentences: The Memoirs and Letters of Italian Political Prisoners from Benvenuto Cellini to Aldo Moro* (Toronto: University of Toronto Press, 1999) 40.

[54] Luigi Monti, *A Reader of the Italian Language, Being Extracts from Some of the Best Modern Italian Authors, Both Prose and Poetry* (Boston: Little, Brown and Company, 1855) vii.

[55] "The Pleasures of the Pen," *Democratic Review* 20 (1847): 29.

[56] Giulio Natali, *Ricordi e profili di maestri e amici* (Rome: Edizioni di Storia e Letteratura, 1965) 205.

[57] Edward Wagenknecht, *Longfellow: A Full-Length Portrait* (New York: Longmans, Green & Co., 1955) 67-68.

Furthermore, Monti's two additional examples of coeval Italian first-rate prose drew upon writers who stood out in the Risorgimento. His choice for a style that was "passionate, imaginative; a 'good hater' of oppression in every form" was Francesco Domenico Guerrazzi.[58] The latter's *La battaglia di Benevento* (1827) was a historical novel focusing on a rather obscure thirteenth-century battle between the troops of the youngest son of the king of France, Charles of Anjou, and Manfred of Sicily. Although Manfred's defeat and death at Benevento in 1266 placed southern Italy under a French monarch, the battle could be construed as an early instance of the Italian people's resistance against the imposition of foreign rule on the peninsula.[59] In addition, Guerrazzi was a follower of Mazzini and a protagonist of the 1848 insurrections in Tuscany.[60] Finally, Monti's selection for "deep, synthetical, and philosophic" writing was Vincenzo Gioberti, whose *Del rinnovamento civile d'Italia* (1850) advocated the political unification of Italy in the shape of a confederation of States under the Pope.[61]

Prevailing anti-Catholic feelings and criticism of the temporary power of the Popes prevented Gioberti, himself a Catholic priest, from becoming a vehicle to spread support for the Risorgimento in United States mainly protestant soci-

---

[58] Monti, *A Reader of the Italian Language*, vii-viii.

[59] For a historical account of the battle of Benevento, see Jean Dunbabin, *The French in the Kingdom of Sicily, 1266-1305* (New York: Cambridge University Press, 2011) 7-8, 25

[60] Nicola Badaloni, *Il pensiero politico di Francesco Domenico Guerrazzi* (Leghorn: Quaderni della Labronica, 1974).

[61] Monti, *A Reader of the Italian Language*, viii.

ety.[62] This, however, was not the case of Pellico, despite his overt Catholic devotion. In particular, Gallenga denied that Pellico was a Catholic "bigot" and pointed to him as a political "martyr" in his own article for the "North American Review."[63]

The inclusion of *Le mie prigioni* in the canon of nineteenth-century Italian literature by Monti and his fellow exiles-instructors of Italian made the volume a quite popular reading either in the original language or in its English translation. Indeed, the English versions circulating in the United States in the 1830s and 1840s were even two: one was a somehow abridged edition that Thomas Roscoe hurriedly prepared under the title of *My Imprisonment* for Harper in New York City in 1833, few months after the volume had come out in Italy in November 1832; the other was translated by Catherine E. Norton – Charles Eliot Norton's mother – and published as *My Prisons* by Folson in Cambridge, Massachusetts, in 1836. In this latter year, Maroncelli – who had been Pellico's cellmate in the Spielberg prison – had his own *Addition to "My Prisons: Memoirs of Silvio Pellico" with a Biographical Note of Pellico* printed by Folson, too.[64] Confalonieri pointed out that "one could find a copy of *Le mie prigioni* in

---

[62] Ray Allen Billington, *The Protestant Crusade, 1800-1860: A Study of the Origins of American Nativism* (New York: Rinehart, 1952).
[63] Gallenga, "Romantic Poetry in Italy," 227.
[64] Silvio Pellico, *My Imprisonment: Memoirs of Silvio Pellico da Saluzzo* (New York: Harper, 1833); Silvio Pellico, *My Prisons: Memoirs of Silvio Pellico* (Cambridge, Mass.: Folson, 1836); Piero Maroncelli, *Addition to "My Prisons: Memoirs of Silvio Pellico" with a Biographical Note of Pellico* (Cambridge, Mass.: Folson, 1836). For the first two U.S. editions of Pellico's memoirs, see Lograsso, *Piero Maroncelli*, 186-200, 207-219.

any log cabin from Alabama to Michigan."[65] Gallenga even argued that Pellico's memoirs "obtained more popularity in this country [the United States] than the original work could ever secure in Italy."[66]

The legacy of Pellico's work long influenced Americans' stand on the Risorgimento. For instance, while invoking "the day-dawn of Italian liberty" in 1851, poet and prominent abolitionist John Greenleaf Whittier celebrated "Pellico's faith [...] to bear / Years of unutterable torment, stern and still, / As the chained Titan victor through his will!"[67] Similarly, as a meeting gathered in New York City in 1860 to express sympathy with the unification of Italy, one of the orators maintained that this outcome would "see the atrocities of Spielberg avenged."[68] Actually, Pellico became so familiar a name as an Italian champion of such values as independence and freedom within U.S. society that a number of American travelers to Italy – including George Ticknor, literary critic and professor of Italian literature at Harvard University, and Joel Tyler Headley, author, clergyman, and future New York secretary of State – visited, or tried to visit, him before he died in 1854.[69]

---

[65] Federico Confalonieri to Camillo Casati, New York, June 13, 1837, now in *Carteggio del Conte Federico Confalonieri ed altri documenti spettanti alla sua biografia*, ed. Giuseppe Gallavresi, vol. 2, part 2 (Milan: Ripalta, 1913) 713.

[66] Gallenga, "Romantic Poetry in Italy," 227.

[67] John Greenleaf Whittier, "The Prisoners of Naples," 1851, now in *The Complete Political Works of Whittier*, ed. Horece E. Scudder (Boston: Houghton Mifflin, 1894) 372.

[68] Marraro, *American Opinion on the Unification of Italy*, 289.

[69] Giuseppe Prezzolini, *Come gli americani scoprirono l'Italia* (Bologna: Massimiliano Boni, 1971) 130, 133-34, 362; Joel Tyler Headley to E.,

"Lingua Esule"

Consequently, in the United States the teaching of Italian language and literature fuelled the flames of anti-Austrian feelings and spread empathy with the efforts for Italy's political unification. In particular, it helped make the Italophiles in U.S. intellectual circles aware of the political problems of the peninsula and contributed to encouraging them to go beyond a vision of Italy that had theretofore been linked almost exclusively to the realms of the arts and culture in general. In other words, Italy acquired a new dimension that was no longer detached from current affairs.[70]

Foresti, for instance, exploited the growing interest of the New England's intellectual elite to gain its support for Italian political unification. For instance, he approached Catharine Maria Segdwick – one of the best-known U.S. female novelists of the 1830s – and persuaded her to contribute to Catherine E. Norton's American translation of Pellico's *Le mie prigioni*.[71] Foresti also managed to turn Segdwick into an ardent sympathizer of the cause of the Risorgimento. As a result, in her own writing such as *Letters from Abroad to Kindred at Home,* based on her travelling to Italy and published in 1841, Segdwick overstressed her negative evaluation of

---

Genoa, February n.d., 1843, in Joel Tyler Headley, *Letters from Italy* (New York: Baker and Scribner, 1848) 59-60.

[70] A. William Salomone, "The Nineteenth-Century Discovery of Italy: An Essay in American Cultural History: Prolegomena to a Historiographical Problem," *American Historical Review* 73 (1968): 1365-71.

[71] Mary E. Dewey, *Life and Letters of Catharine M. Sedgwick* (New York: Harper & Brothers, 1871) 223, 256-59, 262-63; Lucinda L. Damon-Bach and Victoria Clemens, "Introduction," in *Catharine Maria Sedgwick: Critical Perspectives*, ed. Lucinda L. Damon-Bach and Victoria Clemens (Boston: Northeastern University Press, 2003) xiv; Gemme, *Domesticating Foreign Struggles*, 110-11.

the Austrian rule in Lombardy and Veneto in order to have additional means to extol the patriotism of the Italian people in their efforts to unify the peninsula and free themselves from foreign domination, as a coeval but anonymous review pointed out.[72] Similarly, practices of Italian with Foresti made poetess Julia Ward Howe, who was one of his "most avid students at Columbia," into another prominent supporter of Italy's political unification and independence from foreign rulers within the U.S. intellectual elite, as she realized that the peninsula was "so bound hand and foot by Austrian and other tyrants."[73] Following the efforts of the exiles-instructors of Italian, additional learned individuals – such as jurist and lawyer Theodore Sedgwick (Catharine Maria's father), George Ticknor, and writer Henry Theodore Tuckerman – joined the group of the Americans who advocated Italy's unity.[74] The latter became one of the most dedicated U.S. backers of the Risorgimento. For instance, after Garibaldi's Thousand landed in Sicily, Tuckerman attended a meeting in Newport, Rhode Island, on July 28, 1860, spoke in support of the Redshirts, and offered a resolution, unanimously adopted, by which "the present struggle for freedom

---

[72] Catharine Maria Sedgwick, *Letters from Abroad to Kindred at Home* (New York: Harper, 1841); "Miss Sedgwick's Letters from Abroad," *Southern Quarterly Review* 1 (1842): 183.

[73] Luciano J. Iorizzo and Salvatore Mondello, *The Italian Americans* (Youngstown, N.Y.: Cambria Press, 2006) 42 (first quote); Julia Ward Howe, *Reminiscences, 1819-1889* (Boston: Houghton Mifflin, 1910) 120, 206 (second quote 120).

[74] Joanne Pellegrino, "An Effective School of Patriotism," in *Studies in Italian American Social History: Essays in Honor of Leonard Covello*, ed. Francesco Cordasco (Totowa, N.J.: Rowman and Littlefiled, 1975) 101.

in Sicily deserves the earnest sympathy and practical encouragement of every friend of justice and humanity."[75]

This climate of opinion in favor of the Risorgimento in the United States had eventually negligible political consequences. Young America – a progressive wing of the Democratic Party led by Stephen Douglas, with whom Foresti was in contact thanks to his own friendship with the Segdwicks[76] – encouraged the U.S. government to intervene in the 1848 nationalistic upheavals in southern and central Europe to export the American values of democracy and republicanism to the Old World. In theory, such plans included a U.S. contribution to Italy's unification and independence. But the appeals of the Young Americans fell on deaf ears during both the Polk and the Taylor administrations and the U.S. government refrained itself from any involvement in the Italian political situation.[77]

Yet, the *Democratic Review* – the most authoritative mouthpiece of Young America – helped keep alive the glory of the Italian patriots in the United States. For instance, as late as 1852, in an article that reconstructed the events of the 1848 military campaigns in the peninsula, the journal celebrated "Italy rising from the sleep of ages" as well as a land that

---

[75] "Sympathy for Garibaldi," *New York Times*, August 9, 1860, 1.

[76] Edward L. Widmer, *Young America: The Flowering of Democracy in New York City* (New York: Oxford University Press, 1999) 58.

[77] Merle Curti, "Young America," *American Historical Review* 32 (1926): 34-55; Gemme, *Domesticating Foreign Struggles*, 72-82; Yonatan Eyal, *The Young America Movement and the Transformation of the Democratic Party, 1828-1861* (New York: Cambridge University Press, 2007) 93-115.

had "brought forth men worthy of the brightest times in her memorable annals."[78]

The spread of pro-Risorgimento feelings made it easier fund-raisings in American society for the military campaigns aiming at Italy's unification. This goal and the teaching of Italian were strictly intertwined. For instance, the chairperson of one of the two committees that collected funds for the 1860 expedition of Giuseppe Garibaldi's Thousand Redshirts – the Italian National Committee – was Vincenzo Botta, a former member of the Sardinian Parliament and Foresti's successor as professor of Italian at the University of the City of New York[79] Contributors comprised numerous Italophiles in the intellectual circles, including Longfellow and Lowell, who offered 125 lire each.[80] Longfellow's wife, Fanny Appleton, who had used to read Italian authors with Bachi, also came to think of Garibaldi as "a great hero."[81]

---

[78] "Monarchy and the Republic in Italy: Campaigns of Charles Albert and of the Republicans," *Democratic Review* 31 (1852): 195.

[79] Fucilla, *The Teaching of Italian in the United States*, 129-30; Maria Teresa Zagrebelsky Prat, "Botta, Vincenzo," in *Dizionario biografico degli italiani*, vol. 13 (Rome: Istituto della Enciclopedia Italiana, 1971) 379-80; Matteo Sanfilippo, "L'emigrazione italiana nelle Americhe in età preunitaria, 1815-1860," *Annali della Fondazione Luigi Einaudi* 42 (2008): 77-78

[80] Raymond Grew, *A Sterner Plan for Italian Unity: The Italian National Society in the Risorgimento* (Princeton, N.J.: Princeton University Press, 1963) 334-35.

[81] Fanny Appleton Longfellow to Samuel Longfellow, Cambridge, Mass., November 6, 1860, in *Mrs. Longfellow: Selected Letters and Journals of Fanny Appleton Longfellow (1817-1861)*, ed. Edward Wagenknecht (New York: Longmans, Green & Co., 1856) 228. For her readings with Bachi, see *Mrs. Longfellow*, 75.

"Lingua Esule"

The Risorgimento exiles arrived in the United States several decades before the beginning of mass immigration from their native land. Indeed, as few as 4,562 Italian newcomers settled in the country from 1820 to 1850. Consequently, only 3,679 Italians lived in the United States in 1850.[82]

However, although the Italian-American community was quite small in number, the teaching of Italian was an educational force to spread patriotic sentiments among immigrants from Italy, too. For example, until it was dissolved in 1848, the Congrega Centrale of the Giovine Italia operated two schools for the children of destitute Italian newcomers in New York City and Boston on the model of a similar institution that Mazzini had set up in London in 1841.[83] The purpose of these schools was to offer classes in standard Italian. One, however, can reasonably suggest that the ideals of the Risorgimento were taught along with the language as these schools also organized conferences on current events in Italy.[84] New York City's elementary school for the Italian youth of the Five Points district was likely to perform a similar task. Actually, although it was established by the Children Aid

---

[82] U.S. Bureau of the Census, *Historical Statistics of the United States, Colonial Times to 1957* (Washington, D.C.: U.S. Government Printing Office, 1960) 57.

[83] Joseph Rossi, *The Image of America in Mazzini's Writing* (Madison: University of Wisconsin Press, 1954) 24-25. For the Italian School in London, see Michele Finelli, *Il prezioso elemento: Mazzini e gli emigrati italiani nell'esperienza della Scuola Italiana di Londra* (Verrucchio: Pazzini, 1999).

[84] Donna R. Gabaccia, "Class, Exile, and Nationalism at Home and Abroad: The Italian Risorgimento," in *Italian Workers of the World: Labor Migration and the Formation of Multiethnic States*, ed. Donna R. Gabaccia and Fraser M. Ottanelli (Urbana: University of Illinois Press, 2001) 31.

Society – a non-ethnic organization – in 1855 and funded by E.P. Fabbri, an Italian partner of banker John Pierpont Morgan, it listed Vincenzo Botta among the personalities involved in its management.[85] After all, Botta was not only an advocate of the Risorgimento. He was also an education expert, who had initially moved to the United States in 1853 in order to study its school system.[86]

In conclusion, to the exiles of the Risorgimento who chose the United States as their adoptive country at different times in the first half of the nineteenth century, the teaching of Italian was not only a job to make a living. It also offered an opportunity to spread their patriotic ideals and to win supporters for the cause of Italy's independence and unification both in the Italian-American community and in U.S. society as a whole.

---

[85] Robert Ernst, *Immigrant Life in New York City, 1825-1863* (Syracuse, N.Y.: Syracuse University Press, 1994) 274; Frederick M. Binder and David M. Reimers, *All the Nations under Heaven: An Ethnic and Racial History of New York City* (New York: Columbia University Press, 1995) 51.
[86] Giovanni Battista Michelini, "Un italiano in America," *Rivista Contemporanea* 18 (1859): 173-99; Yael Razzoli, "Botta Vincenzo," in Fondazione Casa America, *I primi italiani in America del Nord: Dizionario biografico dei liguri, piemontesi e altri: Storie e presenze italiane tra Settecento e Ottocento*, ed. Chiara Vangelista (Reggio Emilia: Diabasis, 2009) 78-79.

WHAT ITALY GOT FOR HER TWENTY-FIRST BIRTHDAY

Sante Matteo
Miami University

The Kingdom of Italy turned twenty-one in 1882, along with the first generation born as Italian nationals in 1861, the first year of national unification. What did they get to commemorate their coming of age?

A few of them — males with at least two years of school — received precisely that: the status of "coming of age": i.e. statutory enfranchisement as full-fledged citizens, granted by the Depretis government which that very year lowered the voting age from twenty-five to twenty-one. For the purposes of this discussion, this could be seen as a "gift" that came wrapped with metaphorical strings; or more provocatively, with strings attached. The rights and privileges of national citizenship were tied to a corresponding set of responsibilities and obligations that, bundled together, served to bind the newly enfranchised citizens to their country, in the political and cultural endeavor to "make Italians."

But there were other "gifts," or memorable events: a talking puppet that went about without strings; the elaborate funeral and celebration of a national hero, who also refused to have strings on him, and thus came to be considered a pesky gadfly in some quarters; and a mass exodus of fellow "new" Italians, who rather than submit to the process of "being made" into Italians chose to cut the strings that held

From: *Theater of the Mind, Stage of History*. Bordighera Press, 2015

them in their new *patria* and seek a livelihood elsewhere. Metaphorically speaking, these other occurrences were characterized by missing or broken strings and severed ties: characteristic less of Italians in the making than of Italians unbound and unmade.

The puppet was Pinocchio, and the national hero, who for some became an irritating gadfly, was Giuseppe Garibaldi, who died in June of 1882, during the initial serial publication of the puppet's adventures. And both events, the appearance of the unstrung marionette and the death of the "Hero of Two Worlds," coincided with the surge of a massive wave of emigration that would see millions of Italians, as much as a third of the population, abandon their homeland over the next four decades.[1]

Pinocchio's song in Disney's animated film *Pinocchio* (1940), "I've Got No Strings,"[2] could just as well serve as the

---

[1] According to Gian Antonio Stella: "In 27 milioni se ne andarono, nel secolo del grande esodo dal 1876 al 1976" (As many as 27 million left during the century of the great exodus from 1876 to 1976), in *L'orda: quando gli albanesi eravamo noi*, p. 8.

[2] The lyrics allude to Pinocchio's anarchic desire to be free of paternal/familial restraints and societal rules and laws, but they could also be applied, albeit in a less boisterous and boastful vein, to the plight of the emigrant: Pinocchio: "I've got no strings / To hold me down / ... / I had strings / But now I'm free / There are no strings on me!"

In the film, at the end of Pinocchio's boast, puppets from foreign lands join in the song and dance, inviting him to join them, thus making the connection between migration and his condition of being 'unstrung' and not tied to his own customs and traditions more apparent:

> Dutch puppet: "You have no strings / Your arms is free / To love me by the Zuider Zee / Ya, ya, ya / If you would woo / I'd bust my strings for you"

"What Italy Got for Her Twenty-First Birthday"

theme song for the recalcitrant Garibaldi and for the emigrants who felt obliged to expatriate, instead of waiting to be "made into Italians." In their case the oft-cited quip: "We have made Italy! Now we must make Italians!" would be more apt if altered to: "We have made Italy! Now go away!"[3]

Were Italians "made" by Italy's twenty-first birthday? If not, would or could they still be made?

Making Italians and Puppets

During the 1881-82 biennium the adventures of a puppet named Pinocchio appeared serially in the *Giornale per i bam-*

>French puppet: "You've got no strings / . . . / I've got strings / But entre nous / I'd cut my strings for you"
>Russian puppet: "Down where the Volga flows / There's a Russian rendezvous / Where me and Ivan go / But I'd rather go with you, hey!"

"I've Got No Strings": Performed by: Pinocchio (*Dickie Jones*); Music: Leigh Harline; Lyrics: Ned Washington: http://www.fpx.de/fp/Disney/Lyrics/Pinocchio.html#I%27ve%20Got%20No%20Strings.

[3] The celebration of Italy's 150th Anniversary as a nation in 2011 led many to look back at the *Risorgimento,* the movement that led to the wars of independence and the struggle for unification, and to look back at the country's early years, when, in the oft-cited dictum attributed to Massimo D'Azeglio, Italy had been made and the next goal and struggle was to make Italians. D'Azeglio never actually wrote the expression in the way that it is usually cited. The closest he comes to expressing something similar is in the Preface to *I miei ricordi,* written in 1863, where he writes: "pur troppo s'è fatta l'Italia, ma non si fanno gl'Italiani" (unfortunately Italy has been made, but Italians are not being made), p. 5. The sentiment expressed is very different from the oft-repeated dictum. It is not an imperative or a call to action to make Italians, but rather a negative declaration that Italians have not been and are not being made. For the full quotation see note 14 below.

bini. The first fifteen weekly installments, titled *La storia di un burattino*, appeared between 17 July and 27 October 1881. The cycle ended with the death of the puppet, hanged from a tree by thieves: "He closed his eyes, opened his mouth, straightened his legs and, giving a great shudder, hung there as if frozen stiff."[4] The puppet comes to his end shortly after he is created, without ever becoming a "real boy."

If the creation of a puppet who comes to life and starts to explore the world around him is seen as analogous to the process of creating "Italians" out of an ill-defined, uneducated, and mostly illiterate populace that did not share the same language, history, or traditions, the implication seems to be that it was a short-lived experiment that ended in failure: if not an abortion, practically a stillbirth.

In what was meant to be the last chapter of the story, pursued by bandits, Pinocchio "saw amidst all the dark green of the trees, shining bright in the distance, a cottage as white as snow,"[5] and ran to it looking for salvation. Since he is made of wood, the trees represent his origin, and by extension a savage, uncivilized state, and the white house outside the forest represents his destination: society, civilization, civility. The house holds the promise of safety and comfort that the state of Italy might have held for the millions of poor, ignorant, oppressed people within its borders. But the girl with the blue hair who, after a long delay, finally opens an upstairs window in response to his desperate knocking refuses him entry into the house. She says that everyone in the

---

[4] Carlo Collodi, *The Adventures of Pinocchio*, trans. Ann Lawson Lucas (New York: Oxford University Press, 1996), 48.
[5] Ibid., 45.

house is dead, including her: "I am waiting for the bier to come and take me away."[6] Left outside the protective walls of the house, with all doors and windows shut to prevent his entry, Pinocchio is apprehended by the bandits and hanged from a tree, thus forced to return to his original state.

If one were to consider the house as an objective correlative for the Italian state, the implication would be that the state has not only failed the disenfranchised masses looking for protection, as represented by the hapless puppet, but that it has also failed the ruling class that dwells within the house, represented by the equally hapless girl with the waxen face and the blue hair. In this very pessimistic series of episodes that culminate in robbery and death, Collodi's implicit critique of the society that his puppet encounters resembles the disillusionment and the vitriolic criticism of the Italian monarchy that Garibaldi expressed in his post-unification writings, as we will see later.

But the death of the wooden creature and the failure of identity-formation it connotes were not to be final. The puppet would be resuscitated. Despite having put "Fine" (The End) at the end of the episode, the author, Carlo Lorenzini, using the pen-name Collodi, prompted by reader demand and the publisher's insistence, brought the puppet back to life and allowed him to embark on new adventures. The puppet's demise and rebirth thus echo the cycles of periodic reemergence that characterize Italian history: *Rinascimento, Risorgimento, Italia redenta* (Renaissance, Resurgence, Redeemed Italy).

---

[6] Ibid., 46.

The second series of installments, with the title changed to *Le avventure di Pinocchio*, consisted of an additional fourteen chapters (16-29 in today's numeration in the book[7]), published between 16 February and 1 June 1882. This cycle ends on a more positive note: Pinocchio keeps his word to study hard and to be good, indeed gaining "the distinction of being the best pupil in the school"[8]; the Fairy promises to make him a real boy on the morrow; and all his friends are invited for a sumptuous celebratory breakfast: "That day promised to be full of joy and gaiety; but . . ."[9] The narrative ends with a "but" followed by ellipsis that is in turn followed by this final authorial observation: "Unfortunately, in a puppet's life there are always *buts*, which spoil everything."[10]

And, one might add, there might occasionally also be something in the *author*'s life that can "spoil" things. After this installment there is another hiatus, of almost half a year, before the story is picked up again. The last seven chapters, 30-36 (11-18 in the serial numeration), appeared between 23 November 1882 and 25 January 1883.

In these final episodes Pinocchio runs away to the Land of Toys with Candlewick, turns into a donkey, is swallowed

---

[7] In the magazine they were numbered *ex novo*, I-X, published in eleven installments. For an account of the publication chronology see pp. 68-69 in the Feltrinelli edition of *Pinocchio*, edited by Fernando Tempesti and with an extensive introduction and commentary by him, "Chi era il Collodi / Com'è fatto Pinocchio," pp. 7-138.
[8] Collodi, *Pinocchio*, trans. Lucas, 116.
[9] Ibid., 117.
[10] For the English translation see p. 117; For the Italian see, "Disgraziatamente, nella vita dei burattini c'è sempre un ma che sciupa ogni cosa," 238.

by a monstrous shark, in whose stomach he finds Geppetto, swims home with his 'father' on his back, and is finally turned into a real boy, in what is now a well-to-do, flourishing home, thanks to his conversion, not so much from a puppet to a child, but from a bad boy to a good one: "Because," as Geppetto explains, "when naughty children become good, they have the power to bring about a happy transformation at home for all their family."[11] A possible lesson to be derived from this conclusion seems to be that if Italian children follow Pinocchio's example and become obedient, studious, conscientious, and altruistic, Italy, the "home of all their family," will also become industrious, prosperous, and content. If so, then the narrative might be read as a manual for Italian children on how to become good citizens, or as a user's guide on how to "make Italians."

But why did it take another eight months and more disobedience, deception, and betrayals by Pinocchio to reach a point that he had apparently already reached in the installment of 1 June? At that point too he had apparently learned his lesson and had been successfully converted, not yet to a real boy but at least to the behavior expected of a good boy, not only promising to behave better, as he had done before to little avail, but actually succeeding in doing so: "Pinocchio promised and swore that he would study hard, and that he'd always be good. And he kept his word for the whole rest of the year. Indeed, in the annual examinations he had the distinction of being the best pupil in the school. Also his conduct in general was judged to be so satisfactory and commendable that the delighted Fairy said to him,

---

[11] Ibid., 169.

'Tomorrow, at last, ... you will cease to be a wooden puppet, and you'll become a real, good boy."[12] A possible answer is that the author and the publisher wanted to milk the story for all it was worth by extending the installments for as many issues as possible, and that Collodi needed the time to come up with other ideas for adventures.

It is intriguing to note, nevertheless, that the second interruption of the serial publication, suspended after the installment of 1 June 1882, coincides precisely with the death of Garibaldi, on 2 June. Carlo Lorenzini had been a "Garibaldino" of sorts. He had volunteered and fought in the First War of Independence in 1848 and then again in the Second in 1859.[13] It is possible therefore that he was indeed particularly stricken by the General's death. Having also shared Garibaldi's republican and anti-clerical ideals, and in sympathy with the Hero's harsh criticisms of the new Kingdom, it is likely that he continued to be concerned about such issues and that he projected those thoughts and concerns into his writing, including the adventures of Pinocchio.

Upon the death of the figure who had become the very face of the *Risorgimento*, its most widely recognized icon throughout the world, Lorenzini and others who had participated in the struggle for independence and unification would naturally pause to reminisce and to take stock of the results: to ponder what had been gained and what had been lost during and after the wars; what had died with Garibaldi

---

[12] Ibid., 116.
[13] See pp. xii-xiii, xvi-xvii in Ann Lawson Lucas's "Introduction" to her translation of *The Adventures of Pinocchio* and her useful "Chronology of Carlo Collodi" on pp. lvi-lix.

"What Italy Got for Her Twenty-First Birthday"

and what still survived. The final episodes of Pinocchio that followed later that year might thus be informed by these reflections and concerns.

The narrative of Pinocchio's picaresque adventures, even after the episodes were compiled and published as a book in February 1883, only a month after the last serial installment, is too unstructured and anarchic to be read as a straightforward allegory. Collodi seemed to be making it up helter-skelter as he went along, without a pre-conceived plan, theme, or narrative arc, and with no apparent concern for consistency or coherence, whether narrative or logical. Nevertheless, or perhaps precisely because of the loose structure of the text, many of the episodes can be read as metaphorically addressing social and political issues that were being debated in the new nation: such as poverty, class differences, labor, laws, crime, justice, education, and religion. In other words, the process of transforming an unformed piece of wood into a puppet with a boy's features and then into a real boy with a distinct personal identity can be seen as analogous to the national project of transforming the heterogeneous, disconnected population of the Italian peninsula into a unified citizenry, into real "Italians" with a distinct national identity.

After Geppetto has crafted him, Pinocchio is essentially made and is practically whole, as was Italy after the wars of independence. His various parts are joined together into a unified, articulated body, as are those of the new nation. But his character is not yet made, or is not yet fixed and constant. His civic conscience and respect of the rule of law cannot be crafted artificially, by decree or legislation, but must be acquired through experience, education, and acculturation. It is precisely the issue of character that D'Azeglio stresses when he addresses the problem of creating Italians:

> For about half a century Italy has been moving, struggling to become one people and to make itself into a nation. For the most part it has regained its territory. The struggle with foreigners has been successful, but this is not the major difficulty. The major difficulty, the real one, that which keeps everything in doubt, in suspension, is the internal struggle. The most dangerous enemies of Italy are not the Austrians; they are the Italians. . . .
>
> Italians . . . think to reform Italy, and no one realizes that to succeed it is necessary, first of all, that they be reformed themselves, because Italy . . . cannot become a nation . . . until . . . [everyone] does his duty . . . . But to perform one's duty . . . one needs strength of will and a conviction that duty must be fulfilled not because it is enjoyable or rewarding, but simply because it is a duty; and this strength of will, this conviction, is that precious gift that in a word is called *character*; hence, to put it simply, the primary need of Italy is that Italians be created who know how to fulfill their duty. . . . [U]nfortunately Italy has been created, but not Italians.[14]

---

[14] Translation is mine, emphasis in the original. Carlo Collodi, *Pinocchio*, ed. Fernando Tempesti (Milan: Feltrinelli, 1972), 4-5. Here is the quotation in its entirety, including the sections elided and marked with elliptical points [. . .] in the translation above. The elided passages are in italics:

"L'Italia da circa mezzo secolo s'agita, si travaglia per divenire un sol popolo e farsi nazione. Ha riacquistato il suo territorio in gran parte. La lotta collo straniero è portata a buon porto, ma non è questa la difficoltà maggiore. La maggiore, la vera, quella che mantiene tutto incerto, tutto in forse, è la lotta interna. I piú pericolosi nemici d'Italia non sono gli

"What Italy Got for Her Twenty-First Birthday"

As he explores his new world Pinocchio learns what this new state in an old land is like and tries to understand how he can fit into it. In his explorations and misadventures he encounters characters and conditions that embody diverse political ideologies and economic systems, which could serve as possible models of how to create a society or as negative *exempla* of socio-economic-political systems that have failed or are likely to fail, or that should fail: systems, customs, and conditions to avoid. His adventures can thus be read as explorations of the problems and needs that the new nation is facing, the conditions and beliefs of its inhabitants, and various ways in which Italy and Italians can (or cannot) be "made." As such it can be read as a kind of manual on how to make Italians, or perhaps more accurately, an advisory on how not to make Italians, or more in

---

Austriaci, sono gl'Italiani. / *"E perché? /* "Per la ragione che gl'Italiani *hanno voluto far un'Italia nuova, e loro rimanere gl'Italiani vecchi di prima, colle dappocaggini e le miserie morali che furono ab antico il loro retaggio; perché* pensano a riformare l'Italia, e nessuno s'accorge che per riuscirci bisogna, prima, che si riformino loro, perché l'Italia, *come tutt'i popoli,* non potrà divenir nazione, *non potrà esser ordinata, ben amministrata, forte cosí contro lo straniero, come contro i settari dell'interno, libera e di propria ragione,* finché *grandi e piccoli e mezzani,* ognuno *nella sua sfera* non faccia il suo dovere, e non lo faccia bene, od almeno il meglio che può. Ma a fare il proprio dovere, *il piú delle volte fastidioso, volgare, ignorato,* ci vuol forza di volontà e persuasione che il dovere si deve adempiere non perché diverte o frutta, ma perché è dovere; e questa forza di volontà, questa persuasione, è quella preziosa dote che con un solo vocabolo si chiama *carattere,* onde, per dirla in una parola sola, il primo bisogno d'Italia è che si formino Italiani che sappiano adempiere al proprio dovere. *E pur troppo si va ogni giorno piú verso il polo opposto:* pur troppo s'è fatta l'Italia, ma non si fanno gl'Italiani." ("Prefazione," *I miei ricordi,* pp. 4-5)

consonance with D'Azeglio's actual assertion, an account of what is preventing Italians from being made.

Read in this key, the Cricket, for example, could represent acquired, traditional, or "choral" wisdom: conventional beliefs so ingrained in a community as to seem "natural": the knowledge contained in proverbs, customs, and popular traditions: those beliefs that are taken for granted, passed down from generation to generation, indoctrinated into the young by elders, so as to become dogmatic and unquestioned, as if nature itself is speaking to us — in this particular case through one of its noisiest and most repetitive, insistent, ubiquitous creatures.

The puppet theater run by Mangiafoco (fire-eater) might stand for one of the possible forms of government that a new nation could adopt: despotism or dictatorship. The puppet master can be seen as an analog for an all-powerful ruler: a wielder of absolute, pre-ordained power who pulls all the strings to which his subjects must dance. His power is unchecked and arbitrary. He can be cruel or compassionate, may kill or save whomever he wants, or hand out unmerited punishments or benefits, on whim or fancy.

By extension the puppet theater over which he rules can also represent a monarchy, the system of governance opposed by Mazzini and Garibaldi but ultimately adopted by the new Kingdom of Italy under King Victor Emanuel II. The puppet theater, to which Pinocchio is initially attracted only to end up in mortal danger of extinction, can be seen as an analogy of how despotism functions and as a warning to Italians of the dangers it poses to those subjects who allow themselves to become puppets of a dictator's strings.[15]

Geppetto is the product and the emblem of an economic system based on class and economic distinctions. He is a member of the poor working class of the community: disenfranchised from power but not excluded from the common weal. Indeed, the poor are a necessary segment of this society. When Mangiafoco asks what Geppetto's trade is, Pinocchio answers, "il povero," a poor man, a pauper. Pinocchio uses the word "*povero*/poor" as a noun, not as an adjective, thus presenting poverty as a category that denotes one of the normal occupations, professions, or lines of work that exist in this society. The implication is that poverty, the trade of a poor man (*il povero*), is a permanent social structure, a common and accepted category for people to occupy, an occupation perceived by the community as a "natural" option, accepted as such even by those whose lot it is to belong to the lot of the poor.

In chapter 19, near the beginning of the second cycle of episodes, after Pinocchio has been brought back to life, he again falls prey to the Fox and the Cat, who swindle and rob him. Pinocchio is arrested and taken to court, where the Judge condemns him to jail for having been the victim of a crime. Behind the seeming absurdity of this turn of events is the suggestion that the legal system is contrived to benefit those who make and enforce the laws: the ruling class, the

---

[15] Strings, one could add, that four decades later another Mangiafoco-like incarnation, *Il Duce* Benito Mussolini, would learn to control with great dexterity; hence a warning that proved to be both prescient and wasted — as oracles and prophecies often are in myths and stories, in which they are typically misunderstood or ignored.

small percentage of the population who were enfranchised to vote at the time, because they were literate and possessed property. The poor and disenfranchised are those who end up populating the prisons. Like the impoverished puppet, they too are victimized twice: first by the society's economic system that relegates them to the status of have-nots, and then again by that society's system of justice devised to protect the status quo and the interests of the wealthy and powerful. Thus it is not what befalls Pinocchio in Collodi's narrative that is outrageous, but the legal system that the episode adumbrates and mocks.[16]

The Field of Miracles, presented by the Fox and the Cat as a place to multiply one's money, seems to describe a stock market and is analogous to Wall Street, but with a name and image more appropriate for an agricultural society. What they are describing and pitching to Pinocchio is a capitalist economic system: "you can sow your four coins . . .; after a few minutes you'll be able to pick up two thousand, and this evening you'll be back with your pockets full."[17]

The encounter with the mastiff Alidoro, on the other hand, alludes to a system of mutual aid, or a kind of communism. At the end of chapter 27 the dog is sent after Pinocchio by

---

[16] More disturbing cases of the blame-and-punish-the-victim syndrome are those that continue to occur in communities that jail rape victims for adultery or bring charges of vagrancy against homeless people who have been robbed or beaten. The unfairness of such laws and of such "justice" may not be apparent when one reads or hears about them in the news media. It is through the satirical lens of texts such Swift's *Gulliver's Travels* and Collodi's *Pinocchio* that the absurdity and the unfairness of such conditions and behavior are made manifest.

[17] Collodi, *Pinocchio*, trans. Lucas, 61.

the police when the puppet tries to escape arrest. However, in the next chapter, having reached the sea, where the marionette floats but the dog sinks, Pinocchio ends up saving Alidoro, who then tells him: "You've done me a great service, and, in this world, what is given is returned."[18] Once they've reached the sea, outside the confines of their land or country, the laws of society and their assigned roles as prisoner and guard no longer apply, or have no solid foundation, and they resort to a populist-based system of reciprocity that could also serve as the basis for the socialist and anarchist ideas circulating at the time.

And what of the Blue Fairy who makes her appearance in the second set of episodes and proceeds to play a very prominent role in controlling and shaping the events and the outcome of the story? As a figure in the project of "making Italians" she could bear various messages. For example, she could stand for the missing mother figure who is outwardly assigned a secondary role in the commonplace assertions and rituals of a patriarchal society, but who actually wields substantial control and authority within the home and in the sphere of rearing children and future generations. In fact in the book she ends up being more knowledgeable, more resourceful, and more powerful than Geppetto, the father figure. Initially, she is absent from the text, which very absence could betoken a similar absence of female protagonists missing from the political stage of Italian history. Her appearance as a sort of *dea ex machina* is thus a "correction" within the text that proposes a similar correction to society, suggesting that women

---

[18] My translation of "Tu m'hai fatto un gran servizio: e in questo mondo quel che è fatto è reso," (*Pinocchio*, p. 230).

must play a more prominent and visible role in the public arena.

She could also be seen as an emblem of the powerful force of folklore with deep roots in the various regions of the new country: sets of beliefs and practices that conditioned people to believe in magical thinking and superstitions to resolve all problems or to accept them passively and fatalistically as dictated by forces beyond their control. Along this line of reasoning, she might serve as the equivalent of a religious agent, akin to a patron saint or a guardian angel, who can intervene with the Almighty on the supplicant's behalf. By extension, she could even embody the benign face of the "familism" and "clientelism" that are often attributed to Italian society as forms of corruption: the tendency to rely on sponsorship rather than merit, to seek a recommendation from someone with the authority to intercede on an applicant's behalf. Such behavior in other social spheres replicates the practices and rites of Catholicism as widely practiced in Italy, in which mediation is fundamental: to seek a solution or a cure one seldom petitions God directly, but rather appeals to an intermediary, be it one's patron saint, or the saint "in charge" of the particular malady or difficulty in question, or to Mary, the mother figure *par excellence*.[19]

One of the best known episodes in various versions of *Pinocchio* is his excursion to the *Paese dei Balocchi*, the Land of

---

[19] As an enabling intermediary, the Blue Fairy might even be viewed as a descendant of Dante's Beatrice, that is, as a spur and a guide for the journey toward "salvation," in religious terms, and by analogy, in sociopsychological terms, for the journey toward self-fulfillment, insofar as she makes Pinocchio want to become a "real boy" and makes it possible for him to achieve that goal.

"What Italy Got for Her Twenty-First Birthday"

Toys. In chapter 29 Pinocchio goes back to the Fairy's house, and she promises to turn him into a real boy the next day. Instead, lured by the promise of an easy life of leisure and pleasure, Pinocchio leaves for this "promised land," where he does not have to go to school or to work for his rewards or to obey rules. And once there, he does not in fact go to school and does not thereby further his education. Instead he ends up being turned into a beast of burden, a donkey.

What real-life experience can this episode evoke? Where was it that many Italians were indeed being lured with similar promises of bounty and ease, only to find upon arrival that living and working conditions were in many cases worse than those they had left behind? Was it not *l'America*, or *la Merica*, or *Lamerica* (as Gianni Amelio transcribes it in his 1994 movie), where "America" stands for any destination outside of Italy that offered or seemed to offer better opportunities and conditions of life, but in fact turned many of those who went there into exploited, unskilled manual laborers, or little more than beasts of burden? If we see in the Land of Toys an analog of the Italian emigrants' "promised land," Collodi's depiction of it may be read as a warning about the possible dangerous consequences of the lure of emigration that was rapidly and massively developing at the time and that over the following four decades would produce one of the largest waves of migration in history.

The subsequent episode in the sea, where Pinocchio is swallowed by a monstrous fish, to find that Geppetto had himself been swallowed up some time before, might also serve as an allusion to the dangers of setting out on the sea for other shores.[20] Even if they survive the sea voyage, emigrants may end up being swallowed up within foreign communities and institutions, the equivalent of monstrous organisms that are strange to them and that treat them like invading foreign bodies to devour and then to consume or to expel. Those who, like Pinocchio, choose to cut their strings from their original moorings in the desire to find better living conditions elsewhere with little or no preparation risk facing the unknown and being overwhelmed by it.

Some, if not all, of Pinocchio's adventures may thus be read as parables of possible ways to forge the diverse population of the Italian peninsula into "Italians." The very first words of the narrative suggest as much: "Once upon a time there was . . . 'A king!' my little readers will say straight away. No, children, you are mistaken. Once upon a time there was a piece of wood."[21] Pinocchio starts out as an inert yet organic entity that is designed, carved, and animated — or re-animated, since wood was once alive — into new life. He is, to some extent, emblematic of the Italian populace that is starting to assume a new national identity, and as such he also conveys the notion of an *Italia irredenta* (unredeemed Italy), a dormant body with a pre-existing organic unity, whose resuscitation and animation correspond to a kind of resurgence, or *risorgimento*.

The book seems to end with an uplifting, socially acceptable resolution: Pinocchio, having learned the values and codes of correct behavior of his community and having be-

---

[20] The last monthly story, "Il naufragio" (the shipwreck), in the novel *Cuore*, addresses the same issue, albeit in a more direct and realistic manner.
[21] Collodi, *Pinocchio*, trans. Lucas, 1. (Ellipsis in original).

come a real boy, goes to school to further his education and presumably eventually to become a good citizen and a valuable member of society. Nevertheless, because of the episodic structure of the narrative, it is difficult to say if this is the final and definitive resolution or if it is instead only the last in a series of similar resolutions that have reoccurred throughout the narration, each time to be violated shortly afterwards. Indeed, after practically each episode in the book Pinocchio claims to have learned his lesson and vows to reform. Repeatedly he lists all the things he did wrong and resolves never to do them again, only to rebel again as soon as another opportunity presents itself. With that setup, is there any reason to think that it will be different this time? Will Pinocchio remain a "real boy"? Have the Italians he embodies "been made"?

The Hero of the Two Worlds vs. The King of One Nation

The year of Italy's coming-of-age, when Pinocchio came on the scene, when Garibaldi died, and when a great many Italians emigrated, is when Edmondo DeAmicis's novel *Cuore* (heart) takes place: the school year from October, 1881, to July, 1882. Divided into chapters that correspond to the months of the school year, the book consists primarily of diary entries by Enrico, a fourth-grade elementary student from a bourgeois family in Torino. The first diary entry, recounting the first day of school, is dated 17 October (1881). The last entry, dated 10 July (1882), recounts the last meeting of the class to find out the results of the final exam and to say farewell to each other. Interspersed among Enrico's accounts of events at school and descriptions of his teachers and classmates, there are occasional letters and notes written to Enrico by his father and a few from his mother. For each month there is also a transcription of a short story read to the class by the teacher to exemplify and inculcate such personal and social virtues as loyalty, justice, patriotism, altruism, and self-sacrifice.[22]

The book, planned by the author and announced by the publisher Treves in 1878, was finally published on the first day of the school year, 15 October, 1886.[23] Setting it five years earlier, in 1881-82, allows the narrative to conclude with a dramatic historical event of profound national significance. The penultimate chapter, June, the last month of classes, begins with a letter from Enrico's father: "3 June. Tomorrow is a national holiday. / Today is a day of national mourning. Yesterday evening Garibaldi died."[24]

---

[22] As canonical as the entire book became in Italian schools, several of these stories took on an editorial life of their own by being published separately and anthologized in elementary-school textbooks: "Il piccolo patriotta padovano," "La piccola vedetta lombarda," "Il piccolo scrivano fiorentino," "Il tamburino sardo," "L'infermiere di Tata," "Sangue romagnolo," "Valor civile," "Dagli Appennini alle Ande," and "Naufragio." As the titles themselves indicate, themes include patriotism, self-sacrifice, and civic virtues, and the young protagonists to be admired and emulated represent various regions of the new country: Venetia, Lombardy, Tuscany, Sardinia, Campania, Sicily. The last two stories are among the few texts in canonical Italian literature that address the phenomenon of emigration.

[23] This date would have coincided with Italy's and the first generation of Italians' coming of age, if electoral laws had not been changed in 1882 to make the age of majority, or the voting age, twenty-one. Before then it was twenty-five.

[24] My translation. Collodi, *Pinocchio*, ed. Tempesti, 223; "Giugno / 3, sabato / Domani è la festa nazionale. / Oggi è lutto nazionale. Ieri sera è morto Garibaldi."

"What Italy Got for Her Twenty-First Birthday"

The upcoming national holiday that the father announces — which ended up being postponed to the following week because of Garibaldi's funeral — was a commemoration of the *Statuto albertino*, the adoption by King Carlo Alberto of Savoy of a constitution and a Parliament in 1848 to limit the power of the monarchy and introduce elements of a representative democracy. This celebration of an embryonic stage of nationhood coincided with the death of a great founding father of the nation. Thus in the very middle of Italy's twenty-first year Enrico and Italians in general are called upon to celebrate and to mourn at the same time. And the figure that prompts and anchors this double injunction is Giuseppe Garibaldi, ever more aptly named the "Hero of Two Worlds," in this case the ideal world and the real one.

Even in death Garibaldi manages both to support and to disrupt and challenge the monarchy, as he had done in life. At the same time, the Monarchy manages both to defy or ignore his demands and expectations and to exploit his image for their own purposes. The Kingdom ignored his wishes that there be no public funeral for him and instead put on a grand spectacle to celebrate the greatest Hero of the *Risorgimento*, and by so doing to endorse the results of the wars of independence — a unified Kingdom ruled by the House of Savoy.

The relationship between the Hero and the King had always been a problematic one, consisting of conflicts and accommodations. Garibaldi was a Mazzinian Republican, opposed to the aristocracy and the clergy. But he was also a nationalist who sought the unification of Italy as a nation state and who perceived the King of Sardinia and Piedmont as a figurehead who could serve to unite the people of the various states that existed on the peninsula. When at Teano, near Naples, on 26 October 1860, he ceded to Victor Emanuel II of Savoy the land in the South conquered from the Bourbons by his Red Shirts, greeting the monarch as "King of Italy," he sacrificed his republican ideals for the sake of national unification. But he did not abandon them altogether. For the rest of his life, as a parliamentarian, as a speaker, as an indefatigable and prolific writer of letters, and even as a novelist and a poet, he criticized the monarchy, attacked the Catholic Church, and expressed his disappointment at how the new state was governed. He became a highly visible gadfly who, as a world-famous hero of South American rebellions and of Italian independence and unification, had to be recognized and celebrated by the government, but whose criticism had to be muted. Put up on pedestals throughout the country, with piazzas and boulevards named after him in practically every city and town, as a living person he was practically banished from the new nation he had collaborated to create, confined to his private island of Caprera, off the northeast coast of Sardinia.

During the *Risorgimento*, and even more significantly in its aftermath, when Italy had been created but Italians still had to be formed, Victor Emanuel II, the first King of Italy, came to be an incarnation of the ideals of heredity, lineage, continuity, and permanence. In an iconic image of the four "founding fathers" of the Italian nation, he is depicted as standing directly under the statue of the Capitoline she-wolf nursing Romulus and Remus, with Prime Minister Cavour near his side, while the republicans, Giuseppe Mazzini and

Giuseppe Garibaldi, stand to either side, marginalized.[25] The suggestion is that the King is the natural descendant of Rome's founders and rulers and the legitimate executor of Roman power. And yet, though marginalized, the advocates of a different kind of state, a republic, are still in the picture. The alternative has not been completely eliminated from the picture.

The possibility of a national identity based on difference and hybridity, on cultural memes imported from elsewhere,[26]

---

[25] The image is reproduced at the end of Montanelli's and Nozza's *Garibaldi: Ritratto dell'Eroe dei due Mondi*, on p. 596.

[26] Richard Dawkins coined and defined the term "meme" in the last chapter of his 1976 book, *The Selfish Gene*, suggesting that it is the cultural analog of the biological gene, a self-replicator:

> "I think that a new kind of replicator has recently emerged on this very planet. . . . It is still in its infancy, still drifting clumsily about in its primeval soup, but already it is achieving evolutionary change at a rate that leaves the old gene panting far behind. / The new soup is the soup of human culture. We need a name for the new replicator, a noun that conveys the idea of a unit of cultural transmission, or a unit of *imitation*. 'Mimeme' comes from a suitable Greek root, but I want a monosyllable that sounds a bit like 'gene'. I hope my classicist friends will forgive me if I abbreviate mimeme to *meme*. If it is any consolation, it could alternatively be thought of as being related to 'memory', or to the French word *même*. It should be pronounced to rhyme with 'cream'.
>
> Examples of memes are tunes, ideas, catch-phrases, clothes fashions, ways of making pots or of building arches. Just as genes propagate themselves in the gene pool by leaping from body to body via sperms or eggs, so memes propagate themselves in the meme pool by leaping from brain to brain via

is embodied most forcefully and most colorfully in the figure of Giuseppe Garibaldi (Nice, 1807-Caprera, 1882), a sailor, soldier, sometime-pirate, teacher, migrant, international proto-pop star, perennial revolutionary, consummate general, and also a founding leader of the International Peace Conference (1867) and subsequent Pacifist Movement: a world traveler who subsequently introduced international and trans-cultural ingredients into the mix from which a new Italian identity could be forged.

Anti-despotic, anti-slavery, and anti-imperialist, he led volunteer militias in successful wars of liberation in South America and Italy, and came to be known and admired worldwide as the "Hero of Two Worlds." He was French, Italian, Brazilian, Uruguayan: a man of many countries and without a country. He lived and fought in many places and spoke and wrote in many languages.

After he helped to create Italy, Garibaldi in a sense became homeless and an expatriate, because his hometown Nizza (Nice) had been ceded to France,[27] and he chose to

---

a process which, in the broad sense, can be called imitation" (193).

[27] So had Savoia, the city that was homonymous with and was the original home of the royal House of Savoy of the new Italian Monarchy. Thus, Victor Emanuel II, in order to become King of Italy, also ceded his House's own place of origin to France. The fact that he and his Prime Minister, Camillo Benso di Cavour, the other "Founding Father" of the Italian nation, as inhabitants of the Duchy of Savoy, which later became the Kingdom of Sardinia, spoke French both at home and at court, mitigates my argument that they represent a linear, vertical, autochthonous, "rooted" Italian identity, whereas Garibaldi represents a scattered, horizontal, hybrid, "sporadic" identity. Even so, it reinforces the claim that at its very foundation Italy had a split personality, and that

remove himself to his private island, Caprera, situated off the north-east coast of Sardinia, near Corsica: a sort of self-exile to the periphery of national borders that was symbolic of his marginalization, and that of his republican, egalitarian, populist ideals, within the new political and social regime — monarchical, aristocratic, hieratical — that his military conquests had made possible, but from which he was now alienated. He wrote extensively — letters, speeches, proclamations, poems, and novels — to try to rectify the situation and to set the record straight by retelling the events of the *Risorgimento* from his perspective and expressing his republican, anti-clerical beliefs for a new generation. But if he had cause to protest against the new status quo, so did those in power have cause to fear his protests and to try to silence him. He was too popular, both nationally and internationally, to be sequestered in a dungeon or exiled or attacked and vilified directly. So, he was placed high up on a public and historical pedestal instead, immersed in the heroic, epic rhetoric of the *Risorgimento*, where he could be seen by all but no longer heard, because he was already tethered to the glories of the past rather than to the miseries of the present.

Still, the marginality that he represented, the hybridity he embodied as the "Hero of Two Worlds," his polyglotism, his exotic dress in the guise of a *gaucho* from the South American pampas, his perpetual crossing or violation of accepted

---

the process of "making Italians" was a difficult one, and possibly one that was prone to be superficial and somewhat theatrical: based on language, rhetoric, and iconography: essentially a pretense to be something that one is not, through the adoption of a language different from one's own dialect spoken at home and a collective history that does not pertain strictly to one's local experience and culture.

borders, be they geographical, national, linguistic, or sartorial — or even matrimonial, given his various liaisons with women of diverse origins and social stations — presented a model for a possible new Italian identity that could not be completely erased. As the face of Italy is once again changing today, with the influx of immigrants from all over the world, the somewhat exotic, hybrid figure of Garibaldi as border-crosser par excellence may yet find a new resonance among the next generation of Italians, or of Europeans. The old rebel without a pause might yet be enlisted in a new cause.

How to Make Italians: Morphing vs. Cloning

And perhaps so can *Pinocchio*. Pinocchio's transformation from rebellious puppet to obedient, well mannered boy is not an evolution but a doubling, not a morphing but a cloning. At the end of the book the flesh-and-blood boy has appeared and has stepped in for the puppet, which has been cast aside but is still present, there for the boy Pinocchio to see, to recall, and ultimately to disown and reject: "How funny I was when I was a puppet! And how happy I am now to have become a proper boy!"[28] Inert but intact, the erstwhile rebellious and anarchic puppet remains as a potential doppelganger that will continue to shadow the young new "Italian" who has supposedly learned his lesson and has finally become a good, obedient son, and is set on a path to become a dutiful, law-abiding citizen of the new nation state.

Roberto Benigni captures this underlying and persistent dichotomy at the very end of his movie *Pinocchio* (2002) by making the shadow cast by Pinocchio the real-life boy

---

[28] Collodi, *Pinocchio*, trans. Lucas, 170.

resemble the figure of Pinocchio the puppet. As the boy Pinocchio goes to school, hatless and with books tucked under his arm, the shadow he casts on the wall is wearing the cone-like "dunce" cap always worn by the puppet. When Pinocchio the boy reaches the school house and goes in carrying his books, the shadow on the wall, bookless and dunce-capped, remains outside and begins to chase a butterfly through the streets and then out into the countryside, in the same old spirit of anarchical, 'there are no strings on me!' rebelliousness, that characterized his behavior throughout the narrative.

The blue butterfly he chases is the same one that set the whole story in motion at the beginning of the film by upending a cart laden with wood and causing a log to carom wildly through the town, causing chaos and excitement, until it comes to rest at Geppetto's door. A butterfly represents metamorphosis and is proof that an organism can have very different identities at different stages of its life (larva, caterpillar, cocooned chrysalis, fabulously winged being). In this context it is emblematic of the instability of Italian identity, an instability that is further accentuated in the butterfly's fluttering, non-linear flight.

Pinocchio, insofar as he represents the newly formed generation of Italians that came of age when he himself came to life, has a split personality: the good boy who has been indoctrinated with the bourgeois values of the new country, meant to promote the interests of the ruling class, and the rebellious puppet who refuses to have any strings on him to control his mind and body. This same split personality seems to persist in stereotypes commonly attributed to Italians in general: *Italiani brava gente*, kind, hospitable, warm, generous;

but also scofflaws who avoid following rules, obeying laws, or paying taxes whenever it is not in their interest to do so: and somehow endearing in both guises.

That discarded puppet is a little like the ubiquitous presence of Garibaldi, whose image became the emblem of the *Risorgimento* but whose rebellious, non-conformist voice was similarly muted, replaced by a more conformist voice-over. His image and memory were placed on a high pedestal in order to make him visible as a national hero and the symbol of the success of the *Risorgimento*, but also to deflect and hide his nagging criticism of the monarchy, the clergy, capitalism, and the bourgeoisie that had taken control of the country he had helped to bring about. But like that "funny" puppet lying askew on a chair in Geppetto's house, the memory of Garibaldi as perennial rebel also continues to shadow the Italian imagination, keeping notions of rebellion and hybridity on the shelves of the national psyche as available ingredients in recipes for making Italians.

Swinging on the Pendulum

Returning to the string metaphor and to the quotation from the song in Walt Disney's *Pinocchio*, let us reconsider what Pinocchio's string-less nature connotes in light of the nation-building process. In the Disney cartoon, after singing his song in the puppet theater, Pinocchio is followed on the stage by puppets of different nationalities — Dutch, French, Russian — who continue singing and dancing to the same song. Unlike him, however, all of them do have strings on them. They also perform chorally, dancing and singing in step with their fellow puppets, dressed in similar costumes. The implication is that they are tied or bound to established

"What Italy Got for Her Twenty-First Birthday"

national identities that define and control them, whereas Pinocchio, alone and unstrung, has no such ties to uphold or to restrict him. He is different from them because he is a free agent: free to stumble and fall, as he does at the beginning and the end of his performance, since he does not have strings to hold him up, and free to roam about when and where he wants, since he has no strings to restrict his movements; with nothing to confine him, but nothing to support him either.

At the end of the scene, when Pinocchio tries to imitate the gyrating Russian dancers, he ends up swirling into their midst and causes all their strings to get tangled, ending up dangling among them in a cluster of no-longer-operable puppets. His function as a rogue, anarchic free agent has disrupted their customary routine and has rendered them defunct, as puppets and as representatives of their respective national cultures. Analogously, Pinocchio's lack of a national identity, suggested by the fact that he has no strings and no accent in his speech, whether it is due to a failure to obtain such an identity or to a refusal to adopt one, disrupts the nationalism of the other puppets. On the other hand, his own individual freedom, unfettered by nationalist attributes or constraints, is compromised and altered by their example of coordinated, scripted chorality, as he attempts to imitate their movements and ends up taking on some of their characteristics.

When the bundle of tangled puppets is pulled up, he falls down to the stage floor and once again gets his nose stuck in a knot-hole in one of the planks, as happened near the beginning of his act. Simultaneously one of the hats from the removed Russian puppets falls on his head. When he tries to yank his nose out of the hole, as he had managed to do earlier, he breaks off part of the plank instead, so that it dangles from his face, resembling the uniform beards sported by the Russian puppets. Donning one of their hats on his head and adorning his face with something that looks like their beards, he ends up resembling and replacing the puppets that he has inadvertently forced off the stage because he was so different from them and could not successfully join in their chorus and their dance. After the catastrophic mix-up, the difference between them, the nation-less and the nationalists, has been reduced. He still has no strings on him, but now perhaps he is in a position to perceive the value of having strings that tie one to a community, to a set of traditions and customs, and possibly even to desire a shared language and history, or what can also be termed a Romantic notion of nation.

There are two opposite forces at play in this scene and in the Pinocchio story in general: a centrifugal impulse to "have no strings," to break the bonds that restrict one's agency and confine one's identity, and the countervailing centripetal impulse to remain home-bound, within a familiar context that can give individuals a sense of coherence and continuity, both an individual and a collective identity.

These opposite and countervailing forces also characterize the conflicting aims of the *Risorgimento*: independence and unification. Independence means severing strings. Unification entails tying strings. Conceptually the two goals would appear to be mutually exclusive: having one means sacrificing the other. Chronologically, however, it is possible to have them both be true sequentially, one giving way to the other. The Wars of Independence against "foreign" domination became police actions against "banditry" and "sectarian" interests that threatened national unity and sovereignty. In many cases, it was the same soldiers and the same army, reconfigured and renamed, who fought for independence and then for unification; the same politicians and social and cultural agents.

The historical switch from participating in rebellion during the Wars of Independence to fighting to quell rebellion after unification is echoed in Pinocchio's story. Looked at sequentially it seems as if the obedient, dutiful boy has replaced the unreliable, rebellious puppet. Nevertheless, as I hope to have demonstrated, chronology cannot fully eradicate fundamental dichotomies. It can only hide the tension between them temporarily. Looked at systematically, the tension between Pinocchio's desire to "have no strings to tie [him] down," along with the contrary desire to have a home and a family, remains operative throughout the text. Analogously, Italians' desire for independence and for national unification remains operative in Italian history.

Left Hanging

There were other memorable occurrences to commemorate Italy's twenty-first birth year. In March of 1882 Italy acquired its first official African colony, when the government took control of the Bay of Assab in Eritrea from the Genovese industrialist and shipping magnate Raffaele Rubatino, who had acquired it for his and Italian economic interests in 1869. Rubattino had previously supplied ships to Garibaldi for his invasion of Bourbon Sicily with the *Spedizione dei Mille* in 1860. Thus the switch from fighting for independence to imperial conquest takes place on an individual level as well as a national level. The move is in a sense centrifugal since it looks outward and expands the country's area of interest beyond its conventional borders. But insofar as its aim is to enrich and empower the nation state or the economic stakeholders in the state, its thrust is primarily centripetal: to accumulate resources, wealth, and power, rather than to disperse them.

In May the first international train made its initial run through the recently completed Gotthard tunnel, between Lucerne and Chiasso. The event marks a move beyond either independence or unification toward a state of interdependence, and eventually to the globalization of some of the state's economic, industrial, and technological sectors. This step toward trans-national relations points to another irony of Italian nationalism. The nation was created when the viability of nation states as socio-political entities on the world stage was already on the wane. National borders could not contain or restrict the flow of such things as scientific knowledge, technological advances, political ideologies, religious ideas, diseases and epidemics, and capital. Italian politicians and cultural leaders were striving to create a nation and to instill a sense of nationalism in the country's residents at the very time that the role of nations was diminishing in importance, which made the Italian task not only more difficult but potentially counterproductive, keeping it outside of the mainstream of global trends.

Also in May, albeit secretly, Italy signed the Triple Alliance treaty, with Germany and Austria, the latter the very power against which it had fought its Wars of Independence just a few years before. The treaty's and Italy's secret aim was to form an alliance against France, the very country that had fought alongside the Italians in those same Wars of

"What Italy Got for Her Twenty-First Birthday"

Independence, widely and intensively depicted as heroic and glorious. The switch in allegiance happened because France colonized Tunisia, on which Italy had had its own colonial designs. The switch that takes place with this treaty is thus not only a reversal of allegiance between former allies and former enemies, but also a move from a desire for liberation from foreign domination to a desire for conquest of foreign territories, in the form of the acquisition of colonies: from a centrifugal impulse to break away from one empire, the Austrian, to a centripetal impulse to start creating another one, the Italian.

In October and November of 1882 there were national elections. Suffrage more than tripled, from around 600,000 in the previous election to around 2 million. Even with this sizeable increase, suffrage represented less than 10% of the population. If Italians had been and were being made, it was a very slow process that so far had excluded more than nine out of every ten people in the country. Nevertheless, this expansion of enfranchisement also allowed for a slight expansion of the political spectrum represented in Parliament, with the election of the first Socialist congressman, Andrea Costa, from Ravenna, as well as the first laborer, the Milanese Antonio Maffi, of the *Unione Operaia Radicale*.

The election kept Agostino Depretis in power as Prime Minister, allowing him to develop the system of governance known as *Trasformismo*. Despite the name, which suggests change and transformation, the procedure actually served to prevent radical political change or swings of power from one ideological extreme to the other, by persuading parliamentarians to join centrist coalitions in order to retain their seats and their power, making common cause around pragmatic issues on an *ad hoc* basis, rather than on ideological grounds.

This process of marginalizing and thus disenfranchising the extreme elements of political parties and movements that otherwise had distinct political agendas, so as to concentrate and centralize political and economic power, is redolent of the process that marginalized Garibaldian ideas and goals. Upon the Hero's death, the same process of using his image and his legend to bolster the legitimacy of the central government and its major stakeholders was now applied on a larger scale, using and amplifying the imagery and the rhetoric of the *Risorgimento* to squelch all non-conformist voices.

The year of Italy's coming-of-age comes to an end with an event that can be characterized as either pathetic or heroic, as simultaneously emblematic of defeat or of triumph, depending on one's point of view: the execution by hanging of the irredentist Guglielmo Oberdan (born Wilhelm Oberdank) in his native Trieste on 20 December 1882. This story too has an intimate connection with the death of Garibaldi earlier that year. The young Triestine (and as such an Austrian citizen) — at twenty-four not much older than Italy herself — was studying in Rome at the time of the General's death in June. He used the funeral procession to advocate openly for the irredentist cause, vociferating loudly, and visibly, in front of the Austrian Embassy, demanding that the port-city of Trieste be annexed to Italy. He thus made himself known to Austrian authorities.[29]

---

[29] "Nel grande corteo che si tenne a Roma, nel giugno del 1882, per la morte di Giuseppe Garibaldi, fu notato un giovane pallido, bello, biondo, che portava la bandiera abbrunata di Trieste e che, giunto sotto l'amba-

"What Italy Got for Her Twenty-First Birthday"

Later in the year he returned to Trieste with the aim of assassinating Emperor Franz Joseph, or to die trying, convinced that providing a martyr to the cause would help "liberate" Trieste and "restore" it to its rightful homeland. The irredentist rhetoric implies that the city had been recently taken away from Italy and occupied by Austria, after a long history as an Italian city. In actual fact, however, the Emperor was travelling to Trieste to celebrate the city's 500th year under Habsburg rule: half a millennium as an Austrian city, and what is more, a city known as the *urbs fidelissima* of the Empire. Were Triestines to be considered as Italians to be

---

sciata austriaca, emise un urlo terribile: era GUGLIELMO OBERDAN."
"Era nato a Trieste nel 1858 e, avendo, dopo il Congresso di Berlino, l'Austria mobilitato alcuni reggimenti per occupare la Bosnia e l'Erzegovina, lui, che faceva parte del reggimento Weber, per non andare contro gente che si batteva per l'indipendenza, era fuggito in Italia."
"A Roma si era iscritto alla facoltà d'ingegneria e per vivere e per pagare le tasse si era messo a dare lezioni e a rilegare libri, ma nelle ore che lo studio e il lavoro gli lasciava libere frequentava il circolo democratico studentesco, la trattoria dell'Aquila, ritrovo d'irredentisti, e, sostenendo la necessità di liberare Trieste, comunicava ai compagni, il suo entusiasmo, la sua fede, la sua passione."
"Nel luglio del 1882 l'Oberdan si recò a Napoli per conferire con MATTEO RENATO IMBRIANI, capo dell'irredentismo italiano e per informarlo forse della sua decisione di tentar la sollevazione della sua città natale a costo del sacrificio della propria vita. Lui credeva che per la redenzione di Trieste era necessario il sangue di un martire triestino, era d'avviso che con il sacrificio di una vita si potessero scuotere i giovani "liberi e non liberi" ed aveva stabilito di offrire il proprio sangue alla causa della sua città." From the website "Alfonsine": http://alfonsinemonamour.racine.ra.it/alfonsine/Alfonsine/oberdan2.htm.

"made" along with the rest of the peninsula's population or as Austrians who needed first to be "unmade" as Austrians? Who exactly was hanged on that December day: Guglielmo Oberdan, a late hero and martyr of the Italian *Risorgimento*, or Wilhelm Oberdank, a terrorist and traitor of his Austrian motherland?

From the perspective of his fellow Italian irredentists his execution becomes a symbol of the ongoing, unfinished struggle for national independence: the "liberation" of *Italia irredenta*. From the perspective of his Austrian prosecutors and executioners it is instead a symbol of a threat to nationhood and unity that had to be quelled: the just punishment for treason to the homeland. The image of his body swinging back and forth at the end of a rope is grotesquely emblematic of the swinging back and forth between the countervailing forces that drove the *Risorgimento* and the nation-building process that followed: liberation and unification, breaking away and coming together.

Another seed was planted in 1882 that would come to fruition years later. As a life was ending on the gallows in Trieste, an embryo was gestating in the womb of Rosa Mattoni in Dovia di Predappio, near Forlí. Upon his birth the following year his father, a socialist, would name him after three national and international Leftist political leaders: Mexican revolutionary and President, Benito Juarez; Anarchist, revolutionary militiaman, and Parisian Communard Amilcare Cipriani; and Socialist and founder of the Italian Workers Party, Andrea Costa (the first Socialist parliamentarian mentioned above, elected in1882). Benito Amilcare Andrea Mussolini would eventually incarnate all the contradictions inherent in the process of forming Italy into a unified nation, and he too, like Pinocchio at the end of the first cycle of his story, and like Guglielmo Oberdan, would end up strung up and dangling from a rope.

So how does one make an Italian: with no strings, as Pinocchio sang, or by reinforcing the strings that tie Italians to a glorious past, as the Duce proclaimed? Is it even possible? Is it desirable?

I do not know the answers. Italians may always find themselves swinging back and forth between a fear and repulsion of "strings" that bind one to constraints such as nationalism, conformity, blind loyalty to a state and compulsive obedience of state laws, and a countervailing nostalgia and desire for those "strings" that tie one to past glories, to the cultivation of historical roots, and the harvesting of illusions of cultural superiority and of notions of manifest destinies that will lead to the "rebirth," or the "resurgence," or the "redemption" of past glory and lost power.

Works Cited

Collodi, Carlo. *The Adventures of Pinocchio*. Translated by Ann Lawson Lucas. New York: Oxford University Press, 1996.

———. *Pinocchio*. Edited by Fernando Tempesti. Milan: Feltrinelli, 1972.

Dawkins, Richard. *The Selfish Gene*. 2nd ed. Oxford: Oxford University Press, 1989.

D'Azeglio, Massimo. *I miei ricordi*. Florence: G. Barbera, 1908.

De Amicis, Edmondo. *Cuore*. Novara: De Agostini, 1994.

"Guglielmo Oberdan." *Alfonsine*, http://alfonsinemonamour.racine.ra.it/alfonsine/Alfonsine/oberdan2.htm.

"I've Got no Strings." Web site "Disney Song Lyrics" in *FPX*, http://www.fpx.de/fp/Disney/Lyrics/Pinocchio.html#I%27ve%20Got%20No%20Strings

Montanelli, Indro, and Marco Nozza. *Garibaldi: Ritratto dell'Eroe dei Due Mondi*. BUR SB Saggi edition. Milan: Rizzoli, 2002.

Pinocchio. DVD of 2002 movie. Directed by Roberto Benigni. Performed by Roberto Benigni, Nicoletta Braschi. Miramax, 2003.

Pinocchio. DVD of 1940 animated movie. Walt Disney Studios, 1999.

Stella, Gian Antonio. *L'orda: quando gli albanesi eravamo noi*. Milan: Rizzoli, 2002.

Tempesti, Fernando. "Chi era il Collodi," "Com'è fatto *Pinocchio*." In Collodi, *Pinocchio*.

Remittances and Purchases of Emigrants
Resource for the Development of the Unitary State

Mario B. Mignone
Stony Brook University

The title of the conference "Made by Italians" asks the speaker to delve in Italian creativity.* Attention to aesthetics is a *modus vivendi* of Italians: from architecture to music, to design, to cooking, to the way men wear scarves in wintertime, it is a performance to have and give pleasure. Aesthetics are inherent to Italian identity. Italy is usually credited as being the cradle of an almost inborn sense of aesthetics, good taste, and beauty that permeates the nation's art, fashion, design, and food. The "Made in Italy" label is synonymous with refined taste, elegance, and care. Indeed, Italian identity itself is molded by its identification with glamour and sophistication. Fashion, of course, has played and still plays a key role in the discursive construction of what is now recognized as Italian style.

In this country, also, Italians have contributed to the pleasures of life: from painting (imagine the extraordinary paintings of Constantino Brumidi on the Capitol Rotunda dome and many rooms in the Senate and House wings in

---

* This essay was originally written for the conference "Made by Italians," also organized by the D'Amato Chair. Unfortunately, that conference was cancelled due to Super Storm Sandy. Given its content, this essay fits nicely into this collection as well.

From: *Theater of the Mind, Stage of History*. Bordighera Press, 2015

Washington), to sculpture, architecture, sport, and entertainment. No question, Italians have enriched the culture and life of this nation.

But when we look at the core, at the heart of what Italy and this nation are and who contributed to make them what they are, we should look also at what Italian emigrants made and how they contributed to sustain the evolution of those special characteristics of the Italian people. Italian emigration is a phenomenon that must be profoundly tied to work, that is, labor, which is the application of human energy to produce wealth. Italian emigrants left home in search of work and were lured abroad to do work. It was their ability to work that made them a valuable commodity. It was work that defined their personal and national identity. It was their work that changed their social status and that of their families, and it was their work that created prosperity for their host countries and for the homeland they had left. Our emigrants worked to live, but they also lived to work.

The history of Italian emigrants in America is bound inextricably with the history of the working class in the United States. For the most part, our emigrants had to work under hard and dangerous conditions for meager wages. Many of them lost their lives because of dangerous work and unregulated working conditions. Mining claimed the highest number of lives and Italians were regularly among those who had the highest number of victims. That was true on this continent up to World War II and it was true in Europe after World War II. In fact in Europe, the numbers of miners who lost their lives while working is shocking: 17 in 1946, 32 in 1947, 37 in 1948, 41 in 1949, 40 in 1950, 51 in 1951, 75 in 1952, 101 in 1953, 56 in 1954, and 38 in 1955. 1956 was the year of the great disaster. In February of that year, 7 Italians had already died in a mine in Quaregnon. On August 8, 1956, there occurred a tragedy in the Charbonnage du Bois-du-Cazier in Marcinelle. Of the 262 casualties, 136 were Italians. Those miners had gone down underground to get some of the 170,000 tons of coal which that site produced every year, so that in turn, hundreds of thousands of their fellow-citizens could work and live and so that Belgium could prosper and Italy could energize its "economic miracle."

Those Italian miners were in that mine as the result of a Belgian-Italian agreement of exchange: "coal for men." On June 20, 1946, Prime Minister Alcide De Gasperi signed a Belgian-Italian agreement (*accordo uomo-carbone*) that provided 50,000 Italian workers for the Belgian coal mines in exchange for coal: 2,000 workers per week. In exchange, Belgium would deliver coal to Italy. The "guest workers" were obliged to work in the mines for at least their first 5 years in Belgium. As a result, between 1946 and 1957 Italy sent 140,000 men, 17,000 women, and 29,000 children to Belgium. The amount of coal sent to Italy was based on a monthly output, which depended on the number of Italian workers in the mines in increments of 1,000. Overall, from 1946 to 1963, the period for which the agreement "uomo in cambio" of coal lasted, 867 Italians died in Belgian mines, in addition to the thousands who died as consequence of lung disease caused by coal dust.

During one hundred fifty years of emigration, Italy kept culpably quiet, as if those who were driven to leave, either by need or by individual choice, no longer mattered at all. It was a silence so deafening that even tragic events caused by dangerous work or unprotected labor conditions were not registered with the due attention. The history of our emigration is not made up only of enduring sacrifices, but also of wounds and too many deaths as well. The loss of Italian miners in Belgium, to which I referred, must be connected to the hundreds of Italian miners who lost their lives in American mines. In America, half a century earlier, the working conditions were even worse. One need only remember that a United States law permitted each miner to have a child of 8–12 years of age with him to act as a support. In 1907, in a mine collapse that occurred in the Monongah Coal Mine (West Virginia), there were at least 361 victims, of which 171 were Italians, some of whom were children.

When I went to school in Italy, where I completed high school, I never read a page in our textbooks recalling the sacrifice of emigrants. Not a chapter, not a lesson was ever devoted to emigration, as if did not exist, as if Italy was ashamed of those Italians who had left the "patria" in search of "benessere" elsewhere. In the last couple of decades, Italy has made many attempts to recognize the magnitude of the phenomenon and what it meant for the nation: conferences, publications, extraordinary legislative acts (dual citizenship and the right to vote and have representation in Italian Parliament), and recognition of Italians abroad who have achieved distinction. Most important, Italy has finally acquired the courage to recognize the faceless millions of emigrants who left silently, as part of the "silent revolution," to create, with their labor, wealth in other countries and generate some prosperity for the "patria" they had left. The creation of the National Museum of Italian Emigration (*Museo Nazionale dell'Emigrazione Italiana*) located at the base of the Victor Emmanuel Monument, in Rome, was an extraordinary and symbolic act to remove the veil of silence that has accompanied Italian emigration. Very revealing is also the fact that the same entrance leads to the museum of the Risorgimento and the Museum of emigration. It is a museum with many pictures presented, with no theories or pompous rhetoric on emigration, but with simple descriptive narrative to allow the images to give the story and history of emigration. We do not need theories on human sacrifices of such magnitude. A prominent part of the museum is given to emigrants at work. Certainly, it is the correct and proper way to represent the spirit of emigration and of the emigrant experiences. Italian emigrants poured the foundations, in a literal and metaphorical way, of the new nation: they built reservoirs, streetcar lines, subways, railroads, streets, and sewage lines; they literally build new cities from the ground up. A portion of skilled workers were still laborers as well to a certain degree. The skilled artisans, stone cutters, masons, tailors, carpenters, and horticulturists made a perfect marriage of skill, experience, and hard work.

The museum is an official national act to recognize Italian emigration. As an emigrant, I and many of you, should be gratified, after all it is a museum created to honor our parents, our grandparents, and, in many cases, to honor us. We should appreciate the recognition that Italy has given, finally, to the work of emigrants in making Italy.

Throughout world history, there has always been a tendency to "ethnicize" social conflicts. But today, how can we justify the fact that immigrants are scapegoats for problems that are difficult to solve? Invectives against immigrants "that do not want to integrate themselves" (as if it depended only on them) and who depend on aid programs are recurring, and they are particularly convenient in this time of fiscal constraints, when governments are forced to save on social welfare.

In Arizona in July 2010 a deterrent law took effect against all illegal immigrants (mostly Hispanics) who enter illegally and plan to reside on United States territory. The new law gives police the ability to stop, check, interrogate, and even arrest a foreigner for a "reasonable suspicion." The burden of proof regarding one's legal stay in the country is up to the single suspected individual. In addition, anyone protecting or giving work to illegal immigrants risks arrest.

Three months later, in October, to meet the growing anti-immigration and anti-"political correctness" tide, Germany's Chancellor, Angela Merkel said that multiculturalism had failed in her country, or rather, "it has completely failed." Despite repeating that Germany remains open to the world, she declared: "We do not need immigration that weighs on our social system." In short, those who go to Germany must either integrate by accepting European rules, or return home. This event did not blow up by way of some migratory emergency: in 2009, 734,000 people left Germany and only 721,000 arrived. Thilo Sarrazin, ex-member of the board of directors of the Bundesbank, presented this atmosphere well in his racist book (*Deutschland schafft sich ab – Germany is Destroying Itself*), in which he claims that the intelligence quotient is mainly hereditary, and that the IQ of Turkish and Arab immigrants is low. Sarrazin's book sold a million copies in one month. Why is it that in this virulent rhetoric the value of immigrant's work and the wealth it creates is hidden? Why is it that all too often one's sense of memory and history is lost?

"Remittances and Purchases of Emigrants"

Already at the beginning of the 20th century, the "Father of migrants," Giovanni Battista Scalabrini, had shown with great eloquence and profound humanity the emigrant's human rights. His words are still relevant and should be taught:

> Emigration is a natural, unalienable right; it is a social safety valve that re-establishes equilibrium between wealth and the productive powers of a people; it is the source of wealth for those who leave and those who stay, relieving the land of an excessive population and strengthening the workers who remain; it could be, then, an individual or national good or evil, depending on the manner in which it occurs, since it opens new avenues for commerce, facilitates the dissemination of findings in science and industries, it unites and improves cultures and broadens the concept of homeland outside material borders, making the world the homeland of man.

Even in Italy the vitriolic rhetoric against immigrants, especially by the Northern League, is particularly strong. There is no doubt that the immigration phenomenon is of great importance. The Dossier Caritas/Migrantes states that the estimated number of regularly sojourning foreigners has come to 4,919,000, about 7% of residents, a figure that is 700,000 units higher with respect to that of Istat (4,235,000 at the beginning of 2010): this is almost 5 million immigrants, but the League suggests that there are three times this amount. The dossier makes some interesting observations:

- More than one eighth of immigrants, almost 600,000 people, are of second generation immigrants.

- Immigrants are mostly in north and central Italy, and in the north one out of every 10 residents is a foreigner. One fourth of immigrants live in Lombardy (982,225, 23.2%). Rome (405,657) loses the first place with the highest number of immigrants to Milan (407,191).
- The city earns a higher approval rating with respect to the countryside or the small village.
- With foreigners, Italy is demographically less old.
- The immigrant woman becomes the "engine of change" of her community of origin.
- Mixed marriages do not fail more often than those between Italians.

The economic crisis is complicit, and with the growing number of immigrants, the negative reactions towards them by Italians increase as well. Yet, Caritas's data show a favorable framework of the economic contributions of immigrants, authentic producers of wealth for the country that takes them in:

- They contribute 11.1% to the gross domestic product.
- They pay the state treasury almost 11 billion euros in social security and tax contributions per year.
- They account for about 10% of all employees but they are always more active in self-employment and entrepreneurship, where they are able to create new businesses even in this crisis period, being owners of 3.5% of all businesses.

Many Italians are concerned about the presence of "illegal immigrants," because among them there can be some "undesirables." However, they are even more concerned about the impact that immigrants and their specific burden have on the welfare system. Many see remittances of immigrants as an exodus of national resources towards the immigrants' countries of origin. The Dossier Caritas 2010 highlights the important role of remittances, which now represent the primary source of global financial development with direct foreign investments in companies and in the private sector, blatantly surpassing total amounts of public international aid.

Remittances: the Engine of Economic Development

Despite the current economic crisis, the flow of money earned by immigrants abroad continues to grow. Immigrants support families and the familial group, playing a key role in improving the socio-economic conditions of their countries of origin. The total amount of remittances of resident foreign citizens in Italy in 2009 exceeded 6.7 billion euros. 83.2% of this total comes from seven regions and over 50% from five provinces (Rome, Milan, Prato, Florence and Naples). The most important areas are Lazio (particularly the metropolitan area of Rome) and Lombardy, together issuing 47.7% of remittances, confirming the high presence of immigrants in the two regions. In third place is Tuscany, with 13.8% of remittances. Tuscany experienced an increase of +10% during the year, mainly due to the striking increase in remittances by the Chinese community in Prato.

During the year, the principal flow of money from Italy going abroad is towards Asia (together China and the Philippines hold 50.2% of the total), with Europe in second place, 24.2%. On the old continent, Romania, where 824 million euros were sent, particularly stands out. A relevant fact is that

80% of remittances flow through money transfers, a choice motivated by several factors, among them the speed of the actual transfer of currency. Immigrants living in Italy are creating wealth for the nation with their work, and at the same time, through remittances, are having a profound impact on their families left home and on their country of origin. They are doing what Italian emigrants did for a century, sending money home and consequently helping to propel the economy of the nation.

As is the case today with immigrants in Italy, Italian emigrants sent home to their communities a substantial portion of the fruit of their labor, which was often earned in difficult situations and with scarce social guarantee. The emigrants, who already had suffered through complex affective situations, adopted a lifestyle based on renunciations and sacrifice. They lengthened their work-day as long as possible and saved on overall consumption. It is calculated that, especially during the first few years at their new residence, they would send about one fourth of their income to their loved ones at home. These were important figures, far from being marginal for a nation still in its nascent state, during which time territorial and social imbalances were the rule. Money turned out to be critical in improving the living conditions of their families back home, but it also had an impact on the larger population remaining in Italy. The money was not solely a private matter that was used up in the private sphere of sentiments and family relationships. Already at the beginning of the twentieth century, when Italy started to structure its unified economic identity, when certain economic conditions in the south and the northeast were still tragic and money was needed to overcome them, the cash

"Remittances and Purchases of Emigrants"

flow of immigrants' remittances played an enormous economic role, amounting to about a third of the balance of payments.

In what way were the emigrants and their work interpreted and valued in that period? Did the country realize their economic power? On the one hand, the new nation suffered a hemorrhaging of human capital, and on the other the loss of those men and women (who were often among the best, brave, and most courageous) became a source of financial capitalization.

In the years immediately following the unification, the government assumed a substantially repressive position towards emigration, mostly for reasons related to the economic structure of the time, which was founded above all on the primary sector. Among the first regulatory provisions was the "circolare Lanza," sent to the prefects on July 18, 1873. In it, provincial government authorities were invited to stop illegal emigration and to curb legal and spontaneous emigration by any means necessary. It was the general opinion of the politicians of the time that emigration would cause a rupture in the balance between labor supply and demand in the agricultural classes; the decrease of manpower in the countryside would create an increase in wages and changes in contract terms. As we know, however, the flow of emigration intensified: neither the restrictive provisions of the rulers of the Right nor the subsequent ones released by the historic Left able to be deterrents. According to data from Istat, about 4,711,000 Italians emigrated to the Americans: between 1876 and 1913 3,374,000 of them came from the South.

"The desperate and illiterate laborer became the hero of a new and peaceful social revolution," wrote Leopoldo Franchetti. "While books were written, speeches were given, and rules to resolve the problem of the South were compiled, the southern peasants began the solution to their plight themselves, quietly. They go to America to create the capital that is necessary to fertilize the soil of their country."

Work is itself capital, and from the late 1800s and early 1900s Italy forced out a tremendous amount of work capital to produce wealth on the other side of the ocean. We must ask ourselves to what extent the work abroad was a dispersal of useful resources for Italy or a powerful investment.

Giustino Fortunato (1848-1932), one of the politicians who was most sensitive to the migratory phenomenon, fully recognized both the cost and the contribution of emigration:

> We send to the other side of the seas the only commodity of which we have abundance: men; and across the seas comes in exchange a wide band of gold – remittances – that we do not ignore, no, they are made of tears and blood.

With respect to those tears and that blood, it is necessary to ask ourselves what impact remittances have had: in my humble opinion, they provided important financial resources for the industrial development between the end of the 1800s and the beginning of the 1900s, as well as the economic miracle that followed World War II.

At the end of the 1800s the industrialization of Italy was seen as a pipe-dream, impossible to come to fruition. It was said that the peninsula did not have any energy or mineral sources to develop an industrial system. In addition, Italy was lacking the means of production and the accumulation of capital necessary for takeoff. Given these conditions, it was difficult to hope for a growth process that was not tied to the land, sun, and water. It was a physiocratic prejudice of an Italy that had to be relegated to a land of agriculture, and at most, a tourist destination. The prejudice corresponded to the interests of the European powers of that time, who desired to see the birth of a new state only partially "productive" so that it would not be a competitor in the larger world market. European manufacturing could have rightly assumed to export hands down in Italy, without fear of competition.

This prejudicial thinking was not taking into account something important: the factors of production are not only those to be derived from raw energy and mineral materials. In perhaps a synthetic but not a less effective way, classical economists, starting with Adam Smith, taught us that at the foundation of effective productive processes there are three elements: land, capital, and work. Italy was very rich with the third element, human capital and its respective intelligence. The Italian man, raised in free local communities, then organized in many small states that were formed on the peninsular territory, asserted himself over the ages thanks to his own intelligence and his own knowledge, gaining universal recognition not only for his capacity for hard labor and material work, but for his lucid intellectual creativity. He was a man that courts and lords had regularly sought throughout the course of millennia, to acquire intellectual works and pay with the capacity of intuition, work, resourcefulness, and pragmatism.

In the new Italy, politically united by the Casa Savoia, that capacity for work and ingenuity found a historical expression in the emigrant. With his performance, he became the hub of a productive, even industrial system, that made the new nation take off, contributing in a major way to the transformation and modernization of the country.

At the end of the 1800s, Italy found itself in an unexpected situation with respect to the rest of Europe: between 1875 and 1896 the so-called Great European Depression took place; for Italy, still with an eminently agrarian economy, it signified a huge agricultural crisis. When the growth cycle started, which coincided with the "Belle Époque" that in Italy was identified with Giovanni Giolitti's period of government, Italy was experiencing a huge emigration. These are the years of the first Italian take off, an industrial take off that almost exclusively took place in the north-west part of the peninsula, in what became known as the industrial triangle: the Genoa – Turin – Milan triangle.

Coincidentally, this paradoxical and unexpected phenomenon took place when a great stream of the migrant population was flowing towards the Atlantic. It was made mostly by men from the South, from Campania, Calabria, Basilicata, Sicily, or Puglia, who were seeking their fortune abroad. They moved towards North America, the United States in particular. They left with the objective of finding a job that would have allowed them to send money home, to their families. By sending remittances home, they were giving a very valuable economic gift to the country that they had abandoned. By emigrating they had made a "passive" contribution to Italy by both alleviating the social pressure caused by heavy unemployment and by helping the economy of the nation. By emigrating, which was an act of a tremendous self-expulsion of a surplus workforce, they fueled conditions for re-balancing offers of manpower and industrial demand that granted Italy a smoother entrance in the age of partial industrialization. It is relevant to note how the populations of the South, already having gone through enormous sacrifices since the unification, had taken historic form by paying a hefty bill in social and human terms by leaving the country in order to help the industrialization of the Northwest triangle.

Those so-called "passive" contributions will soon be followed by an "active" contribution through a flow of cash that went to fuel the industrial base especially for the purchase of energy abroad (at the time, coal above all) as well as raw materials. The balancing of the budget in Italy, usually realized through exports and financial disbursements, was achieved with the remittance of emigrants. In this critical moment of Italian industrialization, Italian work abroad acquired strategic relevance in Italy's national economic history.

The protagonists of this financial epic, which drains resources from the poor pockets of Italian emigrants and moves those same resources towards families of origin and to the counters of post offices and banks that draw them in, are the men of the South, often dark-skinned with calloused hands. In their regions of origin, they are remembered only by family and friends. In the North of Italy they are called *terroni* or "Napoli." Textbooks and newspapers did not talk about them for their sacrifices and endurances. Repeating the rites and habits that they had to endure at home, those Italians lived in a frugal, austere way in America, often enduring living conditions worse than those they had left back home. Knowing the art of saving, they would scrape together mountains of pennies and *centesimi*, and transformed those savings into substantial nest eggs, sending them regularly to Italy, where families, but also the state and industries of the North, knew how to make them fulfill their potential.

Emigration remained an immense social, political, and human tragedy for Italy at that time. However, from that tragedy emerged something exceedingly positive: profit gain for a balance of national payments, still under stress due to the costs of the unification and the debts incurred by the new state to support the entry process into the concourse of nations. This explains the fact that, with the sole exception of the Fascist period, the country would not further hinder but rather encourage the movement and export of manpower abroad.

Remittances at the Base of Italian Development

There is no doubt that one of the most socially and economically relevant consequences of the intensification of migratory flow was the handling of emigrants' remittances, particularly with respect to the construction of conditions for the Italian boom of the 1970s and the introduction of the North into the virtuous period of European growth. Surprisingly, this issue has not received sufficient attention by economic historians, except for some intelligent exceptions. It is rather obvious that remittances turned out to be a valuable source of hard currency, an element of wealth for the finances of the state, and its spending was prevalently oriented towards the industrial North, the more economically advanced part of Italy. In addition, a good portion of the proceeds of emigration did not find use in consumption, real estate purchases, or other immediately productive investments. Since they were hoarded via deposits at post offices or in the acquisition of public debt securities, they created a pool of money/financial resources that allowed the state to direct them to support the development of the industrial triangle in the form of credits, loans, and public contracts. The savings of emigrants and their Italian relatives were used to contribute to the formation of the capital accumulation necessary for the development of the country.

Remittances during the Giolitti decade (1903 – 1914) were fundamental for the first Italian industrial take off. Between 1901 and 1910 remittances constituted 25% of the balance of payments. According to estimates of the Commission of Immigration in the United States, remittances reached the sum of $85 million in 1907. From almost 132 million *lire* at their current value in 1902, total remittances from Italian emigration exceeded 716 million in 1913 with an annual average of about 450 million. After World War I, a progressive increase brought the total amount of remittances to approximately 5 billion *lire* in 1920, the year that logs the highest point in the curve of remittances of the first decades of the twentieth century. These sums of money for most economists represent only 15% of the total of the remittances. An additional 15% was sent through postal money order (*vagli postali*) or through deposit in saving accounts. But more than 50% of remittances reached their destination through private means.

Even the funds collected only from institutional collectors stood out as truly significant amounts. Adding up remittances made out for one half of the Bank of Napoli with deposits made in the postal savings banks (Casse di Risparmio) and international postal money orders paid by post offices of the kingdom, between 1902 and 1905 average annual remittances obtained amounted to over 160 million *lire* circulating. It was a figure destined to grow during the following years: up to 304 million annually for the next four years, to 404 million during the period of 1909 – 1913, for an annual average that, for the entire period, stands at 290 million.

Remittances helped Italy to face the trade deficit. In the years before World War I, Italy's exports matched only 60-80 percent of its imports, yet the country enjoyed a steady currency and low interest rates. Before 1890, Italy had financed two thirds of its trade deficit with foreign loans, but after 1900, remittances balanced out foreign loans, and counterbalanced Italy's spending on imported foreign goods. From 1901 to 1913, against Italy's commercial deficit of 10,230 million *lire* stood an "invisible credit" of 12,291 million lire. More than half the credit came from remittances, more than a third from tourism, and the rest from shipping. The credit turned Italy from debtor nation into a modest creditor nation. Directly through remittances, and indirectly through exports and shipping, migration became a decisive factor in Italy's favorable balance of payments, by balancing Italy's internal consumption with external input. Thanks to its international credits, Italy was able to industrialize without relying extensively on foreign loans, without serious price tensions, and without lowering real wages.

Overall the official amounts deposited in savings at Italian lending institutions grew from 61% during wartime to 117% between 1918 and 1921, and a further 36% in the four following years, passing from 7 billion 600 million *lire* in 1914 – 1915 to 36 billion 221 million in 1925, for a total increase of 376%. Without intending to, even with these figures, money that the emigrants saved was used to purchase stocks of shares of national debt.

"Remittances and Purchases of Emigrants"

It is important to note that the statistical *Annuario* of Italian emigration, with its collected and carefully drawn up data, does not mention the purpose in cataloging the amounts remitted to Italy from abroad by international money order. Thus a distinction is not made between the emigrants' savings and money sent for commercial transactions taking place in Italy. On the other hand, in the figures reported here, the so-called "invisible" games do not appear; that is, the movement of money from abroad into Italy helped by informal channels.

By injecting hard currency that was otherwise unavailable into the Italian financial system, emigrants' remittances, both official and unofficial, created a fortune for many credit institutions that made a considerable profit on transfers and exchanges. Sending savings to Italy followed a complex and articulate process, and especially in the early days, the bank operators living in Italy were undisputed and privileged protagonists.

It is useful to analyze some of the aspects tied to the remittance phenomenon, as well as regional redistribution in Italian territories, which is immediately linked to the progression of migratory flow as well as to the changes that assume their geographic origin. Between 1907 and 1913 the biggest amounts flowed into Southern Italy (61%), with Sicily, Campania, and Calabria in the lead. In the North, the Veneto region reported the highest percentage. Between 1914 and 1918 the top four regions on the list were all Southern: Sicily (18%), Campania (19%), Abruzzo and Molise (14.5%), Calabria (14%), followed by Veneto, Puglia, Piedmont, Basilicata, Marche, Lombardy, Tuscany, Emilia, and Lazio. Following World War I, between 1919 to 1925, according to documentation furnished by Balletta, the majority of money orders were paid in Sicily and Campania, followed immediately by other Southern regions, and from a distance by the northern and central regions. This is good evidence that, through the course of time, emigration became mostly a Southern phenomenon.

We have already discussed some of the positive macroeconomic effects on a strictly financial level. It must be added that the injection of such large sums of money from abroad, besides providing direct support to the source of capitalism of the northwest triangle, improved conditions of emigrants' families, creating the basis for the greatest availability of money to spend on consumption.

Remittances resulted in the betterment of eating habits and an improvement of the quality of life in general. Affected first were hygienic-sanitary conditions, that translated into a diminished mortality rate, starting with that of infants. Endemic illnesses such as pellagra, and very common diseases such as pulmonary illnesses, diminished rapidly in a noticeable way.

There is a patently recorded increase in inclination towards the purchase of the following goods:

- clothing,
- furniture and cooking appliances,
- tools, machinery, and instruments, either of industrial or artisanal origin.

Quantitative and qualitative increases in productive activities were registered in family businesses, stores, and tailor and shoemaker shops. Donations to devotional activities grew; donations of emigrant families recurred with a certain frequency for patronal festivals, and contributions of the most prosperous emigrants were used for church renovations and/or for the renovation of church ornaments and vestments.

The positive impact that remittances had on the eradication of usury in the countryside cannot be forgotten. With the money *"della Merica,"* emigrants and families of emigrants first paid their debts, especially affecting the mortgage debts of rural properties. In the space of a few years the remittances of emigrants profoundly changed the context of criminal exploitation, which had taken root over the course of centuries and had intensified during the second half of the nineteenth century. Because of this, the credit market was revolutionized, all for the good of the peasant world that finally was able to emancipate itself from a cancer that had corroded its spirit.

Home and land were real estate properties that attracted the majority of investments made with remittances. Old dark cabins with the walls blackened by soot were substituted by small houses with two floors, ample and airy rooms, and balconies or terraces. In many ways, the massive movement from the rural class towards the behaviors and attitudes of the lower middle class, the city-dwelling bourgeoisie, was realized.

The "piece of land" was the other historic aspiration that "American money" satisfied. The race to buy did not corrode the majority of the estates, because they were concentrated on land that was closest to town, which was often already divided into small plots, or on fringe areas. Even with these limitations, small peasant property grew significantly even during the following period, also because the investments of small holders were married with the need of the middle and aristocratic classes to overcome the obstacles of rank and nobility, with the intent of shedding funds that had been turned into a parasitic weight against unexpected costs or financial difficulties. Between 1911 and 1921 the number of farmer-owners grew 412% in Sicily, 309% in Puglia, 306% in Calabria, and 159% in the Veneto region.

Thanks to the remittances of family members living far away, the improvement of the standard of living of those remaining relatives was realized, even if the necessary emancipatory movement and rural democracy were not fulfilled. While emigrants and emigrant families achieved the dream of owning land, they were not able to establish complete economic and social position of respect. In addition, in many cases remittances had an unanticipated negative effect on property value, (especially the abnormal increase of the cost of property for construction, speculations on building materials, increases in food prices) thus generating inflation. The surge in consumer prices of essential goods in particular ended up driving out marginal individuals from the area, increasing, thus, the number of candidates for new forms of migration. The low-income or no-income individuals that did not have emigrant relatives or kin were unable to sustain costs related to the increases on both old and new goods, that for the most part were generated by inflationary demand with roots overseas.

It could be asked why the financial availability of remittances was not utilized by the Southern populations in order to promote their economic and social advancement, and in particular to build a capitalist base for the industrial development of Southern Italy. Among the reasons is the fact that emigration had drained the work force and intellects, directing them towards more developed markets. Moreover, the residual working population lacked the appropriate professional and technical training and a corporate culture. It is not surprising that one half of remittances were spent on common expenditures and family housing, while only 10% of remittances were invested in agriculture. Residual uses went towards traditional and tertiary activities, increasing unprofitable performance and fragmenting the use of savings. Not even land investments were directed towards the consolidation of property capable of capitalist development: the microfund remained the rule, with 60% of families as holders of less than one hectare plots.

Remittances at the Base of the Economic Miracle

Remittances were the fundamental element of the Italian reconstruction and of the country's economic miracle after World War II. The equation designed by the De Gasperi government was effective in its simplicity; a country, impoverished by war and by the shortage of currency, exchanged the overabundance of a young, healthy, productive workforce with raw materials, of which Italy was scarce. Following this reasoning, agreements were signed with countries leading in immigration, such as Argentina and Australia, but also in particular with Italy's European neighbors: Belgium, France, and Switzerland. In two years, between 1946 and 1947, nearly 84,000 Italians left for the French and Belgian mines, most of them from the Veneto region, from Campania and other regions of the South.

The incredible flow of remittances from this work force constituted extraordinary wealth that allowed Italy to pay debt that had been drawn with countries overseas, to acquire raw materials, and to start the economic revival. According to data of the Italian Exchange Bureau, remittances were around $32 million in 1947. With the increase in emigration, in 1949 they jumped to $90 million, to $102 million in 1952, recording a steady increase in subsequent years, up to $246 million in 1959 and $288 million in 1960. In total, through official channels between 1945 and 1960, remittances amounted to $2 billion 40 million, 55% of which went to the South, with 16% to Sicily alone. With the arrival of the 1980s, the Italian laborer that worked abroad was attributed non-resident status: consequently he could transfer savings to Italy in the form of credit in foreign accounts exempt from withholding tax on interest, or as donations to the family.

According to survey statistics, the above-mentioned movements of foreign currencies are the recorded amounts transmitted through official channels. It is difficult to verify the specific contributions of non-resident compatriots. In addition, the sending of money through unofficial channels and remittances sent to families with varied means, particularly the savings transferred from repatriated emigrants, continue to elude the surveys of financial authorities. The Consiglio Generale degli Italiani all'Estero (CGIE) has pointed out that the lack of savings deposits from Italians abroad in Italy is due to the absence of a monetary policy aimed at encouraging investments, but, in reality, actually penalized due to the absence of tax breaks, deductions on interest, risk of exposure, exemptions at the source, and scarce compensation with respect to the inflation tax.

"Remittances and Purchases of Emigrants"

Not Only Remittances

In addition to the emigrants' direct contribution to Italy's development via remittances, three more modalities of financial contribution can be added to the progress of the national economy:

- the promotion of Italian products through direct consumption and the introduction of consumption into the way of life in their communities,
- the promotion of Italian culture,
- the economic impact of returning tourism.

The role of Italians abroad is relevant in the promotion and diffusion of the Made in Italy. Italians abroad favor exports and act as real and true promoters of the Made in Italy. Emigrants retain and spread consumption habits that increase the demand of goods produced by Italian companies (one thinks of food, fashion, and design). Not surprisingly, in foreign countries where the presence of the Italian communities is stronger, the imports of Italian products are greater.

Emigrants make up one of the main vehicles of distribution of Italian products. The case of Veneto, with its 10% of Italian exports, is the most striking. To the ex-emigrants, Veneto is often a much too undervalued and misunderstood debtor. If there were specific findings for the whole period of our emigration, a curve of correlations between the consistency of the Italian communities and the tendencies towards national exports to receiving countries could be established. A formula that reveals the correlation between migratory flows and increases in exports could be established; a testimony, among other things, of the increasing integration of migrant communities into the local social fabric. The direct and indirect market of Italian goods and services abroad has been fueled in large part by communities that still live and eat in the Italian way, creating businesses that import Italian products, and outfitting their own factories with Italian machinery. They "Italianize" the lifestyle of local communities influencing, even indirectly, thoroughly and therefore definitively the tastes of the established society. According to the Consiglio Generale degli Italiani all'Estero (CGIE), it is reasonable to assert that a third of the volume of Italian exports can be attributed to the effects of the network of Italian communities abroad.

The economic impact that emigration has on Italy can be given also by additional data. Throughout the world, there are about 60,000 restaurants that qualify as "Italian" (35,000 in Europe), with a turnover of 27 billion euros and 1 billion customers. Italians in Germany are proprietors of 38,000 companies, especially in the gastronomic sector: mostly operated by Italians originating from the northeast, there are about 2,500 gelato shops. The gelato shops are good showcases of the Made in Italy and they generate about 250 million euro annually for raw material supply and 100 million for investments in furnishings and maintenance.

However, this thriving market poses problems in terms of continuity. In Germany, two thirds of restaurants no longer belong to Italians; in South Korea, while there are over 600 restaurants that qualify as "Italian," only eight are

"Remittances and Purchases of Emigrants"

actually run by Italians. The solution adopted by Italian *gelatai* in Germany could be paradigmatic: with the absence of children able to continue a family business, the net loss could be made up by bringing to Germany thousands of youth of Italian origin from Argentina and Brazil.

The Italian state and regional institutions are aware of the strong commercial potential Italians abroad represent and are making strong efforts in strengthening their ties with them. For example, the underlying idea, strongly emphasized during the second Conferenza Stato-Regioni-Province Autonome-CGIE in 2005 was to utilize Italian entrepreneurs abroad like "consultants" of the "Italy system," of the Made in Italy that they are promoting through their entrepreneurial ventures. It was stressed that in particular the "successful" Italian emigrants can exercise "a sort of lobby activity." In this perspective, some of the regions are taking action (through the Councils on emigration) by approving projects and allocating funds for internalization in countries with the highest presence of fellow compatriots, often aiming for the promotion of specific commodity production, and making the increase in relations with communities of compatriots become the lever of social development. In this regard, ITENETS (International Training and Employment Networks) and PPTIE (Programma di partenariato territoriale con gli italiani all'estero) can be mentioned, designed to guide the regions in the South in the internationalization process.

Italians abroad provide another important contribution to Italy through "returning tourism." The Associazione delle Camere di Commercio confirms that the Italian Diaspora throughout the world is an economic force that hides in the net. Understood as a transnational and globalizing social and economic factor, indifferent to the traditional forms of the nation-state, it is the post-modern idea of the people's identity that extends beyond territory and national boundaries. The flow of return tourism is not to be underestimated because expanded tourism continues to present itself as one of the pillars of the Italian economy.

All these contributions raise a big concern for the future. To maintain or enhance the economic contributions of different Italophile agents is important to nourish a new cultural nexus at the transnational level. Italian language in the world is not an unknown language, as suggested by the widespread, diffuse presence of compatriots and people of Italian extraction. With the exception of the Republic of San Marino, Switzerland is the only country in which, thanks to the Canton Ticino, Italian is the national language, even if the percentage of those who speak it is decreasing. In Australia, Italian is the most spoken language following English. In Argentina, there are about 93,000 students of Italian divided into more than 5,000 classes with 1,359 teachers. In the United States, 60,000 students study Italian, and since September 2005, Italian has entered the Advanced Placement Program (APP). In areas such as Long Island, the population of Italian origin is widespread; Italian is taught in all the schools and has become the second foreign language taught following Spanish. Furthermore, the presence of the Catholic Church in Rome, and the fact that Catholicism has in recent decades abandoned the use of the Latin language, is giving new opportunity to the diffusion of Italian, starting with the fact that foreign popes and cardinals usually communicate with each other in Italian as well as in English, and that the

"Remittances and Purchases of Emigrants"

Pope delivers speeches on Sundays in Piazza San Pietro in the Italian language.

Many initiatives have been taken to satisfy the needs of both Italians and worldwide lovers of Italian. There were 6,519 Italian courses organized in 2004 by Italian cultural institutes, besides 5,000 of those organized in the same year by the Dante Alighieri Society, 16,517 courses taught in public schools (2003/2004 school year), to which 13,181 additional courses were added, thanks to the contributions supplied by the Ministry of Foreign Affairs, for a total of about 600,000 students. These data help to frame the actual situation and to understand the need to put into action assertive projects regarding the promotion and valorization of the Italian language.

In the first place, we need to keep the new generations from forgetting the language of their parents and/or their grandparents. In Switzerland, for example, only a third of children between 6 and 15 years old take Italian courses and obtain an intermediate level of fluency, while a growing number of senior citizens do not speak their native language fluently, which is a detriment also at the various levels of participation.

Cultural initiatives are also, as mentioned, a vehicle for the enhancement of the image of Italy and of Made in Italy. Important sectors exist that "speak Italian": opera, restoration, fashion, cuisine, the world of soccer and automobiles all come to mind. Promoting the language and Italian cultural heritage represents, indirectly, also promoting the industrial creativity and the agricultural-food peculiarities of the nation. Culture has, in fact, important effects on the plane of international relations, on tourism (the vacation to

Italy is a "classic dream") and on marketing. In the process of the internationalization of business, these diverse aspects emerge closely linked together. The Italian language and culture set themselves as "forerunners of an encounter with Italy," an encounter that will also embrace business and positive financial flow for the country.

In Conclusion

Italy's extraordinary economic and social growth of recent decades was not accidental. In the innovative capacity of transformation and of entrepreneurial development, there is also the lifeblood of generations of emigrants who knew how to transfer new potential back home: capital, language, technologies, trades, enterprise, courage, and far-sightedness. All are values that are integral parts of the national cultural substratum. The talent of working and saving, especially during the difficult years, for example, explains the strength of Veneto today. The Veneto model, which could enter into crisis with the progressive expected advancement of Central and Eastern Europe, is an established fact, and it acts as a true and authentic cultural model, as the research of sociologist Ulderico Bernardi has shown.

Precisely to those from the Veneto region who are often at the head of street demonstrations against immigrants and espouse the same racist chauvinism that runs through certain Italian cultural and political forces, it is necessary to remember that emigration has always existed, fortunately for Europe, and it has always produced much fortune and wealth. The old continent could not have experienced industrialization without this safety valve. It was also critical for Italy's economic development. It is emigration that permitted the growth of Italy. We must be profoundly grateful to those who, sacrificing life and feelings (because it is truly difficult to uproot oneself from one's reality only to root oneself in a totally different one) enabled the growth of Italy in an unexpected way. It is also thanks to them that today, for better or worse, Italy is still one of the major economic industrial powers in the world. Recently, the President of the Republic eloquently expressed the recognition that the country owes to its emigrants:

> For decades emigration has been an essential "safety valve" for the persistence of severe economic and social difficulties, and remittances of emigrants have contributed greatly to the development of Italy. Often Italians abroad have led a hard life, full of sacrifices and deprivation, but the work culture of which they were bearers and the values in which they believed permitted them to finally integrate with success into the political, social and economic fabric of the countries that welcomed them. Today, Italians abroad constitute a splendid "calling card" of the image of Italy and they contribute in an often crucial way to the relations between countries of residence and their mother country and to the diffusion of the Italian language and culture.

While we give to emigrants due recognition for their contribution to the economic development of the country and the industrial development to the North, we must warn Italy that ties with grandchildren of emigrants must be nurtured with new lifeblood.

In this context, particular attention must be given to cultural incentives and to the support of the Italian language abroad. Often culture and language are presented as the most efficacious vehicle to enhance the image of Italy and of Made in Italy. Strengthening the quality and the number of the linguistic-cultural promotional initiatives is a tribute to the consistency of any project of the promotion of the Italian system, since even now the demand for Italian culture far exceeds the supply. Promoting culture and the study of the language, which is the DNA of every society, also signifies promoting the Italian economy. The language of a population is certainly its most authentic spiritual manifestation, but in fact becomes the strongest factor in the social and economic promotion of a country.

SELECTED BIBLIOGRAPHY

Balletta, Francesco, *Il Banco di Napoli e le rimesse degli emigranti (1914-1925)* (Napoli: Institut International d'historie de la banque, 1972).

Bernardi, Ulderico, ed., *La societa' veneta: riferimenti bibliografici (1955-1990)* (Padova: Il poligrafico, 1991).

De Rosa, Luigi, *Emigranti, capitali e banche* (Napoli: Edizioni del Banco di Napoli, 1980).

Franchetti, Luopoldo, *Mezzogiorno e colonie, saggio di Umberto Zanotti Bianco* (Firenze: La Nuova Italia, 1950).

Immigrazione: Dossiere statistico-XX rapporto sullimmigrazione, (Roma: Fondazione Migrantes, Idos Edizioni, 2010).

Masullo, Gino, "Economia delle rimesse," in *Storia dell'emigrazione italiana* a cura di P. Bevilacqua, A. De Clementi e E. Franzina (Roma: Donzelli Editore, 2001).

Mittone, Luigi, "Le rimesse degli emigrati sino al 1914," *Affari Internazionali* n.4 (1984).

Nitti, Francesco Saverio, *Scritti sulla questione meridionale*, vol. 1 (Bari: Laterza, 1968).

Serpieri, Arrigo, *La Guerra e le classi rurali italiane* (Bari: Laterza, 1930).

Intellectuals and Expatriates
Bridging the Gap

Vincenzo Pascale
Rutgers University

> *Il compito dell'intellettuale non è quello di suonare il piffero per la rivoluzione dando una veste poetica alla politica, ma quello di raccogliere tutti gli stimoli culturali che la società offre, per rinnovarla dal profondo.*
>
> —Elio Vittorini

Immigration is a complex social phenomena that involves many aspects of a human being's life. It is a phenomenon not only concerned with moving, for whatever reason, to another country, but it also implies a sophisticated process of negotiating a new set of values, life style and acquisition of learning that opens the immigrants to a more creative life with benefits for the hosting society. Immigrants bring with them values, behaviors and a body of knowledge, which serve to enrich the cultural complexity of the host society.

Regarding Italian immigration in New York City (specifically the period between the years 1880 and 1924), there are two main issues to consider when we approach the study of the Italian cultural production and contribution in New York City. The first issue pertains to the high levels of low literacy among the Italian immigrant population during that time frame. The second one concerns the cultural traditions that

From: *Theater of the Mind, Stage of History*. Bordighera Press, 2015

the Italian immigrants brought with them; certainly more music, plays, popular culture than a literate culture would embody. Just to bring a few examples to mind, which may shed light on my research. The structure of a society where oral culture had a predominance upon literary culture is one in which the manifestation of magical thinking is largely considered part of ordinary life of the people.[1] This element of the cultural life of those populations is strictly connected to the form of art *consumed* by those populations in their native regions of Italy. Among these forms of cultural expression, we may include popular representation of holy days. The phenomenon of carnival is one of them, as well as use of musical instruments such as the accordion, guitar, flute, bagpipe, harp, trumpet, etc., with the result that a certain degree of familiarity with musical melodies in many cases entered the everyday life of this population. Therefore, many of these cultural forms of entertainment travelled with the immigrants when they came to America. They came to occupy a public space of ethnic entertainment where the consistency of literary presence as a public form of entertainment was less relevant than those concerning the area of performing arts such as concerts, plays, religious representations and musical performances. For a considerable period of time, they were more popular and better received by immigrants than cultural activities related to the printed word. Indeed, it was the press, in particular newspapers, which

---

[1] For further research on this topic, see: Giovanni Verga, *The House by the Medlar Tree*, trans. by Raymond Rosenthal (Berkeley: University of California Press, 1983); Carlo Levi, *Christ Stopped at Eboli, The Story of a Year* (New York: Farrar, Strauss, 1963); Ernesto De Martino, *Sud e Magia* (Milan: Feltrinelli, 1972).

originally contributed to raising the levels of literacy among immigrants.

Artistic representations among immigrants, in particular Italian immigrants in the New York area, played an important role within Italian community life, when considering the psychological benefits that these artistic forms had in reducing the sense of nostalgia and several mild forms of depression among immigrants. Moreover, when transferred to a different host society, cultural forms produced by immigrants not only enriched a certain cultural field by opening up space for a more culturally diverse society, but were for a considerable period of time, still part of that world which was left behind, and in many cases it remained an important avenue available for the immigrants to relate to that world.

In the case of Italian immigration to the United States, their cultural expressions have been relevant, and in many cases have contributed to increasing and expanding the Americans' artistic world. In this article, I will focus on how the Italian cultural production during the period between 1880-1920 has to be considered in a broader context which does not focus exclusively upon narrative or literary production, but includes other artistic forms which are in some ways an outgrowth of literary production.

A few preliminary and important considerations have to be made. This time period saw a very large number of Italians reaching the shores of United States (the large majority entered to the United States from New York harbor and went through the immigration center at Ellis Island). It must be noted that there were Italians in the United States before 1880, although the great wave of Italian immigration began to arrive around this time period. This mass migration had several causes, which are not always related directly to Italian Unification (1861), although, it did have a certain degree of influence in fostering the migration process with regard to the relationship between shipping companies (mass transportation) and emigration.

What interests us in this study are the strategies and modalities of producing cultural products in the new world. In other words, we aim to point out how immigrants were producers of cultural identities in the world in a way which fostered an Italian cultural industry in the United States, and therefore an important forerunner in the fashioning of an Italian identity abroad. What kind of culture did they produce? How was it reinvented in the new world?

The cultural production of Italian immigrants in the United States has often been overlooked because, among other issues, a prejudice existed towards the literacy levels of immigrants, and prior historical periods held a more narrow definition of the term culture. Cultural perspectives have changed a great deal over the last century, allowing us to reconsider what constitutes our understanding of culture.

A primary cultural factor of early Italian immigrants in New York City was that the majority of them spoke a dialect: that is to say a language restricted in a limited area with a narrow if non-existent circulation of written material. However, in 1879, Carlo Barsotti (1850-1927), a businessman, founded *Il Progresso ItaloAmericano*, which started publication on December 6, 1880 (fourteen Italian newspapers were founded before 1880). The newspaper was published in Italian for an Italian readership focusing on Italian social and political life of Italy and in the United States. A large portion of the paper was dedicated to advertising for jobs, medical services, and business opportunities. The publication of *Il Progresso Italo-Americano* came three years after the *Coppino Law* (1877) enacted by the Italian Government, which made three years of education mandatory for each child of six years of age and older. Although the *Coppino Law* faced difficulties in its implementation, it helped to raise the literacy level among subsequent generations of Italians who later immigrated to the United States.

The role of *Il Progresso Italo-Americano*[2] in the cultural history of Italians of New York was of particular importance in forming the Italian-American identity. It was not only a newspaper used to inform the Italian community of New York, but was a major player in fostering an Italian national identity among Italian immigrants in the United States. A prime example of its cultural influence could be seen in its launching of a campaign to raise funds for a monument to honor Columbus to commemorate the 400th Anniversary of Columbus's landing in the Americas. Constructed with funds raised by *Il Progresso*, the monument consisted of a marble statue of Columbus atop a 70-foot column created by Italian sculptor Gaetano Russo. Another key monument of Dante Alighieri was built in 1911 for the 50th anniversary of Italian Unification, along with other key monuments of Italian personalities and historical figures. Numerous monuments were sponsored by Italian political exiles or by wealthy Italians living in New York City. There is one that was dedicated to Mazzini in 1878, located in Central Park; there is another to Garibaldi dedicated in 1888, located in Washington

---

[2] *Il Progresso ItaloAmericano* is available in microfilm at the New York Public Library.

Square Park; another, as well, erected in 1906, is dedicated to Verdi in Verdi's Square on 72nd Street and Broadway.

We know from newspapers and public chronicles that each of these dedications were attended by crowds numbering from two thousand to ten thousand people. For example, ten thousand people attended the dedication for Verdi's monument. Who were those people attending? For certain, a great number of immigrants, who had a degree of familiarity with the world represented by those statues, Dante and Verdi primarly. The immigrants carried with them a sense of the values conveyed by their cultural personalities and the art they performed. The emergence of an Italian identity abroad was underway. In a sense, this identity was not entirely perceived by Italian authorities in the United States for years to come.

The awareness of this national identity building was acquired by many Italian immigrants in New York more through music, theatre, and food rather than through a process built upon a literary one. Indeed, although the first English translation of *I Promessi Sposi* (*The Betrothed*) dates back to 1828 and was published in Pisa (Italy), three new translations go back to the early 1830s (one of them was printed in New York under the title *Lucia* in 1831), and despite a certain popularity of Manzoni's novel among first generation immigrants, the relationship with Italian literary production was weak, while the relationships with opera, theatre and music was solid and continuous.

In evaluating the impact of *Il Progresso ItaloAmericano* upon the increasing levels of literacy among Italian immigrants in New York, we have to take into account the educational laws passed in Italy by the Italian government, which had a positive impact not only on Italian residents but also on those who migrated. In 1889, the Legge Crispi passed to institute Italian schools abroad. However, in New York City several Italian schools were already in existence, started by the Dante Alighieri Society and by Italian Cultural Associations. Nevertheless, despite the attempt of Italian diplomacy in the United States to foster a national Italian identity through a local educational network, the interest of Italian immigrants towards educating their young in Italian language was low. Education was not a primary factor among the Italian community, as pointed out by several Italian journalists in those years and by the Italian diplomatic authorities. The loss of Italian cultural heritage by Italian immigrants was a primary concern not only of Italian diplomacy, but also of several cultural institutions, among them the Dante Alighieri Society.

Despite the alarming reports from diplomats and journalists, in New York, a sense of Italian identity was well formed within the Italian community. Theatre, poetry, music and political ideas were the leading expressive forms that fashioned an Italian identity (language *in primis*). Language was still very linked to local or regional identities. The same intellectual debate was occurring in Italy during the post Unification years. In Italy the political figure who played a major role in structuring an educational system was Francesco De Sanctis (1817-1883), a literary critic, considered the most important scholar of Italian literature in the nineteenth century. De Sanctis was deeply committed first as educator, then as politician to renew the Italian educational system. He tried to build an educational system based upon a set of values and knowledge which in the past had brought Italy to cultural preeminence in Europe. He was appointed Minister of Education (1878-1880, with Cairoli, Prime Minister). In 1877, the Italian Parliament passed the above-mentioned Legge Coppino, and made elementary education (3 years) mandatory for every Italian child of at least six years of age.

To understand the cultural production of Italians in New York City during the period 1880 to 1920 and how their national identity was fashioned, we have to look more at artistic forms as such as opera, sculptures and newspapers than to literary production. Despite strong local, regional identities, Italians in New York had major cultural references in intellectual characters who were leading figure in building their sense of national identity in Garibaldi, Mazzini, Dante and Verdi. The Italian identity in New York City was strongly anchored to these intellectual and artistic figures without neglecting a local identity. Local and national ties were, and for many reasons still are, the two poles around which Italians negotiated their identities in the New World.

This strong relationship with local identities runs deeply through the Italian cultural history. Francesco De Sanctis, in an article entitled, *Postilla al saggio su Petrarca* (1883) presents a list of values which he considers indispensable for the young Italian nation. Those values are: *la bellezza* (beauty), *la giustizia* (justice), *la verità* (truth), *la famiglia* (family), *la patria* (homeland), *la gloria* (glory), *l'eroismo* (heroism), *la virtù morale* (integrity). These values, according to De Sanctis, were indispensable and would have to enter into the new Italian literature upon which a national identity should have been built. An Italian literature that, for De Sanctis, had to be renewed in view of bringing closer the so called *letteratura colta* to the *letteratura popolare*: a process of democratization of

"Intellectuals and Expatriates"

Italian society. De Sanctis's idea of literature was truly part of the project of building the Italian nation. A literature as a model for life, as a sort of moral and spiritual guide which is grounded in the "Comune" — Municipality. In a speech delivered at the University of Naples on November 16, 1872, De Sanctis presents his ideas:

> L'uomo viveva come abbarbicato al suo suolo, ai suoi avi, alla sua casa, alla sua chiesa, alla sua classe, al suo Comune, chiuso in potenti organismi, che gli rammentavano doveri da compiere più che diritti da rivendicare. Si sentiva non un individuo libero ed isolato, ma parte di un tutto, vivente della vita di quello, figlio, marito, cittadino, soldato, credente, di questo o di quel ceto. E qui era il difetto di quei ferrei organismi, l'individuo non vi aveva fini propri, ma un fine comune che spesso pesava sopra di lui come il fato, e uccideva la sua libertà. A poco a poco il limite soperchiò, cessò di essere uno stimolo, e divenne un ostacolo. L'uomo stretto come in una rete di organismi sopraposti gli uni agli altri, dai quali quali non sapeva come distrigarsi, vi si sentì affogare e intisichire, e prese in odio i sentimenti più cari della vita, la sua religione la sua famiglia, il suo Comune, la sua classe. Volendo rovesciare l'ostacolo soppresse lo stimolo. (De Sanctis, 1959, 1051)

> Man used to live clinging to his ground, his ancestors, his home, his church, his class, his town, closed in powerful organizations, which reminded him more of the duties to perform than what rights to claim. He was not a free and isolated individual, but part of a whole, living the life of the son, husband, citizen, soldier, believer in this or that class. And here was the fault of those iron-clad organisms; individuals had not their own purposes, but a common

goal that often weighed upon them like fate, and killed their freedom." Gradually the limit stopped being a stimulus, and became an obstacle. Caught in a network of superimposed organisms over each other, from which he could not extricate himself, the individual felt drowned, started hating his life, his religion, his family, his town, his class. Wanting to overthrow the obstacle removed the stimulus. (De Sanctis, 1959, 1051)[3]

De Sanctis saw in the Italian local identity a source of values and possibilities upon which to build the literature of the new country (indeed among his favorite writers were Machiavelli and Leopardi, both authors and thinkers grounded in a strong local identity). It seems to me that De Sanctis's ideas found a ground of practicability expressed in the Italian community abroad, particularly in New York City where they had been able to live an identity, which was both local and national. In the case of Italians in New York, their national identity primarily was one lived in public spaces, due to historical monuments placed in public centers. They entered a local public discourse which means they became part of the social history, not only because of the community which decides to install them (those monuments in a public space), but also due to the social and urban history of the city which hosts them. The acquisition of public space to settle cultural symbols or leaders of another country is a sign of mutual acknowledgement between cultures and countries. This process tends (but not only) to reinforce the identity of those to whom the monuments are directly related, but also

---

[3] Francesco De Sanctis, *Opere* (Milan, 1959).

expands their cultural horizon from a local identity to a national one.

Therefore, the acquisition of an Italian identity for the Italians living in New York City, between the years 1880 to 1920 was a long process where the negotiation of local and national identity was at stake. At least in public spaces their identity was recognized entirely as Italian and their historical heritage became part of the life of the city of New York. However, from a linguistic point of view, Italian dialects remained strong and vibrant among the Italian community. Theaters were among the places where dialects were largely used as an alternative to Italian for operas. Therefore, we may conclude that among Italians abroad, the concept of double identity, local and national, remained alive in defining their identity since arriving in the New World.

Stories that Shaped Italian Unification
Ugo Foscolo's *Le ultime lettere di Jacopo Ortis*

Joseph Perricone
Fordham University

As it is easily deduced, the term Risorgimento comes from the verb *sorgere* plus the iterative prefix ri-, meaning therefore to rise again or to resurrect. Both meanings imply a previous stage of death or decadence. Thus the term used for this momentous event reveals both an awareness of a state of dejection and lowliness pervasive in the civic and cultural life throughout most of the Italian territories; but it also suggests a sense of vigor and hope, spiritual resources necessary to deliver the land from centuries of oppression and lethargy caused by indigenous as well as foreign rulers. Both of these components are present in most writings of the period, which were instrumental in revitalizing and regenerating segments of the population, the bourgeois class for the most part. These writings, however, also trickled down among the rest of the inhabitants igniting sentiments that were to lead to the unification of the territories. The term Risorgimento refers mainly to the political, jurisdictional, territorial, and economic spheres, areas that have been explored extensively by historians. However, more questions are still in need of analysis concerning this "vast process" as Gilles Pécout referred to it in his *Naissance de l'Italie contemporaine*.[1] Difficult

---

[1] Gilles Pécout, *Naissance de l'Italie contemporaine* (Paris: Colin,, 1997) 8.

From: *Theater of the Mind, Stage of History*. Bordighera Press, 2015

to establish is for instance the exact beginning of the process especially if one considers primarily its cultural and spiritual aspects, leaving aside the territorial and bureaucratic accomplishments whose chronology is easier to trace. It is generally agreed that the process of Italian unification begins at some point in the Enlightenment, is fueled by the French Revolution, and more specifically by the advent of the Napoleonic reforms gradually enacted between 1796, the year of the invasion of Savoy by the Napoleonic troops, and 1815, the year that marks the end of his era. However, according to a broader meaning of the term, the historical span of the Risorgimento is not limited to the territorial and political unification of the peninsula; rather, it finds its roots in earlier centuries. In the imaginary consciousness of earlier thinkers and literary figures perhaps the notion of a united Italy or at least of an Italy free of foreign rule had been a heartfelt desire shared more or less by a number of writers and artists. It seems that the term was first used in a broad cultural way with some political overtones in a pamphlet written in 1764 by Gian Rinaldo Carli entitled *Della patria degli italiani,* and in 1775 one Padre Bettinelli wrote of *Il Risorgimento d'Italia dopo il mille.* It seems that the term Risorgimento which was borrowed from the romantic nationalism of the 1800s, began to be used only toward the end of the 19th century in a manner that included also the territorial, political and military unification of the peninsula. Gilles Pécout again reports (10) that Francesco De Sanctis, the well-known critic and literary historian, concluded that it was culture that ultimately created the unification of Italy. It is this aspect of the unification process that will be pursued in the next few pages, especially as it operates in the writings of one of the front line protagonists of the early period, the Napoleonic period to be exact, and major literary figure of the Ottocento, Ugo Foscolo. In his *Le ultime lettere di Jacopo Ortis*, Foscolo has left us an invaluable document and radiography of the cultural construct of the Risorgimento.

As is well known, the literature that examines the actual cultural and socio-political conditions of Italy at or around the time of the Risorgimento period, from the Enlightenment onward, or the literature that aims to promote in some ways the ideals of unity, both political and social, is quantitatively impressive and some of it deservedly considered outstanding, representing some of the masterpieces of Italian letters. Alessandro Manzoni's works quickly come to mind, in particular his plays, the *Conte di Carmagnola* (1820) and *Adelchi* (1821), along with his better known historical novel *I promessi sposi*. But there were many more now partly obscure works, such as Pietro Giannone's *L'esule*, which dealt with the vicissitudes of exiles and their relationship to patriotic events in Italy. Actually the exile was treated in several other musical works as well, by Verdi, Donizetti, and Rossini — works that embody part of the massive literature, mostly popular, that celebrated the hopes patriots had for a united Italy.

The rise of modern Italy out of the ashes of centuries of civic inertia brought about by external as well as internal political factors is a startling event, or so it seems to at least one historian, Domenico Fisichella, whose seemingly hyperbolically titled book on the Italian Risorgimento, *Il miracolo del Risorgimento* (*The Miracle of the Risorgimento*), underscores, all things considered, the singularity of that accomplishment. The forces accumulated over the centuries stacked out against the success of the Risorgimento were neither few nor easy to overcome. The debate around the questions that were raised during and after Unification about the merit of its process is still as spirited now as they ever were. Some recent publications leave the reader questioning certain darker moments of that process with books that at times seem to suggest sensationalism with some of their albeit factually accurate affirmations, as do Pino Aprile's *Terroni: Tutto quello che è stato fatto perchè gli italiani del Sud diventassero "meridionali"* (*Southerners: All that Has Been Done so that Southern Italians Would Become "Southerners"* Piemme, 2010); or Gigi Di Fiore *Gli ultimi giorni di Gaeta: L'assedio che condannò l'Italia all'unità.* (*The Last Days of Gaeta: The Siege that condemned Italy to Unity*, Rizzoli, 2008); or *I vinti del Risorgimento: Storia e storie di chi combattè per i Borbone di Napoli,* UTET, 2004) (*The defeated of the Risorgimento: History and Stories of those who fought for the Bourbons of Naples*). Although some might question it, there is no argument valid enough against Italian unification, which is different of course from Italian unity, an accomplishment that lies beyond the realm of any debate. Questions can be raised, however, concerning the factors that delayed Italian Unification or that brought it about at the time when it occurred and not earlier. What were the driving energies, the right combination of emotions and reasons that led to an accomplishment that few thought could be possible? In his book *Il Risorgimento*, Giampiero Carocci relates an anecdote in which to a French diplomat who in 1797 wanted to convince him that unifying Italy was a chimera, Napoleon answered that "nonetheless it is a beautiful idea," underscoring both his design to weaken English domination of the Mediterranean Sea and establish control and primacy in a "united Italy," which nonetheless for sometime risked remaining only a dream.[2]

However weak and vague, and however limited to a circumscribed territory it might have been, a sentiment of patriotism if not of nationalism had been manifested by some intellectuals in the earlier centuries of Italian culture. One need only think, for instance, of Dante's famous invective in *Purgatorio* Canto 6, lines 76-78: "Ahi, serva Italia di dolore ostello / nave senza nocchiere in gran tempesta / non donna di provincia ma bordello" (Servile Italy, hostel of suffering / ship without a helmsman in stormy sea / not mistress of provinces but of brothels), where it is difficult not to note in the apostrophe "Italia" a reference to the entire peninsula, or at least to a larger area than just Florence and its immediate territory. Moreover, in this Canto, Dante is surrounded by a crowd of souls who are eager to ask him to renew their memory on earth with their dear ones whose prayers can help shorten their time spent in the Ante-Purgatory. These souls in their lifetime had been political figures who perished during the civil clashes caused by the hatred of opposed factions that divided cities in Dante's time. While Dante agrees to satisfy their wish, he nonetheless treats these souls with a certain disdainful detachment since they represent a symbol of that hatred that he knew only too well, but that in the end he firmly condemned. Within this Canto in *Purgatorio*, furthermore, is the famous and touching episode where Sordello, a poet from Mantua, meets Virgil and falls to his knees in awe and admiration, not just because Virgil is a great fellow poet, an idol, but also because Virgil too is

---

[2] Giampiero Carocci, *Il Risorgimento* (Newton, 2011) 14.

from Mantua, a fellow citizen from the same city. This episode is often cited as an example of love and brotherhood and a model of that spirit of fraternity that should be a bond among all people of the same place. In his treatise on poetry, the *De vulgari eloquentia*, moreover, Dante argues that the existence of a common language is felt throughout the Italian territories. Although it is clear that he never concludes that the Italian language whose existence he is set on discovering is fully and completely formed anywhere, he does discover its presence in different areas throughout the peninsula wherever there is a poetic tradition of some refinement. The language becomes very important throughout the Risorgimento as a binding factor among Italians, at least among the cultured class, and Dante himself is recognized as a symbol of union, of common heritage, and an emblem of distinction and greatness.

Another case in point is Petrarch, whose canzone *Italia mia*, later echoed by Leopardi in his *O Patria mia*, contains several elements that suggest a sense of common identity with the rest of the people of the Italian peninsula on the part of Petrarch. Unlike Dante, who was still under the influence of a universalist political concept, in spite of his undeniable attachment to Florence and Italy, Petrarch displays a notion of an Italy inhabited by a people of close kinship generally identified as Latin people in opposition to Germanic ones. In particular, in his canzone *Italia mia*, which might be considered the first truly heartfelt, doleful lament for the suffering and destruction that Petrarch witnesses inflicted by foreign armies on the Italian population, the populations that live along the Tiber, the Arno and the Po rivers represent, by virtue of a synecdoche, the people of the whole of Italy. Particularly incisive and insightful is the second stanza of that canzone where the author apostrophizes the Italian princes who are deceived by their narrow sight for personal avaricious gains and permit foreign armies to bring destruction and devastation to the beautiful countryside.

Although the term Italia had been at different times used to indicate various parts of the peninsula, it seems that Petrarch is limiting its use to include the areas indicated by the famous rivers that run through them, in order of importance for Petrarch and historically, the Tiber, the Arno and the Po. Obviously not unknown to Petrarch the accomplished classicist, must have been the famous lines from the *Aeneid*, where the name Italia is repeated three times probably to mean the Southern areas, but not excluding the possibility that Virgil meant the whole peninsula with that term: "Iamque rubescabat stellis Aurora fugatis, / cum procul obscuros collis humilemque videmus / Italiam, Italiam primus conclamat Achates, / Italiam laeto socii clamore salutant" (iii521). (Now the pink Dawn put in flight the stars / when we see the faint hills far away and low lying Italy. / Achate first shouts Italy, Italy the other companions salute with joyful shouts.) Such reminiscences will exert their inspirational virtues in many compositions of the Risorgimento period. Several themes of Petrarch's canzone *Italia mia* will be echoed in later verses by patriots that clearly recall his passionate pleas. For instance, Italy personified as a woman upon whom foreign armies inflict numerous wounds is one such leitmotif; and there is the image of Italy as a beautiful place (le belle contrade). In the sixth stanza there is the motif of the love for one's birthplace, the nest "where I was nurtured so sweetly." The image of the fatherland, the earth that nurtured both parents, introduces the theme of the ancestors that in the Risorgimento will become the metaphoric symbol of the noble minds of great achievers elected as spiritual fathers. The canzone also examines the theme of the ferocious greed of rulers that Fortune has appointed as leaders who take no pity on the population afflicted with suffering as a result of their lust for power. The problem of placing trust in foreign armies composed of mere venal mercenaries who fight only for pay is explored at length. The note of unity is introduced in the last stanza where the author suggests that if union is achieved among the princes, the ancient military valor of the people would once again triumph. These are all themes that would resurface in the Risorgimento period and would make Petrarch one of the spiritual fathers mentioned for instance by Foscolo in his *Le ultime lettere di Jacopo Ortis*, along with Dante, Parini and Alfieri. Petrarch's Canzone *Italia mia* is one of the earliest civic-political analyses of the Italian situation in verse formulated in modern terms. Its echo in Risorgimento literature is relevant in the discourse articulated in the literary texts intended to develop and strengthen a sense of civic and political conscience necessary to bring about the momentous events that set the course for the Unification.

    The construction of a patriotic sentiment was the product of the convergence of several cultural and ideological forces at work that began to exert their positive influence gradually, with a crescendo around the time that the ideas of the Enlightenment found fertile ground among Italian thinkers such as Pietro Verri, Gianluigi Beccaria and Ludovico Antonio Muratori, among others. In the particular area of literature, specifically in the satirical genre, a precursor who contributed to the reawakening of the observation and criticism of social customs especially by the aristocratic classes, who also inspired with his particular blend of gravitas and depth, was Giuseppe Parini. In his narrative poem *Il giorno*, Parini exposed all the parasitic practices of the nobility with implications that these were the cause of social injustice and civic decadence. His book awakened a spirit of responsibility that formed the character of subsequent writers such as Alfieri and Foscolo, both of whom found his figure to be a model of emulation and admiration. The renewed concepts and visions of society and humanity developed by the Enlightenment are an indispensible premise for the events that will bring about Italian unity. Ugo Foscolo's title for his epistolary novel *Le ultime lettere di Jacopo Ortis* suggests homage to the Swiss thinker Jean Jacques Rousseau though not to the followers of the secret society of St. Jacques' church later known as Jacobins. Foscolo was a moderate and like Alfieri believed in freedom, fairness, and justice but not in the excesses of the French Revolution. As a political figure and a political writer Foscolo was engaged in the celebration of Italian intellectual artistic and literary traditions in order to develop a sense of nationalism and civic sensibility that would bring about the cohesion of as many inhabitants of Italy as possible to support the cause of a free and united country.

Foscolo celebrates Giuseppe Parini as a beacon of austerity, sincerity, and integrity around which he hoped many of his contemporaries would group and bring about the resurgence of the country. Foscolo has his hero Jacopo travel to various parts of Italy, after he leaves his beloved Veneto because of the proscriptions after the treaty of Campo Formio, inaugurating the theme of the political exile in modern Italian narrative. In his wanderings, Jacopo goes to Milan where he meets Parini, now a stately octogenarian. Several pages are dedicated to this encounter, which is framed in the style of a devotional pilgrimage. Jacopo in fact has already visited Tuscany and Florence where, in the Church of Santa Croce, the reader witnesses a heartfelt commemoration of several figures, emblems of high minded principles, of greatness and freedom, acclaimed as the national fathers of the Italian nation. Jacopo is moved by the sight of the tombs of Galileo, Machiavelli, and Michelangelo. Earlier Jacopo had expressed a desire to meet Vittorio Alfieri, saying that he was "l'unico mortale ch'io desideravo conoscere." (…the only person that I wanted to know"; p.128). In his patriotic novel, Foscolo also quotes lines from Alfieri's tragedy *Saul*, admiring enthusiastically the courage and valor of the biblical king after whom the tragedy is named. In these pages of the novel, which happen to be the central body of the narrative, Foscolo provides a construct of a national identity whose ingredients are high achievement, dedication, devotion to the fatherland and love of the Italian language. At the time that Foscolo was writing his prose masterpiece the word "patria" had been used primarily if not exclusively to refer to one's immediate birth place and specific state, of which there were eleven constituencies in the Italian peninsula prior to the arrival of Napoleon's armies. In *Jacopo Ortis*, however, Foscolo seems to use it at times to refer to a larger entity, to include the vaster area where Italian culture and civilization had developed, particularly the artistic and literary accomplishments of the past, of which the Renaissance had been the most significant expression. In his desire to write a text in which readers would find inspiration and guidance for the resurrection of Italian civic life, and even for the instigation to find love for their fatherland, courage to defend it and pride in its past valor, Foscolo undoubtedly found inspiration in an already established tradition. This albeit tenuous and sparse tradition, was recognized in the motley make up of the populations inhabiting the Italian peninsula, whereby a cultural unity existed, a commonality of genius shared by all, or at least by all those who partook in the heritage of the arts and learning. There had been already publications in the seventeen hundreds claiming a cultural unity within the people of the Italian peninsula that were not unknown to Foscolo, such as Ludovico Antonio Muratori's *Rerum italicorum scriptores* (*Writers of Italian Deeds*) published between 1720 and 1751; Tiraboschi's *Storia della letteratura italiana* (*History of Italian Literature*) that appeared between 1772 and 1782. Before the end of the first decade of the 19th century Sismondi would publish his voluminous *Histoire des républiques italiennes du Moyen Âge* (History of the Italian Republics in the Middle Ages).

Through Jacopo's meeting with Giuseppe Parini, Foscolo is able to accomplish several aspects of his plan to construct a model for readers to internalize the new ideals and aspirations. First, he is able to draw the portrait of an exemplary figure of the intellectual, artist and citizen of the prospective nascent republic. Foscolo apostrophizes Parini by saying that "Il Parini è il personaggio più dignitoso e più eloquente ch'io m'abbia mai conosciuto; e d'altronde un profondo, generoso, meditato dolore a chi non dà somma eloquenza?" (142-130) (Parini is the most dignified person, the most eloquent that I've ever known; and after all wouldn't a deep, generous and reflexive suffering make anyone eloquent?). Secondly, by introducing Parini in the narrative, Foscolo is able to draw attention to some of the ills that beset his contemporary Italian society as it had been observed by the accomplished testimony of the author of *Il giorno*. The narrative states:

> Mi parlò a lungo della sua patria, e fremeva e per le antiche tirannidi e per la nuova licenza. Le lettere prostituite, tutte le passioni languenti e degenerate in una indolente vilissima corruzione; non più le sacre ospitalità, non la benevolenza, non più l'amore figliale—e poi mi tesseva gli annali recenti e i delitti di tanti omiciattoli ch'io non degnerei di nominare, se le loro scelleraggini mostrassero il vigore d'animo, non dirò di Silla e di Catilina, ma di quegli animosi masnadieri che affrontano il misfatto qualunque e' si vedano presso il patibolo—ma ladroncelli, tremanti, saccenti, più onesto insomma è tacerne. (142)

> (He spoke to me at length of his fatherland, and quivered both for the ancient tyrannies and the new abuses. Literature was prostituted, all passions languished and degenerated in a vile and indolent corruption; no more sacred hospitality nor benevolence, nor filial love—and then he narrated to me recent events and the murders by so many homunculi that I would not deign to name, if their wicked deeds would show some vigor of spirit, not of the sort of Silla and Catilina, but of those spirited ruffians who face up to their misdeeds when brought to the hanging scaffold, but petty thieves, trembling, boastful: more honest in short it would be to be silent about them).

The opening sentence of *Le ultime lettere* introduces the principal theme of the narrative, a patriotic one, the sacrifice of the fatherland, which foreshadows the final theme, the sacrifice of young Jacopo's life. His suicide is the only choice left to him after all his other hopes fail. This gives the novel a sort of circular form connecting the beginning to the end and the end again to the beginning in a powerful bond. Teresa's impossibility to exercise her own free will in choosing her husband parallels Jacopo's own inability to choose a free government for his country, thus leaving him with no other choice but that of taking his own life, it having become impossible for him to go on living in an oppressive and tyrannical world. In that very first sentence are also sounded the other main themes of the novel such as the theme of suffering and of death, of misfortune and shame, of abandonment of the native soil and of exile. That opening sentence with its solemn tragic tones is well worth quoting for the echoes it will have in the remainder of the novel as well as in the other literary works of this period: "Il sacrificio delle patria nostra è consumato: tutto è perduto; e se la vita, se pure ne verrà concessa, non ci resterà che per piangere le nostre sciagure, e la nostra infamia." (Our fatherland's sacrifice has been consummated: all is lost; and our life, even if it is spared, will be left to us only to cry about our misfortunes and our infamy; 15).

In fact, all the major themes elaborated throughout the Risorgimento years are introduced in Foscolo's works, particularly in *Le ultime lettere di Jacopo Ortis*. Prominent in Foscolo's creative universe is the theme of exile, as even the sonnet "A Zacinto" reminds us. But in his Wertherian epistolary novel it looms larger and it earned him the notoriety among his contemporary patriots of being the one who made exile an institution, as one of his great contemporary admirers, Carlo

Cattaneo, announced. It is indeed the most vibrant chord in his works that characterizes his world, so much so that Glauco Cambon named his own study of Foscolo's literary persona "the poet of exile."[3] Jacopo, Foscolo's young idealist persona, after the debacle of Campo Formio, that most disillusioning political act underwritten by Napoleon at the conclusion of his first phase of the invasion of the northern Italian provinces, reflects on the possible consequences that patriots faced, uttering then the most wrenching rhetorical question posed by Jacopo (and by analogy, by Foscolo, who was a Napoleonic soldier and subject), preparing the reader for the final deadly conclusion of the protagonist's life: " Merita poi questa vita di essere conservata con la viltà, e con l'esilio?" (Is this life then deserving of being preserved with cowardice, and with exile?; 15). Jacopo alludes here to the final rejection of either one of these options. At the end of his "confessions" he embraces the worst form of "exile" ever possible, that of self-inflicted death. But Foscolo elaborated further on the theme of exile as Jacopo thinks more on the disastrous outcome of the fate of Veneto orchestrated by Napoleon. Jacopo exclaims:

> Oh! Quanti de' nostri concittadini gemeranno pentiti, lontani dalle loro case! Perchè, e che potremmo aspettarci noi se non è indigenza e disprezzo; o al più, breve e sterile compassione, solo conforto che le nazioni incivilite offrono al profugo straniero? Ma dove cercherò asilo? In Italia? (16)
>
> (Oh, how many of our countrymen will lament regretfully, far from their homes! Why, and what could we expect oth-

---

[3] *Ugo Foscolo: Poet of Exile* (Princeton: Princeton University Press, 1980).

er than need and disrespect; or at the most, short-lived and fruitless compassion, only comfort that civilized nations offer to the foreign refugee? But where shall I find asylum? In Italy?)

History informs us that Foscolo, after the 1815 Restoration, refused to swear allegiance to the Austrian government and, after a short stay in Switzerland, went to live in England where he died in 1827. The exemplary model that Jacopo Ortis offers to his contemporaries is emblematic of the entire Risorgimento period: a dedication to the ideal of freedom and independence that goes beyond the self even to the point of supreme sacrifice. This message is embedded in the literature of the period and informs even the national anthem. Death, sacrifice and self-abnegation in the name of the supreme good, the fatherland, are the themes that populate consistently the popular literature of the Risorgimento. Foscolo inaugurates a literature that, inspired by the example of Parini and other earlier figures, connects again the literature to the actual social and human reality of the times, breaking that dissociation that prevailed in the Seicento and in the Arcadian ideology. If Vittorio Alfieri was the precursor of patriots and advocate of freedom, as Gaudence Magaro argues in his *Vittorio Alfieri Forerunner of Italian Nationalism*,[4] Ugo Foscolo was the first patriot poet and politically committed writer. In his epistolary novel he keeps an ear close to the ground and is ever attentive to observe the life, individuals and society, which surround him. The figure of Odoardo is

---

[4] Gaudence Magaro, *Vittorio Alfieri Forerunner of Italian Nationalism* (New York: Columbia University Press, 1930).

emblematic in this sense and represents a type totally opposite the idealistic and freedom inspired Jacopo. Odoardo represents the insensitive, frigid, calculating, opportunist who politically would support any regime that would defend the conventional rights and privileges of the old aristocracy, divorced totally from the reality in which the rest of the population lives, from the needs of the people. There are several "portraits" that Jacopo draws of this character, but the one close to the beginning of the narrative will suffice to render the ideologically negative dimensions of this figure within the economy of the narrative.

> ...s'egli avrà il cuore sempre così morto, e quella faccia magistrale non animata mai nè dal sorriso dell'allegria, nè dal dolce silenzio della pietà, sarà per me un di que' rosai senza fiori che mi fanno temere le spine. Cos'è l'uomo se tu lo abbandoni alla sola ragione fredda, calcolatrice? Scellerato, e scellerato bassamente (p.11).

> (...if he will have forever a dead heart, and that magisterial face never animated by the smile of mirth nor by the kind silence of pity, he will be for me one of those rose bushes without flowers that make you fear the thorns. What is mankind if abandoned to cold and calculating reason alone? A wicked being, lowly wicked.)

Sentiment and pity/piety are posited as positive ideals in opposition to that of pure rationality exalted by the Enlightenment. Beyond the exemplary models of civic virtues and their antagonist, in his novel Foscolo treats also the theme of the degradation of civic life as well as the lack of enthusiasm that prevails in the society of his times for the language and for the literary accomplishments that it represents. This subject had been introduced already by Parini and especially by Alfieri who was a staunch defender of the Italian literary tradition and of the Italian language, as his autobiography *Vita di Vittorio Alfieri, scritta da esso* will attest, as well as his satirical works, the *Misogallo* in particular, where he explicitly targets the French language as being inferior to Italian. One section of the novel in which past glories and present disappointments are addressed is when Jacopo accompanies Teresa's family on a pilgrimage to Arquà, where Petrarch's home and burial site are found. The description of nature is exuberant, probably one of the most moving examples in all romantic literature that captures the supernatural beauty of pristine nature. Of course Odoardo is totally oblivious to the power of the landscape. He is described as one who goes groping in the darkness of night rather than in the splendors of luxuriant and flourishing nature: "Eterno Iddio! parea ch'egli andasse tentone fra le tenebre della notte, o ne' deserti abbandonati dalla benedizione della natura" (15). (Eternal God! He seemed to be walking blindly in the dark of night, or in the deserts abandoned by the blessings of nature.) The carelessness of insensitive people like Odoardo, the text seems to imply, is the cause of the neglect in which lies the tomb of one of the most sublime Italian poets. Jacopo finds:

> la sacra casa di quel sommo Italiano sta crollando per la irreligione di chi possiede un tanto tesoro. Il viaggiatore verrà invano di lontana terra a cercare con meraviglia divota la stanza armoniosa ancora dei canti celesti del Petrarca. Piangerà invece sopra un mucchio di ruine coperto di ortiche e di erbe selvatiche fra le quali la volpe solitaria avrà

fatto il suo covile. Italia! placa l'ombre de' tuoi grandi (p.21).

(The sacred home of that supreme Italian is crumbling because of the irreligiosity of those who possess such a treasure. The traveler will come in vain from a distant land to seek with devout admiration the dwelling still surrounded by the harmony of Petrarch's celestial songs. He will cry instead atop of a heap of ruins covered by stinging nettle and wild growth where the solitary fox will have made its den. Italy! Appease the shade of your great people.)

Le ultime lettere is a text rich with critical observations and references to the social customs and conditions of the Cisalpine Republic as well as its civic and legal traditions and practices. Brief but significant notations scattered throughout the narrative relate the conditions of the plebs, the ill treatment of lawbreakers, the light judicial processes and the excessive penalties inflicted on transgressors whose primary and only guilt was absolute poverty. Social disparity and consequent behavioral misconduct is a dominant theme aimed at discrediting foreign rule, whether French or Austrian, and at funneling patriotic sentiments in the direction of reform and unity. Of the frequent invectives against misrule, this one on page 114, letter of 12 August, makes the point clear. Jacopo encounters two victims being brought to execution for stealing and breaks out in the following exclamation:

Ahi società! E se non vi fossero leggi protrettrici di coloro che per arricchire col sudore e col pianto de' propri concittadini li sospingono al bisogno e al delitto, sarebbero poi sì necessarie le prigioni e i carnefici?...No no; non voglio più respirare quest'aria fumante sempre del sangue de' miseri—E dove?

(Oh, society! And if there were no laws protecting those who in order to get richer with the toils and tears of their fellow citizens forced them to neediness and crime, would prisons and hangmen be so necessary in the end?... No no; I no longer want to breathe this air always filled with the exhalations of the blood of wretches—But where?)

Jacopo embodies the spirit of the restless fugitive, disappointed wherever he goes because everywhere he finds oppression and corruption, violations against his homeland. He thus represents for his contemporaries mindful of the fate of their country the lot destined for the people who continue to remain victims of oppressors in their own home. This ideological model with variations according to artistic temperament and genres, informs much of the popular literature of the period, becoming the matrix and the archetype of the ideological formative model of the patriot. Jacopo's wanderings through Italy mandated by the proscriptions after Campo Formio give Foscolo an opportunity to comment on the cultural squalor and neglect of civic virtues, which versed various areas of the peninsula. The central letters of the narrative between pages 122-140, are those in which Jacopo visits Santa Croce and Monteaperto where he is able to make a series of reflections aimed at fueling the minds of his contemporary patriots. Jacopo's comments on past divisiveness, on fratricidal wars, which only enhanced the advantage of oppressors are clearly recommendations to his contemporaries of what must be avoided presently. Some of the passages that were re-echoed in other works of the period resound of the inflammatory rhetoric of the times: "I cadaveri intanto d'infiniti Italiani ammazzatisi hanno fatte le fondamenta a' troni degli Imperadori e dei Papi" (The bodies of the dead of an infinite number of Italians who killed one another laid the foundations for the thrones of Emperors and Popes"); or in another passage we read: "I re per cui vi trucidate si stringono nel bollor della zuffa le destre e pacificamente si dividono le vostre vesti e il vostro terreno." (The kings for whom you slaughter one another shake their right hands in the heat of the clashes and peacefully divide among themselves your spoils and your land.") The low ebb to which has sunk the respect for the mother tongue, a lament voiced already by Alfieri, and the admiration of past achievements are disconsolately decried in the letter of 11 November, from Milan, where Jacopo asked: "… *La vita di Benvenuto Cellini* a un libraio – Non l'abbiamo. Lo richiesi di un altro scrittore; e allora quasi dispettoso mi disse, ch'ei non vendeva libri Italiani" (… *The Life of Benvenuto Cellini* to a book vendor—We don't have it. I asked him about another writer; and then he said almost spitefully that he did not sell Italian books; 125). Foscolo's book must have been the fundamental text for all who were involved with the Italian cause considering that it saw over sixty new editions until 1861, almost one per year since its first publication in 1802.

    Foscolo's productivity as a poet spanned two decades coinciding with the Napoleonic ventures. After 1815, he went to live in England, unable to bring himself to adhere to any allegiance exacted by the Austrian government. In England his literary activity was circumscribed primarily to criticism. However, in those twenty years of intense activity as a writer, poet, soldier, and university professor, Foscolo's ideas became seminal for the whole next generation of the most important patriots, especially for Mazzini and for Cattaneo, but also for Ippolito Nievo and many others, down even to Giacomo Leopardi's *Patria mia* poem.[5] Foscolo established the identity patrimony of the nation, creating the worship of noteworthy figures such as those that he celebrates in *Jacopo Ortis* and in his *Dei Sepolcri*. In this poem reverberate the themes and topics that Foscolo had elaborated in *Jacopo Ortis*, with greater emphasis on the importance of remembering great figures for which burial monuments constitute a sort of immortality that will sustain a nation in all its future evolution. Foscolo is thus the archetypal paradigm for all subsequent major and minor writers, poets, and patriots throughout the Risorgimento.

---

[5] See Amedeo Quondam, *Risorgimento a memoria* (Rome: Donzelli, 2011) 125.

Tommaso Bordonaro's *La spartenza*
Between Tradition and Singularity

Anita Pinzi
CUNY Graduate Center

Tommaso Bordonaro's *La spartenza* stands out from the Italian and Italian American literary panorama as a singular literary case. Bordonaro immigrated to the United States from Bolognetta, Sicily, in 1947, and being only functionally literate he handwrote his memoir in three notebooks when he was almost 80. He wrote his text for a literary contest promoted by the Archivio diaristico of Pieve di Santo Stefano in Arezzo, Italy. The Archive gave a prize for the memoir, which was subsequently published by Einaudi in 1990, with an introduction by Natalia Ginzburg. Sicily, Italy, and the U.S. constitute the geographical background of Bordonaro's narration. However, elements such as living between the two countries, migration, old and new life and identity shaping of the writer, are only marginally deposited in his anomalous book, which is more interesting for its linguistic particularity than for its content. The events of Bordonaro's life, indeed, are synthetically reported as in a catalogue. Natalia Ginzburg, too, in her introduction underlines that all the events of Bordonaro's life – such as his birth in an archaic Sicily, his demanding work as a peasant, his two weddings, the birth of his children and his emigration (that 'spartenza' giving name to his narration) – are never described in depth but instead are cursively mentioned as facts. Linguistically, instead, the book is a spontaneous communicative eruption, an alchemy of words coming from different linguistic codes – Sicilian, popular Italian, and English – that, despite significant distance from the norm, is fully able to convey to its reader the emotional life experienced by the author. It is the language, therefore, that reestablishes to the text that emotionality hidden behind the dry catalogue of events, and that can speak up from the margin of what is commonly defined as "literature of silence" – a corpus of unheard narrative voices which failed to reach the visibility of the public and academic spheres. This essay, touching briefly upon such a linguistic alchemy, investigates whether and how *La spartenza* fits, one of three literary traditions: the dialectal one within standard Italian; that of Italian migration literature; or the Italian-American literary tradition. Highlighting the elements that distance Bordonaro's work from all these narrative traditions, this paper will show how the singularity of this work – a singularity originating from its linguistic quality and from the absence of an editorial interest for similar minor narrative experiences – is at the same time a challenge to all traditions to reconsider their own borders, and stands out as a subaltern voice emerging from the marginality of minor literature.

As Ilaria Serra argued in her book *The Value of Worthless Lives; Writing Italian American Immigrant Autobiographies*, the lack of editorial and academic interest in minor forms of expression is the main force confining memories of Italian immigration into the U.S. to that gray zone of drawers in private houses, reducing them to a silence that is difficult to break through. Serra, with her work, listened to several marginal voices. She researched family attic archives, manuscript collections, and regional libraries in order to study the contribution of minor voices to the transmission of memories of Italian immigration to the U.S. Many of the names she collected were unpublished or didn't find widespread distribution, and her research sheds some light on the obscurity of archives, recovering voices that had gone unheard. Thinking about her work, Gayatri Spivak's well-known and controversial question "Can the subaltern speak?" seems to arise once again. Bordonaro, among the names Serra collected, represents the voice of the Gramscian social and cultural subaltern who delivered the narration of his own experience using a language that was not the tool of the mainstream culture. Through that tool he found his way to break through silence. Indeed, his story was not just written, but also bestowed awards and published, gaining some visibility in the process. Therefore, the subaltern question, when applied to Bordonaro, should be transformed into "How can the subaltern speak?" and above all "How can the subaltern be heard?"

Along with these questions, many others arise in approaching Bordonaro's experience. Can he be considered a writer because he wrote this memoir? Is he an Italian writer or rather an Italian-American writer? Can a scholar trace a literary genealogy from which Bordonaro's text springs, or find a literary space that can host *La spartenza*, or is this book instead left orphaned, without any canonized literary experience both in Italy and Italian America? *La spartenza* is the only book Bordonaro wrote, in a popular form of the Italian language that is drenched in dialectal and English linguistic disturbances. The text was conceived and written to reach out to the Italian public, and it was published by Einaudi, a major publishing house in Italy. While the text gained visibility in the U.S., it was also transformed into a play and performed in several theaters in New Jersey as homage to the author, who was active in the church of the Sicilian community in Garfield. The life of the author and the story he narrates are divided between Italy and the U.S.

All these elements seem to be insufficient in defining Bordonaro as either an Italian or Italian-American writer, or even as a writer at all. We therefore need to look closer at the specifics of the text to place it in a specific tradition. Such an attempt might be only partially useful to understand the work itself; however, the parallel with existing narrative traditions helps in understanding the extent to which its singularity can be read as a challenge to those traditions to reconsider their own borders. *La spartenza* distances itself, with its content and language, from the Italian-American narratives that are gathered and analyzed in collections such as *The Italian-American Novel*, by Rose Basile Green, *Beyond the Godfather*, edited by A. Kenneth Ciongoli and Jay Parini, and *Dagoes Read* by Fred Gardaphè, to mention only a few, which all focus on authors of Italian heritage writing in English.

The language issue is at stake here, and we know that the Italian American field of research has been enriched in the previous decades by ground-breaking works such as the academic periodical *Gradiva, International Journal of Italian Poetry* edited by Luigi Fontanella, which published a special issue titled *Italian Poets in America* and the volume *Paesaggio. Poeti Italiani d'America* edited by Peter Carravetta and Paolo Valesio. These works, thanks to the Italian language employed by the authors whose work they gather, are able to give voice to the Italian diaspora in the United States and show the extent to which contemporary Italian America is not monocultural and monolingual. Along with these works, the interest for a narrative written in Italian in a U.S. migratory context was also the basis for the extensive work *Italoamericana*, by Francesco Durante. This work, focusing as it does on the literature of the Great Emigration and the realities of Little Italy, hosts works of different kinds, from the short story to poetry, from play to articles, principally written in Italian or in regional dialects, along with some texts translated from English into Italian for the volume. The writers gathered there included professors, journalists, politicians and political activists, several of whom were unknown before the publication of the collection, and who make conscious use of the language. *La spartenza*, which could fit in Durante's attempt to map the articulations between cultural élite and anonymous multitude, challenges that space because of the cultural subalternity of its author and for its hybrid language, which, with the intrusion of English, breaks with the dialectic between dialect and standard Italian.

Together with the language issue, Bordonaro's narration also breaks with large part of Italian American literature to the extent that it lacks typical narrative elements, which Rose Basile Green earlier identified. In her book *The Italian-American Novel; A Document of the Interaction of Two Cultures*, published in 1974, which maps the evolution of Italian American literature, Green identifies four steps on the immigration and integration process of the Italian community in the U.S. Those steps are 1) need for assimilation, 2) revulsion, 3) counter revulsion, 4) rooting. According to Green, these steps or phases, transplanted from real life into narrative, constitute the specificity of the Italian American narrative in the U.S., a narrative manifesting itself first in autobiographical expressions and later in multiple forms of invented narrative. *La spartenza* doesn't openly delve into all these migratory dynamics, but through occasional clues it becomes clear that the author's migratory experience was a difficult one.

To give an example, Bordonaro synthetically tells the reasons behind his emigration and the expectations that he has from the new world. He considered the U.S. to be the land of education for his children, of social elevation for them and himself, a way out from the hard work and misery that Bordonaro was living in his "cruda e misera terra siciliana."[1] Bordonaro is aware that he will encounter some difficulties that he defines with the word "pegio," worse. This 'worse' he found in the U.S. is described no further, and is one of the few clues informing the reader about Bordonaro's struggle in the new world. He provides few other cursory hints about the obstacles in finding a job, a brief description of the cold and humid basement where his family got sick, and the almost-taken decision to go back to Italy.[2] However, consciously or unconsciously, Bordonaro doesn't consider these knots of his own migratory experience as central to his narration. He doesn't delve into or dwell on these challenges, but instead just names them in passing.

Moreover, Bordonaro doesn't spend time articulating his sense of belonging, an issue central to many migration narratives. He defines himself as Italian and he refers to Italy as to "la [sua] patria dove era stato il [suo] natale," the land where

---

[1] Tommaso Bordonaro, *La spartenza* (Torino: Einaudi, 1990) 46.
[2] Ibid., 52.

he was born.[3] His national consciousness, however, is not strongly enhanced, and he considers himself as above all Sicilian. His native island is a moving and warm memory, the dearest place, even when, late in his life, a few family members or friends are left there.

Bordonaro is also American, after forty years lived in Garfield, New Jersey. Narrating one of his last travels he recounts his pain at leaving Italy. "Quella spartenza mi è stata pure amara," Bordonaro states describing the bitterness of his departure, but he goes on talking about his family in America, that land that was his "ultima patria," his last homeland.[4] This moment is the only one opening up to what might have been Bordonaro's sense of belonging, integration and double identity, all issues never openly described by his narrating voice. The absence of these topics, pivotal to Italian American autobiographical narrative spotted by Basile Green, seems to prevent Bordonaro from being hosted even by this literary category.

At the same time *La spartenza* challenges autobiographical narration. The autobiographical pact described by Philippe Lejeune is clearly recognizable in the opening of the text, where Bordonaro declares his identity: "Io sono Tommaso Bordonaro."[5] The intention to narrate his own life is soon declared and restated at the end of the book, where he thanks God for having lived so long and for having accomplished the narration of his previous life. Despite the already-discussed difficulty of locating Bordonaro's work alongside

---

[3] Ibid., 101.
[4] Ibid., 108.
[5] Ibid., 5.

a codified Italian American tradition, it is his autobiographical desire, and the bi-national flavor of his narrative, that align *La spartenza* with the first phase of Italian immigration to the U.S., despite a delay of almost 30 years. Bordonaro indeed migrated in 1947, while the highest peak of Italian immigration occurred from 1890 to 1920. Along with Green, more recently Fred Gardaphè in his work *Italian Signs, American Streets* – in which he takes into consideration writers who used Standard English language, such as John Fante, Pietro di Donato and Jerre Mangione – describes how the narrative of Italian Americans meets several phases, shifting from an initial moment of autobiographical intent to a following moment of narrative invention. The autobiographical intent, therefore, is the element connecting Bordonaro to a preexisting literary tradition of migration memoir writing that was common to several Italian American writers. However, the autobiographical impulse departs from a specific ethnicity label, and pushes *La spartenza* towards a broader understanding of the process of integration in a host society experienced by other immigrants of many origins. The autobiographical impulse is indeed a pivotal element for books written by immigrants to Italy in the last twenty years. We can name the Senegalese Pap Khouma's *Io, venditore di elefanti*, the Moroccan Mohamed Bouchane's *Chiamatemi Alì*, the Palestinian Salwa Salem's *Con il vento nei capelli*, and the Brasilian Fernanda Farías de Albuquerque's *Princesa*, as few prime examples of this autobiographical tendency.

La spartenza, along with this corpus of autobiographical texts, raises pivotal questions such as: What is migration literature actually about? Can we enclose it in a set of forms and topics? Who defines the borders, and on what terms?

Such questions are central to the on-going discussion in the recent field of migration studies in Italy, where we remark the opening of editorial and academic spaces for the study of migration literature – an expanding field thanks to the rapid transformation of Italy from a land of emigration into a land of immigration. Publishing houses and scholars are mainly interested in the voice of first and second-generation foreign writers adopting Italian language as a literary tool. Bordonaro is therefore ethnographically and linguistically different from them. Though migrant, Bordonaro represents the other face of the coin of migration in Italy, which is often taken in consideration to stress thematic parallels between the Italian emigration to the U.S. and the immigration of foreigners into Italy.

An example of such a tendency can be found in Gian Antonio Stella's book, *L'orda: quando gli albanesi eravamo noi*, where Stella draws parallels in the reasons and modalities of the Albanian emigration to Italy and the Italian emigration to the U.S. despite a temporal difference of 100 years. At a cinematic level, Gianni Amelio's film *Lamerica* (1994) overlays the same two migratory movements. However, besides the attention to parallelism, these two areas of study are usually kept apart, and much work needs to be done to see them as interconnected. A good starting point for this approach was the Oxford seminar, *Migrating In and Out of Italy*, held at the Calandra Institute of CUNY in February 2011, where emigration from, migration across, and immigration to Italy were analyzed in a larger spectrum of articulations and interconnections. Returning to Bordonaro, *La spartenza* doesn't catch the interest of this expanding Italian corpus of migration literature. The reasons of such a distance can be also found in the scarce Italian interest in Italian-language narratives that are produced outside Italy. To give an example, the literary journal *Acoma*, dedicated to the study of North American Literature, shows that references to Italian American literature are lacking.

Having mapped all these branches of literature in Italy and the U.S, we can reach the conclusion that *La spartenza* doesn't find a genealogical space in any of them, remaining an orphan among the canonized literary traditions. *La spartenza* is therefore a singular text, published in Italy as the testimony of a personal experience, in a personal and unique language.

Leaving the path of comparison of *La spartenza* with other literary works, and moving into the singular aspects of it, it is certainly the work's language that constitutes its uniqueness. In her introduction to the text, Natalia Ginzburg defines Bordonaro's language as made of rocky sentences and deformed words, a savage language completely free from any rhetoric device, done of natural truth. It is a language and a style proceeding in a synthetic simplicity of words and images. The reference to a savage language suggests its distance from the linguistic norm. *La spartenza*'s language "scrambles" any norm to the point in which the reader is disoriented and fascinated, pushed to reconsider the limitation of linguistic normativity and the impressive power of a language that breaks free from it. The linguistic norms "scrambled" by Bordonaro's narrative are namely Sicilian, Italian, and English.

The Italian used by the author shows Sicilian terminology and morpho-syntactic aspects as demonstrated by the use of the dialectal form of the verb, "erava" for "era," or the wrong use of the auxiliary verb, such as in "siamo cominciate," instead of "abbiamo cominciato." If Italian is influenced by Sicilian dialect, then the dialect as well is deformed in the attempt to write in a standard language, above all at the level of terminology. To give a sense of it, when talking about the crucifixion of Christ, Bordonaro uses "crocifigio," in an attempt to Italianize the Sicilian noun "crucifio," but he doesn't reach the Standard Italian "crocifissione." In addition to this, Bordonaro's language shows pidgin forms of Italian common among Italian American speakers, such as "carro" for car, "storo" for store, "checchi" for cakes.

Hermann Haller, in his book about the Italian American community of New York, *Una lingua perduta e ritrovata: l'italiano degli italo-americani*, describes the pidgin as a formation "resulting from the contact and exchange between two worlds and from the immediate necessity to communicate."[6] Certain kinds of nouns are mostly used in the part of Bordonaro's narration referring to his life in the U.S., often when speaking about objects or experiences that didn't find an equivalent object or concept in his Italian life.

Many more examples could be drawn up, however, for the sake of avoiding redundancy, let me say that *La spartenza* is a text manifesting cases of pidgin (carro – car), code switching and mixing, loan word (ceac – assegno), misspellings (Estate Unite), doublets (vigitable and verdure), and dialectal attribution of gender (figlie for figli). Therefore, Bordonaro's language is the blend of a ternary system of languages, with which first-generation immigrants find them-

---

[6] Hermann Haller, *Una lingua perduta e ritrovata; l'italiano degli italo-americani* (Firenze: La Nuova Italia, 1993), 30.

selves navigating their migratory context. According to Haller, this convergence of the three languages most often occurs with speakers who are poorly educated at the moment of their emigration; they didn't have consistent exposure to the standard Italian and they didn't properly learn English. Moreover, elements such as those we find in Bordonaro's text are characteristic not only of Sicilian immigrants but also of all Southern immigrants. Haller remarks that the dialect of Italian immigrants is a high variety of language, spoken in the very moment they are asked to communicate in standard Italian, and only partially mastering the standard language. It is a homogeneous language that suggests the formation of a "lingua franca dialettale," born from the necessity to communicate of immigrants coming from different parts of the Italian South and different social groups. Bordonaro transplants this linguistic variety from an oral to a written communication.

Therefore, Bordonaro's language is not an accidental choice, because it grows from converting his intention to be published and reach out to an Italian public into the reality of translating a verbal world into writing and converting his personal life into a public narration. The hybrid language of *La spartenza* is a choice made in the moment that Bordonaro's text stops being a private language and enters the public sphere of a projected narrative. Applying Haller's analysis, Bordonaro's amalgamated language is the highest linguistic form he possessed to render his inner world.

This reconnects to the possibility for the subaltern to speak and to be heard. Bordonaro used the tools he was able to access, probably without being conscious of the social and political struggle underpinning his gesture. He derived from the spoken language shared by his immigrant community in Garfield the written mixture that characterizes *La spartenza*. Orality imbues its narration, and it is clearly brought in at the end of the memoir when Bordonaro thanks his audience for having 'listened' to his story[7] Bordonaro's self-perception therefore is strongly connected to the oral side of communication, and the chance to speak becomes central to his narrative operation. Speaking for him was a possibility, made concrete by the attention that the Archive Pieve di Santo Stefano reserved for his work. The Archive is an active promoter of popular memoirs, which often rest at the margins of canonized literature. The publication drew the text away from the only tradition to which it seems to belong, that of "literature of silence," which Ilaria Serra tried to shed light on with the already mentioned work *The Value of Worthless Lives*. Distant as it is from the Italian canon, from the Italian narrative of migration, from dialectal literature, and largely also from Italian American literature, *La spartenza* also stands apart from the "literature of silence," constituting a singular case in the narratives of Italian American memories, at least while other "spartenze" remain silent.

The major reason for the absence of quotations from the text in this analysis was the difficulty to find the proper English to translate Bordonaro's alchemic language. Therefore, to offer a second conclusion that is more of a second opening, let me give you a taste of this language, making it "speak" a little bit:

---

[7] Bordonaro, *La spartenza*, 134.

Così il 10 marzo 1947 io tutta la mia famiglia lasciammo la bella Italia: la mia prima attraversata a 38 anni di età, lasciando la cruda e misera terra siciliana per andare nei Stati Uniti di America il giorno 12 marzo 1947, distaccandomi della mia famiglia, lasciando i miei amorosi genitori, fratelli e figlio, colpendomi fortemente il dolore della mia mamma e figlio, con un cuore straziande che non voleva distaccarsi di me, con le lacrimi che le rigavano la faccia, fino a tarda ora del 12 marzo 1947, e un mio fratello Luciano è pur buscando dei colpi ma finalmente è vinuto lui a stare a me vicino fino all'imbarco: facendo velo di saluto dalla spartenza amara di me con la speranza di avere un più mediocre avvenire [...].[8]

Works Cited

Acoma. Rivista internazionale di studi Nord-Americani. Milano: Editori Riuniti.

Bordonaro, Tommaso. *La spartenza*. Torino: Einaudi, 1990.

Bouchane, Mohamed. *Chiamatemi Alì*. Milano: Leonardo, 1991.

Carravetta, Peter and Paolo Valesio. *Paesaggio. Poeti Italiani d'America*. Quinto di Treviso: Pagus, 1993.

Ciongoli, A. Kennett and Jay Parini. *Beyond the Godfather*. UPNE, 1997.

Durante, Francesco. *Italoamericana. Vol II. Storia e letteratura degli italiani negli Stati Uniti 1880-1843*. Milano: Mondadori, 2005.

Faría de Albuquerque, Fernanda. *Princesa*. Roma: Sensibili alle foglie, 1994.

Gardaphè, Fred. *Dagoes Read. Tradition and the Italian/American Writer*. Toronto and Buffalo: Guernica, 1996.

---

[8] Ibid., 46.

———. *Italian Signs, American Streets. The Evolution of Italian American Narrative*. Durham and London: Duke University Press, 1996.

Ghermandi, Gabriella. *Regina di fiori e di perle*. Roma: Don-zelli, 2007.

Green, Rose Basile. *The Italian-American Novel; A Document of the Interaction of two Cultures*. Cranbury, N.J.: Fairleigh Dickinson University Press, 1974.

Haller, Hermann. *Una lingua perduta e ritrovata; l'italiano degli italo-americani*. Firenze: La Nuova Italia, 1993.

Khouma, Pap. *Io, venditore di elefanti. Una vita per forza fra Dakar, Parigi e Milano*. Milano: Garzanti, 1990.

Salem, Salwa. *Con il vento nei capelli*. Firenze: Giunti, 2009.

Serra, Ilaria. *The Value of Worthless Lives; Writing Italian American Immigrant Autobiographies*. New York: Fordham University Press, 2007.

Spivak, Gayatri. "Can the Subaltern Speak?" in *Marxism and the Interpretation of Culture*. C. Nelson and L. Grossberg (eds.), Basingstok: Macmillan Education, 1988. 271-313.

Stella, Gian Antonio. *L'orda: quando gli albanesi eravamo noi*. Milano: Rizzoli, 2004.

An Allegorist in America
Cultural Identity in Calvino's Travelogues from the United States

Alessandro Raveggi
NYU Florence

Italo Calvino never indulged deeply in his biography. However, talking about himself in a bittersweet "Nota introduttiva," an Introduction published in the book *Gli amori difficili* in 1970, he wrote that "very *little is known* about *his travels* since he is *one of the few Italian writers who does not write travel books.*"[1] Elsewhere, approximately ten years before, he wrote a so-called *customized portrait*, denying the value of traveling in order to describe a biography.[2] Without neglecting his diffuse skepticism about travel experience and travelogues, I will explore some aspects of what I would like to call the 'traveling-theory' of Italian identity in Calvino, citing a renowned formula by Edward Said[3] that was later im-

---

[1] Italo Calvino, "Nota introduttiva", in *Gli amori difficili* (Turin: Einaudi, 1970), then "Nota biografica obiettiva" in *Eremita a Parigi. Pagine autobiografiche* (Milan: Mondadori, 1999) 170. ["Dei suoi viaggi si sa poco perché è uno dei rari scrittori italiani che non scrivono libri di viaggio né reportages"]

[2] See "Italo Calvino", in *Ritratti su misura di scrittori italiani. Notizie biografiche, confessioni, bibliografie di poeti, narratori e critici*, ed. Elio Filippo Accrocca (Venezia: Sodalizio del Libro 1960, VI) 110-12; then "Ritratto su misura", *Eremita a Parigi*, 23-25, now in *Saggi 1945-1985*, II (Milan: Mondadori, 1995) 2714-2716.

[3] See Edward W. Said, "Traveling Theory", in *The World, the Text, and the Critic* (Cambridge Mass.; Harvard University Press, 1983) 226-247, and "Traveling Theory Reconsidered", in *Reflections on Exile and Other Essays*

"An Allegorist in America"

proved by James Clifford. As stated clearly by the latter, theorizing "is a product of displacement, comparison, a certain distance. To theorize, one leaves home,"[4] but creating a state of *"betweenness."*[5] My topic will be indeed the suggestion and modification of a theory of cultural identity in the American travelogues by Calvino, highlighting the value of betweenness as a form of understanding the meaning of 'homeland' and one's own culture. I am convinced that one can find a specific and apparently ambiguous idea of identity rereading the pages of Calvino's reports of the United States, published between 1960 and 1962 in Italian journals such as *ABC* (*Cartoline dall'America*), *Europa Letteraria* (*Quaderno americano*), *L'Illustrazione Italiana* (*I classici al motel*), *Tempo Presente* (*Diario dell'ultimo venuto*), and *Nuovi Argomenti* (*Diario Americano 1960*), without forgetting the letters *Diario Americano 1959-1960* and "La mia città è New York,"[6] both published posthumously in *Eremita a Parigi*. All of these writings refer to Calvino's trip across the USA from November 1959 for six months with a Ford Foundation grant for writers. It is important to consider that these writings have never been published in the revised but promptly dismissed book *Un ottimista in America*. This book, as Calvino said in a letter to Luca Baranelli in 1985, was, in the opinion of the author, "too modest as a literary work and not enough original to be a reportage."[7] On the contrary, many twentieth century

---

(Cambridge Mass.: Harvard University Press, 2000) 436-452.
[4] James Clifford, "Notes on Travel and Theory", *Inscriptions* 5 (1989): 177.
[5] Ibid., 185.
[6] See Calvino, "Diario americano 1959-1960", *Eremita a Parigi*, 26-128 and "La mia città è New York", Ibid., 265-270.
[7] Calvino, "Lettera a Luca Baranelli – Torino", January 24, 1985, in *Lettere*

Italian writers and intellectuals published their reportages on America.[8] This refusal in Calvino is not only a symptom of formal inadequacy; it also reveals America as a continuous, evident or latent approach to a narration of cultural identity.

I will emphasize in this article some significant encounters with people and also with human artifacts — especially modern cities, museums, roads and also flea-markets, provincial neighborhoods and miserable pueblos — with a background composed by two kinds of nature, as stated by Calvino in *I classici al motel*: "a nature not affected by human time," inheritance of a primordial America, and a nature which is "totally absorbed"[9] by humans. With these relevant meetings, I will trace a narration of identity in Calvino,

---

1940-1985, ed. Luca Baranelli (Milan: Mondadori, 2000) 1530 ["troppo modesto come opera letteraria, e non abbastanza originale come reportage giornalistico"]

[8] For a brief bibliography of Italian intellectuals' travel-writings on America, see: Giuseppe Massara, *Viaggiatori italiani in America (1860-1970)* (Rome: Edizioni di Storia e Letteratura, 1977); Angela Jeannet and Louise Barnett eds., *New World Journeys: Contemporary Writers and the Experience of America* (Westport, CT: Greenwood Press, 1977); Martino Marazzi, *Little America. Gli Stati Uniti e gli scrittori italiani del Novecento* (Milan: Marcos y Marcos, 1997). For a broader bibliography on Italian travel-writings from the XX century, see: Monica Farnetti, *Reportages. Letteratura di viaggio del Novecento italiano* (Milano: Guerini e Associati, 1994), Gaia de Pascale, *Scrittori in viaggio: narratori e poeti italiani del Novecento in giro per il mondo* (Milan: Bollati Boringhieri, 2001); Luigi Marfè, *Oltre la "fine dei viaggi": i resoconti dell'altrove nella letteratura contemporanea* (Firenze: Olshki, 2009).

[9] Calvino, "Sabato 16", *I classici al motel*, *L'Illustrazione italiana*, 88, 1, January 1961, now in *Saggi*, II, 2625. ["una natura non scalfita dal tempo umano" - "interamente assorbita"]

mostly European but ultimately Italian. I acknowledge here that a discourse on identity, in our *post-national constellation*, as Habermas would say, illustrates a form of location in transition across the national identities, a traveler's map used to avoid losing oneself in cultural global fragmentation. It is a condition where the ethnographic Self and the 'ethnographized' *Other* have to negotiate their position in a discourse that is bound to the past but also linked to the contemporary. Using Homi K. Bhabha's words, if in contemporary times national identity "becomes a question of otherness of the people-as-one,"[10] then cultural identity becomes a question of including cultural difference without losing specificity. Identity will be described through Calvino's reports of America as a sort of map where the *roots* of a durable tradition and the *routes* of a contemporary encounter with other cultures, recalling a book by James Clifford, may be found and discussed. This concept confronts the changes of evolving worldwide connections between civilizations, a status both homogeneous and atomized, showing both the disappearance of cultural difference in a consumeristic, touristic, *Americanized* monoculture and the emergence of subaltern cultures. Most of these subaltern cultures — the cultures of a Transnational Third World, as Pasolini said in the *Lettera Luterana* precisely to Italo Calvino[11] — emerge in the context of the progressive fall of the Socialist alternative, still active in the days of the American trip of Calvino. Nonetheless, the

---

[10] Homi K. Bhabha, *The Location of Culture* (London-New York: Routledge, 1994) 215-216.

[11] See Pier Paolo Pasolini, *Saggi sulla politica e sulla società*, ed. Walter Siti and Silvia De Laude (Milan: Mondadori, 1999).

USSR polarity had already been contested by the author, since his resignation from PCI, The Italian Communist Party, in the letter published by *L'Unità* on August 7, 1957.[12]

I also have to consider the condition of traveling as an impossibility of travel, caused by the system of tourism, remembering that "farewell to journeying!"[13] decried by Claude Lévi-Strauss. Even in the first pages of *Tristes Tropiques*, the anthropologist described the dawns of a paradoxical world which is static and monotonous while being on the move, with a humanity "taken to monoculture, once and for all ... preparing to produce civilization in bulk, as if it were sugarbeet."[14] In this homogenized condition, where exploration became a profession, we will notice that to be estranged by the 'unfamiliar' is in Calvino related to what defines the concept of 'being at home': being an Italian and carrying an Italian tradition and territory. Italy has a history as an exploring *and* explored country, an ancient and contemporary locus of migrations in and out, but also a place disfigured by tourism. This particular status, of which Calvino often demonstrates his awareness, frequently comparing Italian and American landscapes and social conditions, suggests a shape of identity on the move, which is both *selective* and *shareable*: where preservation should be related to continuance and modifica-

---

[12] See Calvino, "Lettera di dimissioni dal P.C.I.", *L'Unità*, August 7, 1957, now in *Saggi*, II, 2188-2191. For lack of space in this article, I cannot address Calvino's travelogues to the USSR, *Taccuino di viaggio nell'Unione Sovietica*, published in *L'Unità* and *Rinascita* in 1952, now in Ibid., 2407-2496.

[13] Claude Levi-Strauss, *Tristes tropiques* (Paris: Plon 1955, trans. Jonathan Russell, New York: Criterion Books, 1961) 398.

[14] Ibid., 45.

tion of identity. As Calvino wrote in "Identità," an article published in 1977 in *La Civiltà delle Macchine*, identity is not valuable in its essence. Identity is important in its transferrable and divergent value, as it was a "sort of sack or tube in which swirl heterogeneous materials" carried by a traveler, or "a bundle of divergent lines"[15] which intersects in an individual.

America as an Allegory, *America as a* Myth

America is, in Calvino's travel writings, a prospected future to a European identity. Europe is outlined by the author for its normative role, characterized by a dialectical and questioning mental attitude, in contrast with the accelerated world of pragmatism, full of things and seemingly poor of intellectual capability — almost 'acephalic' — that represents the American Future Land. America as a new continent is presented as a country as promising as it is frightening. Not only lacking an antithetical cognition: it could also be *theocratic*, as Calvino declares, due to the historical absence of conflict between State and Church, an old conflict in a now so-called *polytheistic* Europe. However, the travelogue on America by Calvino changes during the trip — it is, as I previously stated, the ground for a traveling theory of cultural identity. For example, during his American stay, Calvino experiences the continuous shift of ethnicities from one place to another, in a centrifugal space without borders. Quoting him, he declares to meet "the people's cycle of rotations in

---

[15] Calvino, "Identità", *Civiltà delle macchine*, XXV, 5-6, September-December, 1977, now in *Saggi*, II, 2825-2827, ["specie di sacco o di tubo in cui vorticano materiali eterogenei" - "un fascio di linee divergenti"]

an abstract space, which corresponds to an expanded and exploded city, just as the explosion of a celestial body alters the spinning of the planets."[16]

America is an abstract space for an experimental community among different races and different histories that contest a possible ethnocentric vision of the European traveler. If "the European representation of the New World tells us something about the European practice of representation"[17] as Greenblatt said in his book *Marvelous Possessions*, then America in Calvino is also an allegory for Italy, as already stated by the author in the conference *Main Currents in Italian Fiction Today* held in many American universities between 1959 and 1960. In this conference, the author discussed not only the connection between Italian and American literature and culture, especially in Vittorini and Pavese, but he also affirmed that America, during Italian fascism, "was a huge allegory of our problems, of the problems of Italian people of those times."[18]

What is more, America, in these writings, may also be an allegory for Italy with regard to his fellow emigrants. On one hand, in Calvino, they represent Italy as an ancient and ap-

---

[16] Calvino, "La città scompare", *Cartoline dall'America*, *ABC*, June-September 1960, now in *Saggi*, II, 2571. ["il ciclo delle rotazioni dei popoli in uno spazio astratto, che corrisponde alla città dilatata ed esplosa così come la esplosione d'un corpo celeste muove il roteare dei pianeti"]

[17] Stephen Greenblatt, *Marvelous Possessions: The Wonder of the New World* (Chicago: The University of Chicago Press 1991) 13.

[18] Calvino, "Main Currents in Italian Fiction Today", *Italian Quarterly*, IV, 13-14, Spring-Summer 1960, now "Tre correnti del romanzo italiano oggi", in *Saggi*, I, 63-64 ["era una gigantesca allegoria dei problemi nostri, di noi italiani d'allora"]

parently hidden explorative tradition, personified mostly in his work by Marco Polo and Galileo.[19] On the other, these emigrants do not represent an open-minded posture, but they embody the Italian shadows of backwardness and archaism, linkable with that diffused Italian parochialism, mixed with that "paternalistic tendency on popular-vernacular style,"[20] frequently criticized by Calvino. The Italian emigrants are included by him in what he calls "calderone americano"[21] of ethnicities, as observed in the 1961 collection *Quaderno americano* published in *Europa Letteraria*. However, they have a singular characteristic: they had come to America, in the opinion of the author, without any deep experience of civilization, moving from a background of an Italian semi-pagan semi-Catholic rural world and transferring deeper problems of their underdeveloped territory to this new horizon. Thus, the allegory of America is a dislocation of Italian identity concerns into a new global context. Calvino at this point confirms himself as the *allegorist*, as found in Todorov's *On Human Diversity*: a traveler who speaks of other people's problems in order to discuss a conflict concerning their culture.[22] A traveling Italian identity,

---

[19] See Calvino, "Due interviste su scienza e letteratura", partially in *L'Approdo letterario*, 41, January-March 1968, now in *Saggi*, I, 229-237.

[20] Calvino, "Lettera a Pier Paolo Pasolini – Roma", Turin, May 9, 1955, now in *Lettere*, 430.

[21] Calvino, "La scuola della durezza", in *Quaderno Americano, Europa Letteraria*, II, April 8, 1961, now in *Saggi*, II. 2613.

[22] See Tzvetan Torodov, *Nous et les autres. La réflexion française sur la diversité humaine* (Paris: Seuil, 1989). Translated into English by Catherine Porter, *On Human Diversity* (Cambridge, Mass.: Harvard University Press, 1993).

through the lens of this American allegory, confronts, in Calvino, its problems of conservation of a past, but also its understanding of the new form of modern urbanization, of including difference without losing specificity. In America, Calvino declares, traveling in such vast dimensions, or being bewildered in a chaotic city like Los Angeles, "provokes an aching homesickness,"[23] the need for familiar dimensions. However, this sense of the familiar, of being at home, has to be set in a wide inter-local perspective, where the conservation of cultural difference challenges a world that tries constantly to homogenize and dissipate difference.

Note: I use the term *allegory*, as Calvino did, and not the common term in Italy for America, *myth*. Obviously, he cites in these travelogues the myth of an adventurous America, a dream of freedom and wilderness that had fascinated many Italian intellectuals under the repression of fascism. Calvino also declares himself, as he writes, "the last loyal to a 'tough,' brutal and lively Myth of America."[24] "Is this myth still present?" he asks, questioning himself. While he acknowledges that those European stereotypes of mass culture or *Americanization* aren't a widely spread phenomenon in America, the author is aware of the metamorphosis of the United States. This is a nation, he says, where the nomadic "instinct of Ulysses"[25] seems faded and a car is a symbol of roots and stability more than mobility. This is a nation of commodities, easy enrichment and the culture of *frigidaire*. It is no more

---

[23] Calvino, "Il collegio delle ragazze", in *Cartoline dall'America*, *Saggi*, II, 2506. ["suscita [...] il senso dolente di una patria"]

[24] Calvino, "Le lettrici di Joyce", in Ibid., 2545. ["ultimo fedele del Mito dell'America «tough», brutale, movimentata"]

[25] Calvino, "I nomadi privilegiati", in Ibid., 2552. ["l'istinto ulisside"]

"An Allegorist in America"

the savage land of adventurers and pioneers, of Melville, Sherwood Anderson, Poe, or Hawthorne. It even seems that for Calvino the American myth was meant to have the same decadent ending that Ernest Hemingway had, whom he defined as a tutelary deity of his early writings, but gradually became a grotesque puppet of "bloody tourism."[26] After the farewell to journeying by Levi-Strauss and now a possible farewell to mythologizing America by Calvino himself, this new allegoric continent is not only a land of flourishing urbanism and development, but also a land with sudden "provincial *dullness*, the dull banality of productive and consumerist small towns,"[27] a scenario where one can encounter fanaticism and conservativeness. This conservativeness is clearly portrayed by the Texan folklore of Western-style cowboys seen by Calvino during a rodeo, as described in *Cartoline dall'America*. The Texan rodeo atmosphere is not only the "manifestation of a practical and anti-intellectual habit,"[28] but even an exaggerated example of how preservation of a tradition can be harmful as well. Indeed, this chauvinistic scene reminds Calvino of a still vivid experience of fascist nationalism.

---

[26] Calvino, "Hemingway e noi", in *Il Contemporaneo*, November 13, 1954, now in *Saggi*, I, 1312-1313 ["cruento turismo"]

[27] Calvino, "L'istituzione dei «beatniks»", *Cartoline dall'America*, *Saggi*, II, 2591 ["«dullness» della provincia, l'opaca banalità delle piccole città produttive e consumatrici"]

[28] Calvino, "Mitologia del Texas", in Ibid., 2533 ["ostentazione di un costume pratico e anti-intellettuale"]

The Geographical Pattern

I will propose now a pattern or model to describe the journey of identity in Calvino's multifarious allegory of America, starting from a trend that I can identify in the aforementioned 'section' *Cartoline dall'America*. I call this structure the Geographical Pattern. First of all, we have to remember that Calvino, as a traveler, defines himself as a sort of "European historicist."[29] As we can see, he is wearing this *habitus* while he is also trying to dismiss it during the journey. Calvino talks specifically about America as a geographical solution to historical problems of European populations, as much as, in that period, Socialist Russia still represented an historical and dialectical solution. Calvino's historicist attitude evidently clashes with the Geographical Pattern, while it splits into a variety of ethnic histories, in an urban space of surfaces but also repressed depths of a conflictual peripheral world.

This Geographical Pattern is, to be specific, marked by two correlative paths: one is the classic Coast-to-Coast path, the other is a North-South path. The first resembles the linear historicist progress of modernity from East to West, the progress of the Eurocentric *Weltgeist* as described by Hegel's *Lectures on a Philosophy of World History*. In these lectures, Hegel presented America as "the country of the future," with a world-historical importance, which lies ahead "in a conflict between North and South America."[30] We will later

---

[29] Calvino, "Il diavolo nel paese di Dio", in Ibid., 2536 ["uno storicista europeo"]

[30] Georg Wilhelm Friedrich Hegel, *Lectures on The Philosophy of World History: Introduction, Reason in History*, ed. Johannes Hoffmeister, trans. Hugh Barr Nisbet (Cambridge MA: Cambridge University Press 1975) 170.

"An Allegorist in America"

see the relevance of this North-South duality. The Coast-to-Coast path is announced, on the East side, by the anachronistic arrival of Calvino after a transatlantic voyage from Le Havre, a trip to New York filled with old and unsophisticated Americans spending their time playing *bingo*, with the substitution of the ship's wood for cheap metal, symbolically attesting again the end of a pioneering era. New York is the city that Calvino sees as a continent distinct from America, where he decided to gallop amongst skyscrapers and in Central Park, ideally retracing the historical evolution of American transportation, from a horse to a Cadillac. It is the city Calvino declares to blindly love, as the love for Milan in Stendhal, which leads the author to forecast his epitaph imitating it from the Stendhal's *Arrigo Bayle Milanese*: *Calvino Newyorkese*. His love seems *blind* because the Big Apple can also be a superficial city, where it is impossible to genuinely connect with people, where the same *calderone* of ethnicities generates criminality and conflicts. It is the electric city which reminds him how much America could be full of conductive and vivid things, but also of opaque humanity. Meanwhile, as recounted in *Quaderno americano,* since his relationship with Joan, the Russian-American woman he dates in the city, New York stands also for the city of all people, where everyone has come from abroad. It is a community where every *native* is in fact an *alien,* as Calvino says,[31] where Joan is the prototype of an authentic citizen, with a father from Kiev, mother from Odessa, and resembling a girl from Čechov.

---

[31] See Calvino, "La newyorkese", in *Quaderno Americano, Saggi,* II, 2613.

On the opposite side, on the West Coast, Calvino encounters San Francisco, the city that overlooks the Orient. Calvino describes San Francisco as the "key-city of a new relation among civilizations,"[32] as the liminal city, the Last Thule of the next foreseen cross-cultural Mediterranean Sea, the Pacific Sea. This city, he continues, gives us a cue in the "search for a new humanism that forges the experience of two worlds,"[33] the East and The West, in a new civilization. We can also find many other significant but not as cardinal cities during his East-West journey: on one side, for example, the decayed Venice represented by New Orleans, where Calvino surprisingly finds the second-hand carnival floats of Viareggio. On the other, there is Los Angeles, where Calvino finds himself lost in a kind of exile from one hotel to another.

These American cities are meeting points where the author comes across a wide assortment of people, from conservatives to liberals, from upper-class women to Jewish families of writers, and of course, Italians. Declaring that an ideal method for traveling in America is formulating an opinion on the country based on human relations ("set all my cognition of America on human relations"[34]), Calvino also maintains that, in traveling, nobody is insignificant for a real traveler, but "each one may bring the spark of a general illumination"[35] on larger problems about civilization. An ex-

---

[32] Calvino, "Alle porte dell'Asia", in *Cartoline dall'America*, Ibid., 2597 ["città-chiave di una nuovo rapporto tra le civiltà"].
[33] Ibid. 2599. ["ricerca d'un umanesimo nuovo che fonda le esperienze dei due mondi"]
[34] Calvino, "Il sindacato dello spogliarello", in Ibid., 2574. ["impostare tutta la mia conoscenza dell'America sulle relazioni umane"]
[35] Calvino "Il sabba delle streghe", in Ibid., 2572. ["da ciascuno può

"An Allegorist in America"

ample of this hypothesis was the monsignor of the Catholic clergy of New York, whom Calvino met in Connecticut. As a result of this controversial meeting, he verifies the aforementioned absence of antithetical spirit in America; its weakness to accept, as Calvino says, "its internal or external contradiction as a necessary element"[36] of evolution. This accent on the value of contradictions can help us move on to a second category of the Geographical Pattern.

The North-South path is recognizable because of the gradual vanishing, or as Calvino says, "pulverization,"[37] of the city in a web of highways, throughways and suburbs, as when the author takes the highway from Chicago to New Orleans, coming to a provincial world that reveals a new tribalism in its middle-class families, gathering around the modern fireplace: the television. This North-South path ideally transforms a trip that starts on a metropolitan and developed world, represented at its extremes by New York and San Francisco, into a trip through a conflicted and peripheral provincial world as discovered in Texas, Alabama, and New Mexico. However, the pulverization of the metropolitan space in America does not mean the disappearance of significant stops and encounters. First of all, in the South, Calvino finds a growing demand for cultural recognition, delineated by the Black movement. In 1960 the author has, indeed, the chance to witness the peaceful protests in the town of Montgomery, Alabama, spurred by the ideas of Martin Luther

---

scattare la scintilla d'una illuminazione generale"]
[36] Calvino, "Il diavolo nel paese di Dio", in Ibid., 2537. ["la propria contraddizione interna o esterna come elemento necessario"]
[37] Calvino, "La città scompare", in Ibid., 2570.

King Jr., the leader of a movement admired by Calvino for its dignity in posture. Moving down to a deep Indian-Native and Spanish South, Calvino finds again recollections of Italy, e.g., in the territory around Taos, New Mexico, which to him resembles Lucania and Calabria, or portrayed by the pueblo of Santo Domingo, near Albuquerque. Its small and drab houses made of *adobe* remind Calvino of the hapless neighborhood of Pietralata in Rome. In the same pueblo, Calvino discovers a Navajo museum of ritual paintings. This local museum motivates him to ponder on the American custom of preserving ancient cultures, a common concern, as Calvino says, in modern lands where apparently "everything that is old, everything derived from another civilization, is rare and threatened with extinction."[38] This observation is relevant for an Italian writer clearly aware of Italian folkloric diversity but also of the underdevelopment of Italian territory at that time, only a few years after the end of World War II. This Navajo museum becomes even more relevant when compared with a hyperbolic and hypothetical museum that he discusses further on in these travel writings, a Museum on Mars, where the radical problem for the terrestrial settlers would be how to preserve the memory of civilization on Earth, and also how to narrate a continuance of the same terrestrial tradition. Quoting Clifford again, folkloric (but also national) museums could be seen as "specific places of transit, intercultural borders, contexts of struggle and communi-

---

[38] Calvino, "I villaggi degli Indiani", in Ibid., 2548 ["dove tutto ciò che è antico, tutto ciò che è derivato da un'altra civiltà, è raro e minacciato d'estinzione"]

cation between discrepant communities."³⁹ This emblem of the museum, as a place for preservation, collection and narration of identity, and also acknowledgement of other identities and minorities in a conflictual territory, is what is worthy of emphasis now, if we want to enjoin the North-South path with the Coast-to-Coast one. As we will see, the exploration of a museum as the exploration of an encounter between civilizations in America will return later in Calvino, in an article collected in *Collezione di sabbia*.

A Mirror of the Future, a Shifting Form of the Present

To sum up, in the Geographical Pattern I have described, we find the form of preservation of identity represented by the museum as a zone of recognition, narration and conflict, and also the decentralized city, crossed by routes, emigrants and travelers, where every *native* is in fact an *alien*, which represents a condition of identity at the crossroads of cultures. Here the urban scenario could be a dissipative and centrifugal condition, although it can reveal a possible substantial identity, as happens in *La poubelle agréée*. In this autobiographical story set in Paris, originally published in 1977 in *Paragone*, Calvino mentions his first trip to America and his encounter with Antonio Barolini, who gives him the instructions on the *garbagio*, the garbage, in the Anglo-Venetian tongue of Barolini. Calvino notices that in the experience of garbage's administration in Paris, "only throwing away

---

³⁹ James Clifford, *Routes: Travel and Translation in the Late Twentieth Century* (Cambridge MA: Harvard University Press 1997) 213.

something of mine I can make sure that something remains and perhaps it will never have to be thrown away."[40]

These two results — preservation and dissipation or conservation and dislocation — have to be combined in order to describe a location-form of identity in Calvino starting from the American otherness. In fact, the atomized city and the museum represent in Calvino two tendencies of America: that America which throws away everything in a consumerist and centrifugal dissipation of things, and the America which conserves and recycles everything, as he discovers in the flea markets of the Jewish community in Orchard Street, New York, described as a sort of Porta Portese. In this bifid America, where ancient times and new times are, as Calvino says, "branches of the same plant,"[41] like an organism that grows by accumulating its dichotomies, the Italian traveler arrives with a historicist and skeptical attitude, but also carrying the controversies of an underdeveloped Italian territory. The traveler gradually adapts his/her 'theory' of American otherness, while encountering a new global condition, where spatial movement and preservation of identities, traveling and provisional residence, are equally crucial in the definition of what is a *moving* and *trans-local* homeland, in a world which seems to obliterate the distances and our encounter with the unfamiliar.

---

[40] Calvino, "La poubelle agréée", *Paragone*, Letteratura, XXVVIII, 324, February 1977, now in *Romanzi e racconti*, III (ed. Mario Barenghi, Bruno Falcetto and Claudio Milanini, Milan: Mondadori 1994) 65 ["soltanto buttando via posso assicurarmi che qualcosa di me non è stato ancora buttato e forse non è né sarà da buttare"]

[41] Calvino, "II. Siamo noi gli americanizzati", in *Quaderno Americano*, *Saggi*, II, 2609. ["rami della stessa pianta"]

"An Allegorist in America"

Reading another short collection of American travelogues by Calvino, *Diario dell'ultimo venuto*, I identify, confirming my discourse, three masks of this European and Italian traveler in America.[42] The first could be called the mask of the *conqueror*: the traveler, in the first months of his/her journey, is persuaded that their advanced civilization has to, speaking metaphorically, *conquer* the United States, a land too young to know how to manage its future by itself. However, the mask of the conqueror, after a few months of residence, Calvino notes, gives way to the mask of a *connoisseur*, a traveler that recognizes the singularity of the American nation in comparison with Europe. The third and last mask, coming almost at the end of the journey, is that of an *American-oriented European*. This traveler probably thinks that America is a land without a vision of the future. At the same time, he thinks that America suggests the shared and relevant future of a new civilization, as stated at the end of the third document of Calvino's travelogues, *Diario Americano 1960*. In these writings, we find again the dialectics between History and Geography, in the contrast between Europe and America, as in a ping-pong match: "in Europe concerns are born before facts happen. In America the facts happen before the concerns are raised,"[43] and so on.

After the last goodbye, after covering a circular trip and departing from New York by jet, Calvino proposes the synthesis between a geographical consciousness and a still alert

---

[42] See Calvino, "Tre atteggiamenti verso gli americani", in *Diario dell'ultimo venuto, Tempo presente*, VI, 6, June 1961, now in Ibid., 2635-2636.

[43] Calvino, "Nostalgia della dialettica", Ibid., 2654. ["In Europa prima si pongono i problemi, poi avvengono i fatti. In America prima avvengono i fatti, poi si pongono i problemi"]

sense of European questioning, with an allegory of identity which is almost a mirror. At this point, the author is already in Europe, across a table from Sartre. While the French philosopher seems fascinated by the Cuban revolution, Calvino summarizes his experience with America: a diverse reality with a different logic, now apparently remote, "which cannot think of the future but has in itself much of the future of all people"[44].

As stated by Calvino in an essay written later for a French art exhibition on the American Conquest, collected in *Collezione di sabbia*, America has become a mirror for Europe, rather than an allegory. The said exhibition was an exploration of European representations of America. What did Columbus *actually* see in America? What did the first European explorers *actually* see? A denial or a confirmation of affinities or biases? Could a *New* World still be discovered in our days? For the sixteenth-century English cartographers and for the seventeenth-century Dutch painters, Calvino observes, America was a figural scheme to "conceptually define what was and remained the *difference*, maybe the American irreducibility."[45] But, the author continues, nowadays Europe has so much of America that the experience of looking at America is no more an allegory but "resembles more and more looking into a mirror: a mirror with the power of revealing some-

---

[44] Calvino, "L'Europa", Ibid., 2679. ["che non sa pensare al futuro eppure ha in sè tanta parte del futuro di tutti"]

[45] Calvino, "Com'era nuovo il Nuovo Mondo", in *Collezione di sabbia*, Milan: Mondadori, 1994, now in *Saggi*, I, 424 ["rendere concettualmente definibile quella che era e resta la *differenza*, forse l'irreducibilità americana"]

thing of our past and future."[46] Paola Castellucci, in her work on America in Calvino, correctly said that in the first contact with America, Italo Calvino discovers an attractive and repulsive world at the same time, especially because "the American lifestyle is for him just the moment that precedes the catastrophe."[47] Moreover, in my opinion, the first American experience anticipates his future reflections, as we have seen, on a new trans-local humanity, ever since *Le città invisibili*, where the catastrophe is *now* and literary space is seen as, quoting again Lévi-Strauss, that "precarious arch that points towards the inaccessible"[48] in the midst of an entropic universe, a bridge between written and unwritten worlds that also gives voice to the difference between cultures in a global melting pot. A narration of identity, as a result of this relationship with this American Future Land, is located between preservation of tradition, represented in these writings by the Navajo and the Martian museum, and the travel encounters in the urban form, represented by the quasi-European New York and quasi-Oriental San Francisco. To be an Italian for Calvino means to go *through* this looking-glass, this threshold of the future of provisional residence

---

[46] Ibid., 425. ["l'Europa porta in sé oramai tanto d'America [...] che l'interesse a guardarsi [...] somiglia sempre più a quello che si prova di fronte a uno specchio: uno specchio dotato del potere di rivelarci qualcosa del passato e del futuro"]

[47] Paola Castellucci, *Un modo di stare al mondo. Italo Calvino e l'America* (Bari: Adriatica 1999) 137 ["la vita statunitense è per lui il momento che precede la catastrofe"]. See also: Nicola Bottiglieri, *I luoghi di Calvino. Guida alla lettura di Italo Calvino* (Cassino: Edizioni dell'Università di Cassino, 2001); Anna Botta and Domenico Scarpa eds., *Italo Calvino newyorkese* (Cava de' Tirreni: Avagliano, 2002).

[48] Lévi-Strauss, *Tristes Tropiques*, 432.

and necessary preservation, without losing diversity in the transition.

In another incarnation of Calvino in America, Mr. Palomar walks in Amherst, Massachusetts, a town haunted by ghosts of Indian massacres. Reflecting on his homeland, "a nation of the Old Europe," Palomar suggests another traveling figure of identity, declaring to be attracted by those "forms that persist through changes ... minimal marks of a civilization ... traces of a narration as the continuation of a project, that emerge in the midst of the universal avalanche of history as pillage and massacre."[49] Identity as a form on the move, which is a map of orientation, a sack or a tube of fragments of experience carried by a traveler, a bundle of lines or histories, resisting cultural entropy and the violence of History.

WORKS CITED

Bhabha, Homi K., *The Location of Culture*. London-New York: Routledge, 1994.

Calvino, Italo, *Romanzi e racconti*, III, ed. Mario Barenghi, Bruno Falcetto and Claudio Milanini. Milan: Mondadori 1994;

_____. *Saggi 1945-1985*, Milan: Mondadori, 1995, volume I and II;

_____. *Eremita a Parigi. Pagine autobiografiche*. Milan: Mondadori, 1999.

_____. *Lettere 1940-1985*, ed. Luca Baranelli. Milan: Mondadori, 2000.

---

[49] Calvino, "Nei boschi degli indiani", *Corriere della Sera*, April 18,1976, now "Palomar nel Massachusetts", *Saggi II*, 2699. ["forme che persistono attraverso i cambiamenti . . . contrassegni minimi d'una civiltà . . . tracce di una storia come continuità d'un progetto che affiorano in mezzo alla frana universale della storia come saccheggio e massacro"]

Castellucci, Paola, *Un modo di stare al mondo. Italo Calvino e l'America*. Bari: Adriatica, 1999.

Clifford, James. "Notes on Travel and Theory," *Inscriptions* 5, (1989): 177.

_____. *Routes: Travel and Translation in the Late Twentieth Century*. Cambridge, MA: Harvard University Press, 1997.

Greenblatt, Stephen. *Marvelous Possessions: The Wonder of the New World*. Chicago: Chicago University Press, 1991.

Hegel, Georg Wilhelm Friedrich. *Lectures on The Philosophy of World History: Introduction, Reason in History*, ed. Johannes Hoffmeister, trans. Hugh Barr Nisbet. Cambridge, MA: Cambridge University Press, 1975.

Lévi-Strauss, Claude. *Tristes Tropiques*. Paris: Plon, 1955; trans. Jonathan Russell. New York: Criterion Books, 1961.

Pasolini, Pier Paolo. *Saggi sulla politica e sulla società*, ed. Walter Siti and Silvia De Laude. Milan: Mondadori, 1999.

Said, Edward W. "Traveling Theory," in *The World, the Text, and the Critic*. Cambridge, MA: Harvard University Press, 1983.

_____. "Traveling Theory Reconsidered," in *Reflections on Exile and Other Essays*. Cambridge, MA: Harvard University Press, 2000.

Torodov, Tzvetan. *Nous et les autres. La réflexion française sur la diversité humaine*. Paris: Seuil 1989; trans. Catherine Porter, *On Human Diversity*. Cambridge, MA: Harvard University Press, 1993.

See endnotes 8 and 47 for additional bibliography.

IL MUTUALISMO DEI SICILIANI D'AMERICA

Marcello Saija
University of Messina

1. *I caratteri generali*

Certo, non è una peculiarità dei siciliani d'America quella di creare Società di mutuo soccorso tra emigrati. Altri italiani delle regioni settentrionali, sin dai primi decenni postunitari, avevano percorso tale strada prima in Italia e poi all'Estero[1]. Agli occhi dello storico, appare, tuttavia, singolare e preziosa quella straordinaria varietà di sodalizi trinacrini che permette di comprendere molti degli approcci all'integrazione sociale, economica e politica usati dalle comunità di riferimento. Ci troviamo di fronte ad un fenomeno di notevoli dimensioni quantitative, ed il molteplice impiego che viene fatto di queste spontanee aggregazioni ci indica con chiarezza che le ragioni di esistenza delle *Mutual Aid Societies* vanno ben oltre

---

[1] Per il mutualismo italiano si veda il saggio e la vasta bibliografia contenuta in L. Tomassini, *Mutual Benefit Societies in Italy, 1861-1922* in M. van der Linden (ed), *Social Security Mutualism. The Comparative History of Mutual Benefit Societies*, Peter Lang, Bern 1996, pp. 225-271, parzialmente riprodotto in L. Tomassini, "Il Mutualismo nell'Italia liberale (1861-1922)" in *Le società di Mutuo Soccorso italiane e i loro archivi*, Ministero per i beni e le attività culturali. Ufficio per i beni archivistici, Roma 1999, pp. 15–53. Per il mutualismo degli italiani d'America si veda S. Bugiardini, *L'associazionismo negli USA*, in P. Bevilaqua, A. De Clementi, E. Franzina, *Storia dell'Emigrazione Italiana. Arrivi.*, Donzelli editore, Roma 2002, pp. 551-577.

From: *Theater of the Mind, Stage of History*. Bordighera Press, 2015

"Il Mutualismo dei Siciliani d'America"

la conclamata necessità di assicurare ai soci assistenza medica, sussidi per malattia e spese funerarie.

Diciamo, però, subito che, sotto il profilo delle origini geografiche, non c'è uniformità. Esistono profonde differenze tra le diverse zone della Sicilia. Pochi sono i sodalizi mutualistici prodotti dagli emigranti delle zone interne non guerreggiate dai Fasci siciliani. Chi parte dalle impenetrabili aree del latifondo e della mafia, va via già nell'ultimo ventennio dell'Ottocento, quanto si apre la stagione migratoria. Porta con se la cultura dell'atavica subordinazione feudale che, nel tempo, ha impedito la modernizzazione e, adesso, non permette ad uomini e donne di sentirsi comunità e di realizzare, nelle zone di destinazione, ciò che in patria non hanno conosciuto[2]. Generalizzando, è possibile dire che ogni emigrante di queste zone ha una storia individuale che non contempla iniziative solidali. In America non c'è chi l'accoglie, e, soltanto se ha fortuna, finisce sotto l'ala protettiva di una parrocchia o nell'orbita di altre strutture aggreganti. Talvolta, invece, un destino perverso lo introduce nei tunnel di una nuova mafia dove il *caporale*, garante del suo viaggio prepagato, gli dà il lavoro, trattenendogli una parte della busta paga fin molto oltre il soddisfacimento del prestito bancario. Su questa strada, capita che il malcapitato incontri il locale boss della mafia italoamericana che lo recluta per impiegarlo nelle attività criminali. Alcuni si adattano, altri rifiutano l'offerta e, dopo poco, fuggono allungando la lista degli "sconfitti".

---

[2] M. Saija, *Breve manuale di storia dell'emigrazione siciliana*, Regione Sicilia, Palermo, 2005.

Marcello Saija

Certo, per fortuna, questa non è la vicenda di tutti. Ci sono paesi della Sicilia interna che, nonostante i condizionamenti di una cultura tardo feudale, riescono a fondare società di mutuo soccorso. Ciò accade per Alimena, Bolognetta[3], Casteltermini, Gagliano Castelferrato, Contessa Entellina, Limina[4], Marineo, Milocca[5], Nicosia, Polizzi Generosa[6], Salemi, San Cataldo e Santa Margherita Belice; ma a ben guardare, in parecchi di questi casi si trovano spesso ragioni particolari che giustificano l'eccezione. Le identità socioculturali delle comunità galloitaliche di Nicosia[7] o la comune appar-

---

[3] S. Lombino, *Mutuo soccorso, società religiosa, social club. Il clobbo dei bolognettisti d'America*, in NEOS, a. II, n. 1, Dicembre 2008, pp 221-230.

[4] Ampia documentazione sulla Società liminese di Mutuo soccorso di Brooklyn è custodita nel Museo dell'emigrazione jonica di Savoca (Messina)

[5] Di questa società fondata nel Wyoming conosciamo soltanto lo statuto del 1915, posseduto in copia dal sindaco di Sutera, dott. Gero Di Francesco e riprodotto da chi scrive.

[6] Brevi cenni sulla storia della società di mutuo soccorso di Polizzi Generosa a Brooklyn, con due foto degli anni '10, sono apparsi nella mostra fotografica e documentaria (curata da chi scrive) *Sicilian Crossings to America and Derived Communities*, esposta ad Ellis Island di New York dal 2 novembre 2007 al 3 febbraio 2008. Alla Società, denominata "U clubbu" è dedicato un capitolo del romanzo di V. Schiavelli, *Bruculino America*, Sellerio editore, Palermo 2003, pp. 27-38.

[7] Gli abitanti del comprensorio nicosiano (90% di latifondi incastonati tra i Monti Nebrodi e le Madonine), da nove secoli parlano e scrivono servendosi del caratteristico idioma galloitalico che serve da collante per tenere unite tutte le comunità nicosiane sparse per l'America. Così a New York, Chicago, Boston, Washintgton, Norfolk, Philadelphia e Hoboken, già alla fine dell'ottocento i nicosiani imboccano la strada del mutualismo. A Chicago fondano persino una esclusiva Cassa di risparmio, prestiti e consumo di generi alimentari. Si tratta dell'*Unione Economica Erbitense (1890)* ed una *Società Siciliana di tutti i Paesani di Nicosia sotto il*

"Il Mutualismo dei Siciliani d'America"

tenenza etnico-religiosa degli abitanti di Contessa Entellina e Piana degli Albanesi[8], per esempio, appaiono fattori più che sufficienti a generare in modo del tutto naturale le spinte alla creazione di fiorenti società di mutuo soccorso.

2. *Le società politiche generate dall'esperienza dei fasci siciliani.*

L'eccezione più rilevante viene, però, da quei paesi interni, protagonisti delle battaglie sociali di fine Ottocento che riescono a proiettare oltreoceano strutture associative, cariche del corposo fardello ideologico e politico maturato. E non è raro trovare, tra gli uomini di queste terre, chi riesce a porsi alla testa dei movimenti radicali d'America. E' il caso di Santa Ninfa.

La vicenda di questo piccolo lembo trapanese[9] è certamente indicativa della capacità di proiezione politica di quel fenomeno conosciuto come *movimento dei Fasci*. Per la verità, l'influenza maggiore delle agitazioni occorse in Sicilia nei primi anni Novanta dell'Ottocento, si registra sul movimen-

---

Titolo del Crocifisso (10 febbraio 1899). A New York, nel 1901, fondano la *Gioventù Nicosiana* e nel 1905, quando i sodalizi superano la decina, nasce persino una *Confederazione delle realtà erbitensi d'America,* destinata a coordinare l'attività dei singoli nuclei presenti nella grande metropoli. Su tutto si veda A. Micalizzi, *Il cuore nella valigia. Nicosia nell'Emigrazione verso gli Stati Uniti d'America*, Editrice "Il Quadrifoglio", Livorno, 2006.

[8] Sin dal 1886, gli emigrati italo-albanesi di Contessa Entellina vantano a New Orleans una società con 590 membri e ben 133.221 lire di capitale sociale (stima del 1908). Si veda *Le Società italiane all'estero nel 1900*, in "Rivista di Emigrazione", anno II, fasc. 3, 1909, pp. 22-27. Si veda anche l'aggiornamento pubblicato dalla medesima rivista nel 1908, anno IX, fasc 2.

[9] Si veda M. Saija-G. Bivona (a cura di) *L'esperienza migratoria dei santaninfesi in America. 1894-1924.*, Trisform, 2009

to cooperativistico che fiorisce negli Stati Uniti del Sud, ma mentre tali vicende maturano in ambiente agricolo ed hanno un conseguente sviluppo in questa direzione, la storia dei santaninfesi d'America sboccia in ambiente fortemente urbanizzato.

Certo, anche a Filadelfia, troviamo una *Società di Mutuo soccorso* fondata dalle comunità ennesi ed intestata a *Napoleone Colajanni* che dei fasci era stato uno dei massimi sostenitori; ma qui, già nel primo decennio del Novecento, la matrice politica originaria appare un lontano riferimento ideologico, ormai privo di risvolti operativi. La composizione societaria sembra prevalentemente borghese e le stesse attività ci portano ad identificare più un social club che non una political society[10].

Diverso è, invece, il caso dei santaninfesi d'America che, partiti dalla Sicilia, all'indomani della sconfitta contadina nel 1894, ai primi del Novecento, creano nel Greater New York, due sodalizi, per raccogliere, maestri artigiani, l'uno, e contadini e piccoli conduttori, l'altro. Tra i membri della prima società i sarti sono parecchi, ed è più che naturale che trovino sistemazione nelle locali industrie tessili. Il metodo di lavoro utilizzato negli Stati Uniti è naturalmente diversissimo da quello manuale usato nel paese d'origine. Quasi tutti sono adesso alle prese con sofisticati macchinari. L'attitudine ai lavori di cucito, tuttavia, rendeva comunque appetibile per le locali industrie questo tipo di manodopera, e ricorda un

---

[10] Alla Società di Mutuo soccorso "Napoleone Colajanni" di Castrogiovanni (Enna) è stato dedicato un pannello della citata mostra fotografica e documentaria *Sicilian Crossings to America and Derived Communities*. Si veda adesso M. Saija, *Breve manuale di storia dell'emigrazione... cit.*, p. 48.

"Il Mutualismo dei Siciliani d'America"

anziano testimone che il padre, vantando l'abilità dei sarti santaninfesi, rammentava i nomi di coloro che erano capaci di valutare i metodi di confezione e le taglie suggerendo persino le correzioni da apportare ai processi di lavorazione[11]. Il frizzante ambiente radicale di Williamsburg e di Brooklyn risveglia, soprattutto in costoro, represse istanze d'impegno politico scolpite nella sentenza che Vanni Sala, uno di quelli che aveva guidato il primo massiccio esodo, aveva pronunziato: *"La Sicilia non cambierà mai. E' meglio mangiare pane e libertà in America che pane e cipolla condito con il veleno delle soperchierie al paese"*[12]. Ed è lo stesso Vanni Sala che in breve tempo diventa leader di primissimo piano nei movimenti sindacali del settore tessile come delegato dell'*Amalgamated Workers*, il più grande sindacato di operai tessili d'America[13], mentre il suo amico Augusto Billanca, fonda e dirige l'*Italian American Labour Movement.*[14]

Attraverso i sindacati, le società si procurano un discreto potere contrattuale nei confronti degli imprenditori tessili e diventano canali privilegiati per il reclutamento degli operai. Trovano, quindi, la forza per alimentare la catena di richiamo dal paese d'origine e provvedono in proprio agli atti di garanzia per i biglietti prepagati, preparando anche la prima accoglienza.

A far data dal 1919, maturano l'ambizioso progetto di realizzare una casa comune finalizzata ad indirizzare i paesani verso la costruzione di una società socialista. Ed in effet-

---

[11] M. Saija – G. Bivona (a cura di)… cit., p. 17.
[12] Ibid., p. 19.
[13] Ibid., p. 18.
[14] Ibid., p. 23.

ti, facendo sacrifici ed indebitandosi con le banche, riescono ad approntare una grandioso edificio che, dedicato al martire del libero pensiero, viene inaugurato il 27 maggio 1928 con l'impegnativo nome di "Galileo Temple".

Racconta il diario di uno dei protagonisti che, dal settembre di quell'anno, prende avvio l'Università popolare con conferenze ritualmente fissate ogni venerdì; si forma subito un gruppo con l'intento di incrementare la propaganda politica radicale per la crescita delle masse lavoratrici; ma, soprattutto, si preparano quadri istruiti a combattere il fascismo sia in America che in Italia. L'organizzazione interna rispecchia un ordine massonico con comparti separati. Una sezione per gli ex artigiani (soci della prima società), ed un'altra per gli ex contadini (soci della seconda), una loggia femminile, aperta anche alle adolescenti, ed un Ufficio di Oratore che viene affidato al sindacalista Vanni Sala. Con l'aiuto di uomini e donne di altre comunità siciliane, si costituisce, poi, una filodrammatica che offre una stagione teatrale su un palcoscenico attrezzato nel salone e talvolta utilizzato anche per le attività programmate dall'associazione "Amici del canto e della musica."[15]

Particolare importanza, sotto il profilo finanziario, hanno, infine, i balli, le feste e le celebrazioni di matrimono, eventi tutti indispensabili per mettere insieme gli introiti necessari a pagare gli interessi del prestito bancario.

Nonostante l'entusiasmo ed il grande attivismo, però, le difficoltà economiche, intervenute dopo il crollo del 1929, provocano una crisi finanziaria irreversibile che in otto anni,

---

[15] Il diario del santaninfese Francesco Maggio è ampiamente riprodotto in M Saija – G. Bivona (a cura di)… cit, p. 43e segg.

nel 1937, porta la Banca creditrice ad impossessarsi dell'edificio.

Seppure sfortunata negli esiti, questa vicenda ha una notevole influenza sulla vita della comunità santaninfese d'America che, nonostante gli inevitabili contrasti, prima, durante e dopo gli esperimenti associativi, mantiene i vincoli di solidarietà e conserva un forte legame con il paese d'origine. Al suo interno, nel tempo, per iniziative individuali, sorgono altre strutture di carattere sociale e ricreativo e, da ultimo, il *Senior Citizen Center* di Peter Cardella che ancora oggi a Williamsburg è punto di riferimento per molti.

3. Le altre società costiere

Se per le comunità dell'Interno, la realizzazione delle *Mutual Aid Societies*, politiche e/o non, è una mera eccezione; per quelle delle città costiere, delle piccole Isole e dell'area Iblea è, invece, la norma, ed è difficile trovare comunità che ne siano sprovviste. Si tratta di un fenomeno imponente che, nella stragrande generalità dei casi, vede uomini e donne impegnati a trasportare oltre oceano quella cultura della solidarietà ampiamente conosciuta in patria. Si tratta, talvolta, di vere e proprie gemmazioni delle società esistenti in Sicilia (è, per esempio, il caso dei ragusani); altre volte, invece, si tratta di creazioni autonome che, pur esemplate sui modelli classici, rispondono a peculiari esigenze avvertite dagli emigranti nei luoghi d'arrivo. Non è quindi possibile la *reductio ad unum* delle fattispecie con l'iscrizione ad una sola tipologia. Tenteremo, quindi, un approccio per piccoli gruppi, trascurando gli scopi meramente mutualistici che, almeno fino al 1935, sono una costante per tutti.

Questa esperienza definita, *plurale*[16], dove il mutualismo si intreccia quasi sempre con ragioni di altro tipo, ha i suoi esempi più antichi nell'attività degli agrumari siciliani che creano in America il proprio centro di commercializzazione e trovano utile promuovere una società di accoglienza per gli emigrati, spesso reclutati per i lavori d'azienda. E', per esempio, il caso di Michele Crisafulli di Santa Teresa di Riva (Messina) che, intorno al 1885, decide di spostare a Brooklyn la centrale commerciale della propria attività e, dopo pochi anni adotta la decisione di fondare e pagare da solo le spese notarili per la costituzione della Società "Figli di Santa Teresa". Ciò vale degli imprenditori agrumari e di alcuni benestanti di cittadine della costa palermitana, come Cefalù che, ben presto, formano a New Orleans, nel 1887, una rigogliosa *Società Italiana di Mutua Beneficenza Cefalutana (Italian Benevolent Association of Cefalutans)* che, nel regolamento del 1893, struttura in maniera minuziosa l'erogazione dei benefici mutualistici e funerari per i soci, tutti cefaludani o parenti prossimi.

Più articolata è, invece, la storia della Società di Mutuo Soccorso "Riposto" di Brooklyn[17] dove, l'iniziativa non è più di magnati, ma di emigranti poveri che si associano volontariamente. Nonostante la previsione rigidamente mutualistica dello statuto, la vita associativa, si intreccia con la politica, le attività commerciali, l'assistenza, la promozione economica e sociale, la protezione sindacale e quant'altro. Il sodalizio si forma il 21 settembre 1919 e viene incorporato il 13 marzo

---

[16] S. Bugiardini, *L'associazionismo negli USA…cit., p. 552.*
[17] Si veda A. Micalizzi, *Da paese a Paese. Riposto nell'emigrazione: percorsi, figure, immagini*, Editrice Il Quadrifoglio, Livorno 1999, pp. 57-85.

"Il Mutualismo dei Siciliani d'America"

1920 con il nome di *Society Riposto inc*. Nei primi anni, i ripostesi erano per lo più di condizione disagiata, trovavano impiego nei lavori portuali e abitavano nei casermoni di Degrow Street di Brooklyn. Molti di loro erano nel tunnel del *Padron System* che, insieme all'alloggio forniva loro il cibo, operando anche considerevoli trattenute sulla busta paga a soddisfacimento del debito per il passaggio transoceanico. In queste condizioni, la società non poteva permettersi una sede stabile e le riunioni, di norma, avvenivano in casa dei due fondatori, il lavoratore portuale Salvatore Denaro ed il venditore di occhiali Pietro Sottile. Poi, con l'afflusso di nuovi soci e con le prime disponibilità finanziarie, veniva presa in affitto una sede provvisoria sulla sesta strada di Brooklyn. Più tardi, compatibilmente con le condizioni finanziarie, giungeva finalmente il trasferimento in una lunga sala al pianterreno di uno stabile poco distante, al n. 563 di Henry Street, nei pressi di Montrose Avenue. Come abbiamo visto nel caso dei santaninfesi, era questo il centro pulsante del radicalismo dei siciliani d'America, ed è proprio questo clima che accoglie, nel 1923, il ventiquattrenne ripostese Salvatore Sturiale, espatriato in America per sfuggire alle prime persecuzioni fasciste. Di idee socialiste, il giovane Sturiale fa compiere un primo salto di qualità al sodalizio ripostese, dando a questo la forza contrattuale che gli proveniva dal fatto che, appena giunto, aveva trovato lavoro in una azienda tessile ed aveva immediatamente aderito al I.L.G.W.U. (International Ladies Garment Workers Union) guidato dal connazionale Luigi Antonini[18]. Scrive Alberto Micalizzi:

---

[18] L'avellinese Luigi Antonini legò per la prima volta il suo nome al sindacato durante lo sciopero degli operai tessili del 1913. La sua oratoria

Sturiale si buttò a capofitto nella difesa dei diritti sindacali di quella parte dei lavoratori che per molteplicità di fattori – a cominciare dalla barriera della lingua fino all'innata ritrosia a rivendicare maggiore tutela in un paese da molti considerato non proprio – costituivano l'anello più debole della classe operaia. Deciso a contribuire all'affermazione di quei principi di democrazia e libertà per il quali era stato costretto a lasciare il paese natio, egli sviluppò una capillare opera contro il diffuso crumiraggio a favore della piena coscienza collettiva da parte dei lavoratori delle stirerie. Non furono poche le occasioni in cui, negli accesi contrasti verbali, egli rischiò di doversi difendere dalle minacce dei boss locali che monopolizzavano vaste schiere di emigrati[19]

La Società di Mutuo Soccorso ripostese, sotto la guida di Sturiale comincia ad assumere l'onere di garantire i prestiti bancari per i passaggi prepagati dei nuovi emigranti, esauto-

---

e la sua passione lo trasformarono in poco tempo nel paladino dei lavoratori italiani e in rappresentante autorevole del sindacato tessile. È grazie al suo attivismo che nello stesso anno nacque l'International Ladies Garment Workers Union (ILGWU). Egli fondò anche il settimanale "L'Operaia", foglio con il quale fece crescere la coscienza sociale di tante lavoratrici e grazie al quale riuscì a trasformare l'associazione in un vero e proprio sindacato, cui diede il nome di Local 89 (con riferimento all'anno della Rivoluzione francese) che attirò ben 25000 membri e rappresentò la sezione più importante dell'ILGWU, che contava in tutto 450000 donne lavoratrici nel settore tessile. All'età di 30 anni, diventò vicepresidente dello stesso ILGWU, che con lui assurse a uno dei più importanti sindacati americani. Negli stessi anni fondò l'American Labour Party e la locale sezione del Liberal Party dandogli una chiara matrice anti-comunista.
[19] A Micalizzi, *Da paese a Paese...cit.*, p. 65.

rando il potere di reclutamento dei bosses; ma fa di più. Spinge con decisione i suoi membri ad una attività politica militante.

Negli anni Trenta, Sturiale diventa un punto di riferimento negli States del movimento *Giustizia e Libertà* dei fratelli Rosselli ed una confidenziale del 1933, spedita quando operava nel *Sindacato sarti italiani,* lo segnala al Consolato come "pericoloso sovversivo professante idee socialiste ed avverse al regime".

Nonostante il forte impulso politico, il sodalizio continuava, comunque, a svolgere egregiamente anche la consueta attività aggregativa attraverso i dinner & dance e le rituali feste commemorative della data di fondazione. Nel biennio 1924 – 25, accadeva, però, qualcosa destinata a turbare la vita associativa. Una società immobiliare, la *"Roosevelt City Land and Homes Corporation"* diffondeva un'offerta finalizzata ad installare, in una zona meridionale dello Stato del New Jersey, una città capace di accogliere una colonia agricola di italiani. Per *captatio benevolentiae*, la ditta promotrice indicava "Roosevelt City" – così si chiamava il progetto – come un sito dotato di caratteristiche similari a quelle lasciate dagli emigranti nelle regioni d'origine:

> Il clima di questa sezione – si leggeva nel depliant – è uguale al clima dell'Italia meridionale ed è considerato come uno dei migliori e dei più salubri dell'Est ed è molto raccomandato dai medici.

La società appaltatrice offriva 3080 lotti per la costruzione di case, 150 acri di terreno adatto per impiantarvi fattorie e 3193 acri di terreno per i piccoli *farmers,* ideali per le famiglie che desideravano avere una piccola e lucrosa industria di pollami, un frutteto ed un orto. Era quindi la promessa di una piccola Sicilia che non poteva non accendere la fantasia di chi ancora pativa una struggente nostalgia. L'invito all'acquisto era, inoltre, corredato dalla promessa di facilitazioni finanziarie e la compravendita, perfezionabile con il versamento di un modesto anticipo, era agevolata da un mutuo mensile a tasso favorevole.

Così, confidando nella onnipossente America, molti soci si convincevano della bontà del progetto e, con il denaro raccolto dopo anni di sacrifici, si decidevano a comprare i lotti. Unica sentimentale condizione che ponevano alla ditta appaltatrice era quella che la strada di limite alle proprietà dei ripostesi, nel nome, avrebbe dovuto essere a loro dedicata. Naturalmente la richiesta trovava terreno talmente fertile che, dopo la prima visita domenicale sul luogo, interamente spesata dalla ditta, una foto di gruppo con l'inaugurazione della *Riposto Avenue* veniva inserita nel nuovo depliant pubblicitario.

Non si trattava, probabilmente, di una truffa. Il progetto non era, però, destinato a vedere un grande sviluppo a causa dell'eccessivo peso fiscale imposto ai proprietari nel corso degli anni. I raccolti, del resto, non si sarebbero rivelati bastevoli per mantenere livelli di dignitosa esistenza, e le ristrettezze economiche complessive non avrebbero permesso ai piccoli proprietari di effettuare una programmazione per gli anni a venire[20]. In queste condizioni qualcuno si sarebbe deciso a vendere, altri avrebbero accettato un livello di sopravvivenza, ma nel complesso il disegno iniziale avrebbe registrato un sostanziale fallimento.

---

[20] A. Micalizzi, *Da paese a Paese...cit.*, p. 83.

"Il Mutualismo dei Siciliani d'America"

Così, a metà degli anni Trenta, la società ripostese riaccoglieva nel suo seno gli sconfitti che, però, ritrovavano uno scenario un po' diverso da quello che avevano lasciato. Alcuni soci storici avevano fatto fortuna e gestivano adesso un'importante ditta di import – export dall'Italia. Erano in parecchi che avevano trovato occasioni di lavoro in questo piccolo impero commerciale e, nella sede della Società, in seguito al *Social Security Act*, non si svolgevano più attività mutualistiche, ma riunioni di social club. Le attività prevalenti erano, adesso, opere di beneficenza verso il martoriato e impoverito paese d'origine e raccolti di donativi per le chiese ripostesi. Nel dopoguerra, la società registrava la nascita di un sodalizio femminile, destinato a rafforzare usi e costumi della terra d'origine soprattutto durante le feste rituali, ma anche per i ripostesi giungeva l'ora della americanizzazione e le ultime generazioni di emigranti trovavano nel club più uno strumento di integrazione nella società d'accoglienza che una casa rifugio. Il social club, ancora attivo, si prepara a celebrare tra otto anni la cadenza centenaria.

Meno impegnativa e più squisitamente mutualistica è la vita delle società fondate dagli emigrati di Termini Imerese che, tra gli ultimi anni dell'Ottocento ed i primi del Novecento, creano la *Società Imera Croce Bianca* (1894 a.f.), che a Baltimora, già nel 1908, vanta 105 soci e 7000 lire di capitale sociale; *la Società Imerese del Beato Agostino* (1902 a.f.) che a Cleveland, nel 1908, vanta 80 soci; la *Società Imera* (1905 a.f.), che a Boston, nel 1908, riunisce 100 soci con 4000 lire di capitale e la *Società Terminese* (1904 a.f.) che a New Orleans, nel 1908, raccoglie 70 soci con 11500 lire di capitale sociale[21].

---

[21] *Le Società italiane all'estero nel 1900*, in *Rivista di Emigrazione*, anno II,

Attivissime nel mutuo soccorso sono pure le *Grandi fratellanze palermitane* intestate a *Santa Rosalia* che, nel 1908, a New Orleans (1906 a.f.) raccolgono 55 soci con 5000 lire di capitale sociale ed a Boston (1907 a.f.) contano ben 250 soci e 4000 lire di capitale sociale[22].

Tra le Comunità dell'Area trapanese particolare rilievo hanno le Società di Mutuo Soccorso fondate dai marsalesi[23]. Un *"Fascio dei Siciliani"* nasce nel Greater New York nei primi del '900 e diventa ben presto un sodalizio consistente che alimenterà la principale catena di richiamo da Marsala. Nasce più tardi la *Società dei Figli di Marsala* che pubblica il periodico *"Marsala agli Eroi della Guerra di Liberazione"* dove vengono affrontati i principali problemi della comunità marsalese d'America oltre che di quella rimasta in patria. Alla fine degli anni '10, i marsalesi assumono le massime cariche della cattolica *"Società Patronato San Michele per gli Italiani del Sud emigrati in America,* fondata a Palermo e a New York nel 1893. Il sodalizio diventa a tutti gli effetti un luogo privilegiato di incontro degli interessi marsalesi in patria e fuori e, nel 1923, accoglie come presidente onorario il sindaco di Marsala. A Brooklyn nasce, ai primi del secolo la Società *"Fior di Marsala"* che annovera diversi piccoli imprenditori disponibili ad aprire uno sportello di credito per gli emigranti marsalesi che non potevano avere alcun rapporto fiduciario con le banche americane.

---

fasc. 3, 1909, pp. 22-27. Si veda anche l'aggiornamento pubblicato dalla medesima rivista nel 1908, anno IX, fasc 2, pp.
[22] Ibidem
[23] Abbondante documentazione in Archivio Comunale di Marsala, Fondo emigrazione, ff. 1-3, 7.

"Il Mutualismo dei Siciliani d'America"

Tra le altre società trapanesi che hanno finalità esclusivamente mutualistiche, vanno, infine, annotate, la *Società di mutuo soccorso "Monte San Giuliano"*, costituita, nel 1907, da 80 ericini, la Società *Maria SS. di Trapani* fondata a Brooklyn, nel 1920, e la *Società di mutuo soccorso "Calatafimi"*, fondata a Glendale (NY), nello stesso anno. Una particolare menzione merita la *Società Concordia Partanna*, che fondata a Ridgewood (NY) nel 1905, crea subito uno sportello bancario nella sede sociale per permettere agli emigranti poveri del paese di giungere in America. Lo sportello, attivo fino a pochi anni fa, è ancora visibile nella sede sociale di Ridgewood e viene mostrato con orgoglio ai visitatori[24].

4. Dalle piccole Isole

Straordinariamente compatto è il fenomeno del mutualismo eoliano nell'area di Manhattan e nel Greater New York. E non tanto per la circoscritta area geografica di provenienza di ben sette società che insistono nella zona, quanto per il corposo intreccio degli interessi.

L'emigrazione eoliana verso le Americhe comincia molto presto, quando ancora il modello di sviluppo dell'Arcipelago, basato sulla produzione e commercializzazione di vini pregiati e sulla escavazione ed esportazione della pietra pomice era ancora in pieno fulgore. Sono i giovani marittimi, imbarcati sulle navi transoceaniche, a portare le notizie sul "nuovo mondo" e già, negli anni '70 ed '80 dell'Ottocento, una nutrita colonia di commercianti di vini e di pomice, ma anche di giovani intraprendenti ed avventurosi, si sposta da Salina e

---

[24] Interviste ai soci della *Concordia Partanna* effettuate da chi scrive durante una visita alla sede sociale di Ridgewood nella primavera del 2007.

da Lipari a New York. Parecchi fanno i venditori di frutta, ambulanti o stanziali, importano prodotti dall'Italia ed alcuni giocano la carta delle piccole imprese di costruzione edile. Il palcoscenico dove si muovono è quello di Little Italy e di Brooklyn, all'epoca incontrastato dominio di quella protomafia siculo – americana che viene ricordata con il nome di *black hand* (mano nera). E si comprende benissimo come la piccola laboriosa comunità eoliana attragga l'attenzione dei mafiosi e, suo malgrado, diventi protagonista passiva nel piccolo teatro della protezione e delle estorsioni. Racconta il giudice prof. Edward Re[25]:

---

[25] Eduardo Domenico Re nasce a Salina il 14 ottobre 1920 ed emigra con il padre negli Stati Uniti nel 1928. Si diploma alla New Utrecht School di Brooklyn e nel 1941 riceve il suo Bachelor of Science Degree dalla Saint John's University. Qui, si specializza in discipline giuridiche nel 1943 e viene, poi, ammesso alla New York University School of Law dove, nel 1950, consegue il Dottorato in Juridical Science. Dalla St. John's University riceve il suo primo incarico d'insegnamento in Diritto romano e, nel 1958, il sindaco di New York, Vincent Impellitteri lo chiama come componente del Consiglio per l'Istruzione superiore della città. Nel 1961, J. F. Kennedy lo nomina Presidente della Commissione statunitense per le transazioni delle richieste estere di risarcimento dei danni di guerra e quasi contemporaneamente diventa membro della Delegazione della Santa Sede all'ONU per il controllo di droghe e narcotici. Nel 1963 il presidente L. B. Johnson lo nomina Assistente Segretario di Stato per gli Affari Culturali e di Istruzione con delega alla Fulbright e, nel 1968, lo nomina Giudice del Tribunale doganale degli Stati Uniti Nel 1977, il presidente J. Carter lo nomina Presidente del Tribunale doganale degli USA. Nel 1980 diventa Presidente della Corte preposta alla guida del Tribunale del Commercio Internazionale. Sempre nel 1980 viene nominato Cavaliere della Repubblica Italiana. Dal 1987 presta servizio come Presidente in otto Circoli federali di Corte d'Appello e quattro Tribunali Distrettuali. Come capo della Corte, nel 1990, diventa componente statutario della Conferenza giuridica degli Stati Uniti. Fa quindi parte del Comitato consultivo

"Il Mutualismo dei Siciliani d'America"

> Cuntava me ziu Ciccu Re ca certi mali genti di Palermu cuminzaro a circari assai sordi pirchì dicianu c'America cumannavanu iddi e cu vulia travagghiari avia a pagari "u pizzu", comu fannu oggi cca a Sicilia, ma magari a New York. E si nun pagavi...(il giudice Re porta entrambe le mani al collo). A polizia americana sapia tutti cosi, ma addri tempi nun ci nteressava. Dicia ca chisti eranu cosi chi s'avianu a spidugghiari i taliani. Taliani eranu i mafiusi e taliani eranu chiddi c'avianu a pagari. All'americani nun ci interessava nenti[26].

Stretti nella morsa dell'indifferenza da parte dell'autorità di polizia americana da un lato e del ricatto mafioso dall'altro, gli eoliani intuiscono che l'unico modo di venir fuori da quest'empasse è quello di suscitare in qualche modo

---

della Pianificazione a lungo termine. Nel 2002 va in pensione come docente della St. John's University e nel 2004 diventa professore emerito di Diritto Internazionale. Ritorna alla Conferenza dell'ONU quale esperto di Diritto Commerciale Internazionale e finisce la sua attività lavorativa quale Componente del Comitato delle Ricusazioni straordinarie del North American Free Trade Agreement (NAFTA). Muore nel 2007 nella sua casa di Neponsit a Queens.

[26] *"Raccontava mio zio Francesco Re che gente malavitosa di Palermo cominciò a chiedere molti soldi, perché sostenevano che in America erano loro a comandare e chi voleva lavorare doveva pagare il "pizzo", come fanno ancora in Sicilia ed anche a New York. E se non pagavi* (il giudice Re si porta entrambe le mani al collo)*... La polizia americana sapeva tutto ma a quel tempo non gli interessava nulla. Diceva che queste erano cose che dovevano sbrigarsi gli italiani. Italiani erano i mafiosi e italiani erano quelli che dovevano pagare. Agli americani non riguardavano queste cose"*. Intervista di chi scrive al giudice Edward Re, nella sua casa di Salina, fatta il 9 agosto 2001. Il racconto ci è stato ripetuto dal giudice Re, più o meno negli stessi termini, il 15 febbraio 2002, nella sua casa di Neponsit, New York.

l'interesse della politica e delle istituzioni locali. In questo senso la tappa obbligata era quella di diventare cittadini americani e gruppo di pressione. La naturalizzazione di massa diventava quindi l'obbiettivo da cogliere. Si trattava di riunire i connazionali sparsi nella grande area di New York e di dar loro la prospettiva dei vantaggi di una Mutual Aid Society.

> Di sugietà ci nn'eranu tanti 'America — prosegue nel racconto Edward Re — e tutti davanu sussidi ppì malatia, assistenza medica e pagavanu spisi di funerali e campusantu e n'avia puru una dill'Isuli. C'eranu genti di Lipari e cci n'erunu puru da Salina, ma, ntra d'iddi, cuminzaru subitu a sciarriarisi pi cu avia a cumannari[27].

La prima società eoliana a cui fa riferimento Edward Re si chiamava "Lega eolia". Era stata fondata nel 1887 a Brooklyn ed incorporata nell'anno successivo. I fondatori erano effettivamente delle due isole maggiori e nei propositi iniziali, come si legge nello statuto, si fa cenno soltanto alla necessità di coltivare la fraternità eoliana e stimolare l'unione per conservare lo spirito di patria. In realtà, come si evince dai ricordi tramandati dal giudice Re, liparoti e salinari avevano cominciato a litigare per il controllo del sodalizio provocando, per conseguenza, veti incrociati per l'ammissione di nuovi soci. Nella testa dei più non albergava ancora la ne-

---

[27] "*Di Società ce n'erano tante in America* – prosegue nel racconto il giudice Re – *e tutte davano sussidi per malattia, assistenza medica e pagavano spese funerarie. E ce n'era una pure delle Isole Eolie. Qui, c'era gente di Lipari, ma ce n'era pure di Salina. Tra di loro cominciarono a litigare per chi doveva comandare.*" Ibidem.

cessità di allargare il raggio d'azione. L'obbiettivo dei due gruppi sembrava essere soltanto il controllo dei posti di comando e mentre i salinari (in minoranza), spingevano per far entrare nuovi soci, i liparoti tentavano di cristallizzare la loro superiorità numerica. Molte cose, tuttavia, andavano rapidamente cambiando. Mentre in America il ricatto mafioso si faceva più incombente, a Salina, a partire dal 1888, i vigneti venivano attaccati dalla fillossera ed a Lipari una grave crisi di commercializzazione metteva in ginocchio l'industria della pomice[28]. A partire dal 1892, cominciava, quindi l'esodo di massa che in otto anni quadruplicava il numero di eoliani che imboccavano la via dell'America[29]:

Tab.4 – Espatri di cittadini eoliani negli U.S.A., 1892-1899

Luogo di provenienza	Anno di arrivo								Tot.	%
	1892	1893	1894	1895	1896	1897	1898	1899		
Lipari	36	47	16	0	10	7	98	35	249	48,16
Salina	7	33	0	7	11	11	93	79	241	46,61
Stromboli	0	0	0	0	0	2	16	9	27	5,22
	43	80	16	7	21	20	207	123	517	100

Così, nel 1897, a dieci anni esatti dalla fondazione della prima società, alcuni salinari insieme ai liparesi di buona volontà, prendendo coscienza dei veri problemi, decidevano lo strappo e creavano un'altra società di Mutuo Soccorso con il nome di *Isola di Lipari Lega Salina* che, pur riproducendo la commistione tra gli immigrati delle due Isole, apriva le porte a nuovi soci ed affrettava i tempi per aprire una campagna

---

[28] Si veda M. Saija – A. Cervellera, *Mercanti di Mare. Salina 1800-1953*, Trisform, Messina, 1997.

[29] La tabella che segue è stata elaborata sui dati di Ellis Island da A. M. Fuda, *Emigrazione Eoliana negli Stati Uniti 1892-1924. Un campione di 5266 emigrati*, tesi di laurea a. a. 2007-2008, relatore M. Saija.

di naturalizzazione su vasta scala[30]. Qualcosa, però, continuava a non funzionare e, a pochi mesi di distanza, i salinari decidevano di fondare una terza società, questa volta, riservata solo ai nativi della loro isola madre. Così, nei primi mesi del 1898, gli esponenti di spicco della comunità salinara di New York e di Brooklyn[31], si riunivano per affrontare il serissimo problema del taglieggiamento mafioso[32]. Parecchi di loro erano proprietari o gestori di negozi di frutta e verdura a Manhattan e quotidianamente si trovavano a fare i conti con la "Mano Nera" che controllava i mercati generali. Secondo la testimonianza di Edward Re, a nessuno di loro era consentito il rifornimento quotidiano senza il pagamento di un "onerosissimo pizzo" che rendeva pressoché nullo il margine di guadagno dei piccoli commercianti. La mafia imponeva poi l'assunzione di garzoni e di mano d'opera generica e l'eventuale rifiuto comportava lettere minatorie e conseguenti atti di sabotaggio nei negozi e nelle bancarelle di esposizione[33]. Preso finalmente atto di questo stato di cose,

---

[30] I pochi frammentari documenti di questo sodalizio sono custoditi nel Museo Eoliano dell'Emigraziopne di Salina.
[31] Rileviamo dallo Statuto della Società custodito dal Museo Eoliano di Salina i nomi di Bartolo D'Albora di Giovanni, Giuseppe Favaloro fu Giovanni, Bartolo D'Albora fu Giuseppe, Giuseppe Giuffrè di Giovanni, Gaetano De Luca di Luigi, Giuseppe Palisi di Gaetano, Antonino Giuffrè fu Gaetano, Francesco Re fu Francesco, Felice D'Albora di Giovanni, Giovanni Bonanno di Antonino, Bartolo Buttà fu Bartolo.
[32] Che questo fosse il vero scopo della riunione lo confermava ad Edward Re, Francesco Re fu Francesco (cugino del padre) che della riunione fu uno dei promotori.
[33] Intervista di chi scrive al giudice Edward Re, nella sua casa di Salina, fatta il 9 agosto 2001. Il racconto è stato ripetuto dal giudice Re, più o meno negli stessi termini, il 15 febbraio 2002, nella sua casa di Neponsit

"Il Mutualismo dei Siciliani d'America"

i salinari convenivano che l'unica soluzione possibile per attirare l'attenzione delle istituzioni americane era quella di insistere sulla strada della creazione di un nuovo sodalizio forte di uomini e mezzi. Per essere credibili con i propri conterranei, naturalmente, bisognava offrire loro anche i vantaggi della mutualità, quali quello di assicurare l'assistenza medica alle famiglie dei soci; un sussidio a chi, per malattia o per invalidità permanente conseguita sul lavoro, perdeva l'occupazione e una indennità alle famiglie dei soci defunti. Ed in questa direzione si decideva. Così, dopo una adunanza convocata per il 27 marzo 1898, al n 4 di Horatio Street, ed una successiva, in casa di uno dei promotori, dove 57 persone decidevano di nominare un comitato direttivo provvisorio[34], ai primi di aprile, nello studio del pubblico notaio Frank Zanolini, i salinari fondavano la *Italian Mutual aid Society Salina Island*, che veniva, poi, ufficialmente incorporata, secondo le leggi dello Stato di New York, il 16 maggio 1898[35]. La sede ufficiale, registrata nel certificato d'incorporazione, veniva fissata al 149 di Bleeker Street[36], ma una testimonianza raccolta da George E. Pozzetta, indica che la Società, già nel 1915, era ubicata nell'arteria principale di Little Italy, in

---

nel Long Island di New York.
[34] Rileviamo dalla introduzione al citato Statuto della Società di Mutuo Soccorso Isola di Salina che il primo consiglio direttivo viene composto con Antonio E. Marchetti, Bartolo D'Albora, Giuseppe Favoloro, Antonio Strangio e Giovanni Bonanno. Lo statuto è custodito in originale nel Museo Eoliano dell'Emigrazione di Salina.
[35] Ibidem.
[36] Ibidem.

quella Mulberry Street, che era il centro della vita italoamericana del tempo[37].

L'adesione dei salinari alla nuova Società è subito massiccia e sono in parecchi ad abbandonare le associazioni nate in precedenza per ritrovarsi in una casa comune che più delle altre dava il senso di appartenenza alla patria d'origine. Gli organi direttivi iniziano subito a promuovere ripetute campagne di naturalizzazione e molto presto, secondo i ricordi tramandati da Edward Re, spunta il primo referente politico:

> Cuntava me ziu Ciccu Re chi u primi a daricci cuntu contra e mafiusi ha statu Theodore Roosevelt, chiddu chi poi fu presidenti, ma addri tempi era u boss da New York City police. E fu iddu a ntricari Joe Petrosino chi era u primu nnemicu di dri mafiusi chi poi u mazzaru 'nPalermu[38].

In effetti, il repubblicano Theodore Roosevet era all'epoca in rapida ascesa politica. Membro della Civil Service Commission di New York dal 1889, nel 1895 era stato eletto Presidente del New York City Police Board. All'epoca della forma-

---

[37] G. E. Pozzetta, *Il Mulberry District di New York City negli anni anteriori alla prima guerra mondiale*, in R.F. Harney e J. V. Scarpaci (a cura di) *Little Italies negli Stati Uniti fra Ottocento e Novecento*, numero monografico di "Storia Urbana", V, 16 (1981) pp. 11-49.

[38] "*Raccontava mio zio Francesco Re che il primo politico ad occuparsi di loro contro i mafiosi fu Theodore Roosevelt, quello che poi fu presidente, ma che a quel tempo era soltanto il capo della polizia di New York. E fu lui a coinvolgere Joe Petrosino, primo nemico di quei mafiosi che poi lo ammazzarono a Palermo*" Intervista di chi scrive al giudice Edward Re, nella sua casa di Salina, fatta il 9 agosto 2001. Il racconto è stato ripetuto dal giudice Re, più o meno negli stessi termini, il 15 febbraio 2002, nella sua casa di Neponsit.

"Il Mutualismo dei Siciliani d'America"

zione della Società Isola di Salina puntava alla carica di Governatore dello Stato di New York alla quale verrà eletto proprio nel novembre del 1898. Nel giugno del 1900 verrà poi designato dal partito repubblicano come candidato alla vicepresidenza degli Stati Uniti e, il 4 marzo 1901, vincerà le elezioni con il presidente McKinley. Meno di un anno dopo, con l'omicidio di quest'ultimo, diventerà il più giovane presidente degli Stati Uniti d'America. Rieletto nel 1904, resterà in carica fino al 1909.

I salinari avevano quindi scelto il carro giusto per la loro attività lobbistica. Non siamo in grado di dire quanto la protezione di Theodore Roosevelt e l'azione di Joe Petrosino avesse funzionato per risolvere i problemi di taglieggiamento mafioso, ma la scelta compiuta era stata certamente un notevole passo avanti sul loro percorso di integrazione nella società americana se, ancora nel 1909, i salinari sentivano il bisogno di esprimere la loro riconoscenza al presidente, contribuendo a stampare e diffondere un manifesto di ringraziamento per gli aiuti concessi dal Congresso alla città di Messina distrutta dal terremoto[39].

Con il trascorrere degli anni, anche la comunità salinara andava diversificando gli interessi e al suo interno c'era chi sgomitava per affermare il proprio ruolo economico in settori diversi da quelli dei commercianti di ortofrutta. Era il caso dei fratelli Paino che con la loro impresa di costruzioni ricevevano, all'epoca, piccole commesse per i lavori ferroviari e

---

[39] Secondo la testimonianza di Edward Re, l'iniziativa venne adottata dalla comunità messinese di Brooklyn ma le società eoliane, tra cui *l'Isola di Salina Society*, contribuirono sia alle spese di stampa che alla diffusione del manifesto. Copia del manifesto è custodita nell' Ellis Island Museum di New York, da qui riprodotto ed esposto nel Museo Eoliano di Salina.

minerari da un altro Roosevelt, vice presidente della *Rail Road Company* e proprietario di miniere della *Springwood Estate* di New York. Costui era lontano cugino del presidente in carica, ma, soprattutto, padre di quel Franklin Delano Roosevelt che nel 1933 diverrà presidente degli Stati Uniti d'America. Nel 1909 il giovane Franklyn decideva l'avvio della sua carriera politica con la candidatura democratica al Senato dello Stato di New York, e, per forza di cose, i Paino avevano fatto scelte politiche conseguenti. Accadeva così che pur attivi membri della Società Isola di Salina, si trovavano a perorare una causa elettorale incompatibile con la loro appartenenza societaria. Da qualche anno, peraltro, erano al centro di accesi contrasti di interesse con i commercianti di ortofrutta che egemonizzavano la mano d'opera, che copiosamente continuava ad affluire da Salina. Nei primi tempi, erano riusciti a trovare un faticoso *modus vivendi*, equilibrando la presenza delle diverse categorie produttive negli organi direttivi e dividendosi la manodopera disponibile Adesso, però, l'opzione democratica dei Paino generava nuovi contrasti, destinati a divenire particolarmente aspri proprio alla vigilia elettorale. Così, mentre F. D. Roosevelt, nel 1910, vinceva la sua battaglia diventando senatore dello Stato di New York, Angelo Paino, il maggiore dei fratelli, con la benedizione dell'omonimo cugino, da poco diventato vescovo di Lipari[40], decideva di concentrare i suoi amici in un'altra So-

---

[40] Secondo la testimonianza di Edward Re, Angelo Paino raccontava spesso che in occasione della nascita della *Stella di Salina Society*, il cugino vescovo gli aveva inviato una lettera raccomandandogli che la nuova società contribuisse sopra tutto a diffondere in America, terra di protestanti, il vero verbo del Signore, secondo i dettami di Santa Romana Chiesa. Il medesimo concetto mons. Angelo Paino avrebbe ripetuto nel

"Il Mutualismo dei Siciliani d'America"

cietà di Mutuo soccorso, la "Stella di Salina Society" che veniva, così, fondata nei primi mesi del 1911 ed incorporata il 18 agosto successivo[41]. Certo, la scissione indeboliva la società madre, ma in certo modo, rendeva più ampia la rosa delle opportunità di inserimento nella società americana. E, di lì a poco, anche i commercianti della *Salina Society* si rendevano conto che, considerato il rapido divenire degli eventi politici americani, forse la scelta dei Paino era la più giusta. Era accaduto, infatti, nel 1909, che T. Roosevelt, chiuso il suo mandato presidenziale, era partito per l'Africa, mentre la stella politica di F. D. Roosevelt era in continua ascesa. Così, quando, nel 1914, Angelo Paino, interpretando l'intenzione dei fratelli separati, organizza un *dinner dance* in onore del giovane Roosevelt, invitando anche la Salina Society, Roosevelt non solo interviene al party ma rivolge a tutti i salinari un caloroso invito all'unità. Era quanto bastava per convincere la Società madre ad avvicinarsi al giovane politico emergente. A distanza di poco più di un decennio da quegli

---

1922 in occasione della inaugurazione della Chiesa di Santa Marina, appena restaurata con i munifici doni della famiglia Paino d'America. In tale occasione il prelato, da pochissimo nominato Arcivescovo di Messina, avrebbe detto nell'omelia ai suoi cugini americani che la Chiesa rispetto all'Emigrazione aveva un sentimento bivalente perché da un lato non poteva non comprendere il dramma della separazione di tante famiglie, ma dall'altro non poteva non rallegrarsi pensando che gli emigranti italiani rafforzavano in America la forza del cattolicesimo e diffondevano la vera Chiesa di Cristo.

[41] Sulle ragioni che determinavano la nascita della Società Stella di Salina, Edward Re conserva ricordi più circostanziati per la testimonianza del padre che, giunto con lui a New York nel 1928, in breve tempo diventa manager dell'impresa Paino e attivissimo membro della Stella di Salina Society.

eventi, nel 1926, rileviamo dal bilancio della *Isola di Salina Society*, che metà della spesa societaria era stata destinata a contributi elettorali per Franklin Delano Roosevelt[42]. In quello stesso anno, peraltro, i sodalizi salinari si ramificavano in California, fondando a San Francisco, dove esisteva un'altra corposa e ormai ricca comunità salinara, una branca dell'*Isola di Salina Society* che, pur adottando il medesimo statuto della società madre, si dedicava in prevalenza ad attività sociali, politiche e ricreative. A New York, tuttavia, il più attivo nel sostegno a Roosevelt, restava comunque Angelo Paino che in previsione delle elezioni a governatore dello stato di New York, assumeva l'iniziativa di fondare altre tre società con lo scopo di raccogliere e naturalizzare i pescatori di Alicudi e gli eoliani di Panarea e Stromboli. Ed è così che con una forte inclinazione a preservare i principi della fede cattolica (come gli aveva raccomandato il cugino, ormai arcivescovo di Messina[43]), ma con lo scopo dichiarato di formare altri buoni cittadini americani, promuove la nascita a Brooklyn della "Alicudi society" (1926, inc. 1928), della "Panarellese society" (f. e Inc.1928) e della "Strombolese society" (1928 inc.1929)[44]. I propositi venivano nitidamente scolpiti nel certificato di incorporazione della Alicudi Society che così recitava:

> To foster and advocate the principles of citizenship conformably with the Institution and Government of the Uni-

---

[42] Copia del rendiconto finanziario della Isola di Salina Society nell'anno 1925 è custodito in Salina da Felice Lopes nella sua casa di Leni.
[43] Vedi *supra* nota 41.
[44] Abbondante documentazione sulle tre società è custodita nel Museo Eoliano dell'Emigrazione di Salina

ted States, to unite in fraternal groups persons of good, moral character for the improvement of the moral, mental and social condition of its members and expecially those formerly residing on the Island of Alicudi, Italy, and to foster and maintain the precepts of the Roman Catholic Church in and among the members, to the end that they may all be good and law-abiding citizens of the United States of America[45].

Nel 1929, F. D. Roosevelt viene eletto governatore dello Stato di New York e nel 1933 varca il soglio della Casa Bianca. Le quotazioni di Paino nel partito democratico salgono notevolmente. La sua impresa di costruzioni riceve adesso commesse pubbliche più consistenti per la costruzione delle arterie stradali di collegamento nel Greater New York e nel Long Island[46] e la cronaca giornalistica di un ricevimento predisposto in suo onore al hotel Baltimore, lo descrive come il maggiore "prominente" della comunità eoliana, mettendo in piena evidenza le solidarietà politiche ed economiche che poteva vantare[47].

A partire dal 1935, qualcosa cambia radicalmente per tutte le società di mutuo soccorso d'America. F. Delano Roosevelt, con il Social Security Act, vara una forma di stato sociale per fornire sostegno ai cittadini a basso reddito ed a quelli

---

[45] Certificato di Incorporazione riportato come introduzione allo Statuto della Alicudi Society di Brooklyn stampato a New York nel 1928. Copia del documento è esposto nel Museo Eoliano dell'Emigrazione nell'Isola di Salina.
[46] *Vita degli Eoliani all'Estero. Da Brooklyn. Le nuove opere dell'Impresa Paino*, in "L'Avvenire Eoliano", a. III, n. 3, S. Marina Salina 1 febbraio 1920
[47] *Vita degli Eoliani all'Estero. Da Brooklyn. Un Banchetto al Cav. Paino*, in "L'Avvenire Eoliano", a. III, n. 7, S. Marina Salina 1 aprile 1920

più anziani. La legge, che operava in parte con il finanziamento dello Stato e in parte con i contributi di datori e prestatori di lavoro, faceva fronte ai sussidi di disoccupazione e malattia prima erogati dalle Mutual Aid Societies. In conseguenza, parecchie delle vecchie società, esautorate nei principali scopi, cessano l'attività, e le rimanenti restano attive come social and political clubs. Tra queste anche le due salinare che seppure distinte continuano ad organizzare congiuntamente, negli anni, le rituali feste e i banchetti per gli anniversari di fondazione, con la corale partecipazione di tutta la comunità isolana, indipendentemente da quale fosse il sodalizio promotore dell'iniziativa. Negli anni cinquanta, i tempi erano, però, più che maturi per la fusione e, il 4 febbraio 1956, con lo scioglimento della *Stella di Salina* nella società madre, nel corso di un banchetto ufficiale promosso dal comm. Angelo Paino in onore del prof Edward Re, veniva affidata a quest'ultimo la presidenza della nuova *Società Isola di Salina*. Il mondo politico americano, però, andava profondamente mutando ed anche il lobbismo si stratificava su specifici gruppi d'interesse. Le ultime generazioni di eoliani d'America, del resto, non avevano più il legame emozionale che legava i padri e i nonni alla terra d'origine. Così, anche la Società Isola di Salina, nel 1960, chiude le attività. Questo, però, non impedisce ad Edward Re, unico erede della tradizione democratica dei salinari d'America, di essere nominato da Kennedy, nel 1961, *Chairman of the Foreign Claims Settlement Commission of the United States* e, pochi anni dopo, da L. B. Johnson, *Assistant Secretary of State for Educational and Cultural Affairs*.

Una storia in parte diversa hanno invece, le due società eoliane create nell'*upstate* di New York dai liparesi e dagli

"Il Mutualismo dei Siciliani d'America"

strombolani, rispettivamente a Norwich e ad Oswego. Qui, appaiono prevalenti le ragioni classiche della mutualità e dell'assistenza ai nuovi arrivati, con l'aggiunta, però, di pregnanti ragioni commerciali nel caso di Oswego.

A Norwich, già a fine ottocento giungono, dalla maggiore delle isole, gli scavatori di pomice che trovano impiego nelle locali cave di *bluestone* a Oxford e a West Hill. La pietra che estraggono è molto più dura di quella bianca e spugnosa lavorata a Lipari, ma ai fratelli John e Frank Natoli, già titolari, nel 1898, di una drogheria e di una rivendita di frutta nell'area, sembra che quello sia un mestiere congruo per i loro conterranei abituati a scavare montagne. John si offre, quindi, alla proprietà mineraria come mediatore di mano d'opera e apre, così, nei primi anni del Novecento, una catena di richiamo dall'Isola madre. A Newton Lane, dell'East Main Street, dove risiedevano, i fratelli sistemano un vecchio fabbricato per accogliere gli immigrati e ampliano così la gamma delle loro attività. Secondo la Directory comunale del 1902, nel fabbricato, abitavano già 14 persone, tutte provenienti da Lipari[48]. Scrive Maria Taranto:

> Natoli became a labor contractor and brought many men from Lipari over to work. He had bought the boarding house that ran along Steers Lane to Newton Lane and turned it into a place where the arriving immigrants could

---

[48] I nomi erano Francesco e Giuseppe Famularo, Antonio Fazio, Giuseppe Ferro, Bartolo, Felice, Giuseppe, Gaetano e Giorgio Natoli, Angelo Mirabito, Bartolo Maiorano, Antonio Merlino e Angelo, Antonio, Domenico e Giuseppe Scafidi. M. Taranto, *Le Società eoliane*, in "NEOS, Rivista di Storia dell'Emigrazione Siciliana", Anno II, N. 1, Dicembre 2008, p 248.

come to live. Natoli helped arrange for their ship's passage, helped the men find jobs and even sponsored many for American citizenship, while instructing them in the process of naturalization[49].

Nella seconda metà degli anni '10, infatti, cominciano i ricongiungimenti familiari ed in breve la comunità liparese cresce notevolmente. In una piccola casa di Norwich, viene organizzata una chiesa dedicata a San Bartolomeo e, per risolvere i problemi di assistenza medica e di mutualità, i liparesi creano una prima organizzazione societaria intestata nel nome al *Principe di Piemonte*. Con la americanizzazione degli immigrati, giunge inevitabilmente anche l'interesse dei politici americani e, alla fine del decennio a Norwich, giunge persino la visita del presidente degli Stati Uniti d'America Theodore Roosevelt.

Quando i *Sons of Italy*, uscendo dal primo periodo di crisi della loro storia, nel 1914, adottano il nuovo statuto federale e rastrellano gli Stati Uniti per trasformare in logge le piccole comunità italiane organizzate, portando a ben 400 il numero dei sodalizi attivi[50], i fratelli Natoli accettano di fondare in Norwich la loggia n. 115 dello Stato di New York e favoriscono la confluenza in massa di tutti i liparesi presenti nell'area. La comunità eoliana è ormai più forte di quella irlandese, preesistente nella zona, e decide di dare un segnale della propria supremazia staccandosi dalla parrocchia istituzionale gestita dagli irlandesi. Chiedono ed ottengono dal vescovo di Syracuse l'erezione in parrocchia della piccola

---

[49] Ibidem.
[50] E. L. Biagi, *The Purple Aster. A History of Sons of Italy in America*, Veritas Press, N.Y., 1961, pp 18-19.

chiesa, da anni allestita in una casa privata[51], e, poco dopo, riescono anche ad avere un prete in grado di celebrare in lingua italiana i riti e le confessioni. E non è tutto. Alcuni anni appresso, con uno sforzo corale, i lavoratori delle cave, finito il turno quotidiano, portano con loro pesanti blocchi di *bluestone* fino ad un terreno del centro città acquistato dalla chiesa alcuni anni prima e dedicano le ore serali alla costruzione della Cattedrale di San Bartolomeo. Nel 1923, finiscono l'opera che ricorda nella tecnica costruttiva e nelle sembianze i muri liparitani e la inaugurano con grande solennità. La nuova chiesa diventa il centro pulsante della vita comunitaria, mentre la loggia continua ad assolvere agli scopi mutualistici. Negli anni, i liparesi arricchiscono la parrocchia con vistose opere d'arte e strumenti d'arredo di notevole pregio e tutti gli eventi che scandiscono la vita sociale continuano a ruotare intorno alla Cattedrale di San Bartolomeo. Oggi, a Norwich, gli uomini e le donne di discendenza liparese sono più di 4000 e tra questi il sindaco, il capo della polizia ed il parroco. Il 26 agosto di ogni anno si porta in processione per le strade la statua del santo e tutto questo contribuisce non poco a conservare negli anni i legami con la terra d'origine.

Poco distante da Norwich, ad Oswego, sulle rive del fiume Ontario, proprio all'estuario con l'omonimo lago, nel 1895, si ferma Antonio Ferraro che, rileviamo dalle liste di Ellis Island, è un sailor man di Stromboli. Come Ferraro capiti in quel luogo è difficile stabilirlo, ma dagli eventi successivi è possibile affermare che probabilmente il suo interesse sia quello di trovare impiego sui battelli commerciali che da

---

[51] La piccola chiesa era ospitata nella casa di Angelo Biviano, all'angolo tra Birdsall Street e Front Street.

Oswego fanno la spola con il Canada. Di lì a poco, infatti, nella cittadina dell'Ontario si forma una piccola colonia di strombolani, tutti uomini di mare, che hanno alle spalle un corposo trascorso mercantile sui velieri che dalle Eolie percorrevano l'intero Mediterraneo. Quest'esodo così precoce non è un fatto episodico nell'emigrazione strombolana se si pensa che, già negli anni '80 dell'Ottocento, una colonia di marinai della stessa Isola raggiunge Wellington in Nuova Zelanda per dedicarsi alla pesca d'altura. Così, alla fine della prima decade del Novecento, gli strombolani ad Oswego sono già più di cento e, appare perfettamente comprensibile come, nel 1912, si celebri la fondazione della *Mutual Aid Society Isola di Stromboli*. I soci, tutti della medesima origine geografica, sono annotati come *merchant sailors* e negli scopi sociali dello statuto iscrivono come obbiettivi prevalenti l'assicurazione per malattie, la previsione delle cure mediche, l'assistenza alle famiglie dei soci deceduti, le spese funerarie ed il supporto sociale e morale ai nuovi arrivati dall'isola madre[52]. Nulla di diverso, quindi, dai fini classici che accomunano le società siciliane d'America, ma se tentiamo di comprendere qualcosa in più sulla cultura associazionistica dei soci fondatori di questa società, rileviamo che in patria, oltre che padroni marittimi e naviganti, erano tutti membri del "Circolo Progresso Stromboli", un sodalizio a base democratica che conduceva le sue battaglie con una forte carica rivendicativa nei confronti del Governo italiano, a cui, ripetutamente chiedeva la creazione di un molo d'attracco per i

---

[52] Statuto della società di mutuo soccorso Isola di Stromboli, pp. 9-10. Il documento è custodito in originale da Peter Tesoriero nella sua casa di Melbourne

velieri, una struttura assicurativa per i carichi dei natanti, la creazione di scuole d'istruzione primaria, la realizzazione delle strade di collegamento nell'Isola e quant'altro fosse necessario per il progresso della comunità[53]. Sono quindi, pienamente credibili le poche notizie raccolte da fonti orali di Norwich secondo cui gli strombolani di Oswego utilizzavano il sodalizio, oltre che per i classici fini mutualistici, anche come struttura di supporto alle attività commerciali e di trasporto marittimo delle merci da e per i porti lacustri canadesi[54]. Qualcuno afferma, in particolare, che i mercanti strombolani avessero la sede sociale sulle rive del fiume e che, da questa, avessero accesso diretto ad un piccolo molo d'attracco dei natanti ormeggiati in attesa del carico. Qui svolgevano le contrattazioni, acquisivano le committenze e c'era chi, nella società, si occupava di tenere in ordine i libri di carico e scarico delle merci[55]. Non siamo riusciti, purtroppo, a trovare riscontri documentari di questa attività, ma le

---

[53] C. Russo, *The Società mutuo soccorso Isole Eolie. From the Eolian Islands to Melbourne*, tesi di laurea discussa al Dipartimento di storia dell'Università di Melbourne nel 1986, pp. 26-28. Le considerazioni sulla nascita e la natura della SMSIS sono dovute al fatto che da questo sodalizio ha origine la Società di Mutuo Soccorso Isole Eolie di Melbourne, fondata da un Salvatore Tesoriero, membro della SMSIS che, nel 1924, decide di lasciare Oswego per raggiungere i fratelli in Australia. L'autrice di questa tesi ha avuto modo di intervistare i figli dei protagonisti della vicenda e vedere i documenti in loro possesso.

[54] Con maggiore o minore chiarezza, nel ricordo, tale circostanza viene riferita a chi scrive da Angelina Maiurano e Carmela Amendola nel mese di maggio 2008, a Norwich.

[55] Testimonianza, raccolta da chi scrive l'11 maggio 2008 a Norwich, di Bartolo Maiorana (83 anni), nipote per via materna di Vincenzo Di Mattina, membro della Società di Mutuo soccorso Isola di Stromboli.

poche notizie raccolte, per tradizione orale, ci sembrano ampiamente compatibili con una verità semplice e perfettamente comprensibile che vuole gli strombolani, uomini capaci di trasportare nelle terre d'accoglienza la pregressa esperienza acquisita nel mercantilismo mediterraneo. Della Società di Mutuo soccorso Isola di Stromboli, ci restano, oggi, poche vestigia conservate nel Museo Eoliano dell'Emigrazione nell'Isola di Salina[56]: lo Statuto, il budge societario e alcune foto raccolte, nella sua casa di Melbourne, da Peter Tesoriero[57] e il banner di rappresentanza, custodito in originale nella Chiesa di San Bartolomeo a Norwich.

Per chiudere il panorama delle società di mutuo soccorso eoliane, dobbiamo, infine, dar conto dei sodalizi sorti nell'area di Boston. Diciamo subito che i primi migranti verso il Massachussets non sembrano avere le caratteristiche economiche e sociali di quelli giunti nell'area newyorchese. Si tratta di una emigrazione più povera, fatta di braccianti ed operai generici che non hanno possibilità di investire capitali. Non devono, quindi, fare i conti con la piccola criminalità organizzata, tipica dell'area newyorkese, e, per conseguenza – almeno nel caso dei due sodalizi presi in esame – riescono a conservare a lungo un'identità che non si riferisce ad un isola in particolare, ma prevede una membership allargata a tutti gli immigrati dell'arcipelago. Si tratta della *Società italiana di mutuo soccorso e beneficenza Unione Eolia (Union Eolia inc.)*, nata il 1 luglio 1899 e incorporata il 3 settembre 1903, e

---

[56] Si tratta di una statua della Madonna rivestita delle insegne del Presidente onorario della Società di Mutuo soccorso Isola di Stromboli di Oswego.
[57] P. Tesoriero, *Memorie eoliane tra Stati Uniti ed Australia* in M.Saija, (a cura di), *L'emigrazione italiana transoceanica tra Otto e Novecento e la storia delle comunità derivate*, Trisform, Messina 2003, pp. 539 e segg.

"Il Mutualismo dei Siciliani d'America"

della *San Bartolomeo Eoliana (Saint Bartolomew Eolian Mutual Aid and Benefit Society),* nata il 15 aprile 1910 ed incorporata il 1 agosto successivo[58]. Dall'analisi degli statuti ed in particolare, dalla tassativa disposizione che il numero degli aderenti non poteva superare le 200 unità, ricaviamo che gli scopi della fondazione fossero soltanto quelli di assicurare ai soci i benefici mutualistici (fino a $10 la settimana per malattia e fino a $200 per il funerale) e proprio la soglia massima di adesione e le cifre predeterminate per la mutualità indicavano quantità rigidamente calcolate per poter far fronte alle quotidiane domande d'intervento. Queste disposizioni non esistevano negli statuti delle società newyorkesi proprio perché, al contrario di quelle bostoniane, queste prime avevano l'interesse politico ad allargare più possibile la membership; nella realtà bostoniana, invece, le seconde avevano soltanto l'esigenza di un equo rapporto finanziario tra le entrate ed i fini mutualistici previsti dalla carta di fondazione. Tant'è che quando il numero degli aspiranti ai benefici cresce con l'incremento degli immigrati, sono alcuni degli stessi fondatori dell'Unione Eolia a creare, nella vicina Brighton, nel 1910, la *San Bartolomeo Eoliana*. Certo, a motivare la nascita del nuovo sodalizio sembrano concorrere anche ragioni di provenienza geografica. Non è forse un caso che la quasi totalità dei soci fondatori del nuovo sodalizio sono originari di Malfa, nell'Isola di Salina; e, anche se lo stemma sociale scelto e ricamato nel budge continua a riportare in grande evidenza i simboli della municipalità liparese, l'omaggio che la

---

[58] Su entrambe le società si veda il saggio di M. Taranto, *Le Società eoliane*, in "NEOS, Rivista di Storia dell'Emigrazione Siciliana"... cit, pp. 245 e segg.

Società porge al comune di Malfa, nel 1911, in occasione della sua autonomia amministrativa (una grande bandiera italiana con le cifre ricamate Malfa 1911)[59], appare certamente come una dichiarazione di affezione se non di appartenenza. La prevalenza malfitana non modifica, tuttavia, le regole di ammissione e, nello statuto, la membership resta aperta a "tutti i figli delle Isole Eolie". Al di là di questi elementi che sembrano in qualche modo distinguere le due società, è però necessario rilevare che la condizione sociale e lavorativa dei membri di entrambe non sembra differire in alcun modo. C'è chi lavora come muratore o capomastro nell'area di Commonwealth Avenue e Beacon Street nella Back Bay e nelle imprese che operavano a Mount Vernon Street. Qualcuno vende frutta per conto dei grossisti californiani e col tempo riesce ad assicurarsi uno stand al Quincy Market di North End. Soltanto uno diviene tipografo e si sposta in California. La maggior parte, però, continua a fare lavori saltuari e cambia spesso occupazione. La sede sociale della S Bartolomeo Society appare decorosa e serve prevalentemente per il ritrovo serale di chi intende passare un po' di tempo giocando a carte o conversando con i paesani. Ed anche se i bostoniani non rinunziano ai rituali *dinner and dance* ed al banchetto annuale per l'anniversario della fondazione, la celebrazione degli eventi, a giudicare dalle foto, appare decisamente più modesta di quella usualmente praticata a New York. Negli anni '40, entrambe le società vedono la gemmazione di sodalizi femminili, ma, dal dopoguerra in poi, sembrano proseguire per inerzia la loro vita associativa, fino alla chiusura

---

[59] La bandiera è custodita, in originale, nel Museo dell'Emigrazione Eoliana di Salina.

"Il Mutualismo dei Siciliani d'America"

dei battenti che avviene tra la seconda metà degli anni '50 ed i primi anni '60.

Per taluni aspetti, simile a questa, ma con alcune peculiarità che assicurano una più lunga durata, è la vicenda delle società generate dall'emigrazione filicudara a Waltham ed a Newton[60], due piccole cittadine poste a pochi chilometri da Boston. Secondo una consolidata tradizione orale, ancora presente nella comunità, la prima società nasce a Waltham, intorno al 1909, quando alcuni emigrati dalla piccola isola dell'Arcipelago decidono di intervenire in soccorso di una povera famiglia di conterranei priva dei mezzi necessari per dare dignitosa sepoltura ad un povero Cristo, da poco giunto in terra americana. Nella leggenda delle origini, nulla di nuovo, quindi, rispetto all'intenzione di assicurarsi i classici *benefit*. Gli è però che la Filicudi Society, che verrà incorporata a Waltham nel 1911, sin dalle origini presenta alcune singolarità che appare necessario rimarcare. Il primo elemento che balza agli occhi è il connotato di appartenenza societaria, geograficamente marcato dallo statuto di fondazione, che riserva la membership soltanto agli uomini nati nell'Isola di Filicudi ed ai loro discendenti maschi. La ragione di questa così rigida disposizione diventa comprensibile non solo alla luce di altre norme statutarie che estendono i benefici mutualistici anche a soci e parenti ancora residenti sull'Isola madre, ma soprattutto per la prassi, documentata nel primo libro dei verbali, di mandare oltreoceano aiuti economici, talvolta impegnativi, diretti a sostenere uomini e famiglie, ma anche a dotare il paese o la chiesa di opere e strumenti di

---

[60] Si rimanda al saggio di M. Taranto, *Le Società eoliane*, in "NEOS, Rivista di Storia dell'Emigrazione Siciliana"…cit, pp.245 e segg.

crescita civile e religiosa. E quasi sempre, i donativi vengono accompagnati da accorate petizioni al sindaco di Lipari o al Governo italiano perché intervengano a beneficio della piccola isola mediterranea, sempre al centro dell'attenzione da parte degli espatriati.

Più in generale, leggendo i libri dei verbali[61], sembra emergere un sentimento diffuso per il quale l'atto migratorio del singolo non era soltanto un fatto individuale diretto a migliorare le condizioni personali o della propria famiglia, ma piuttosto un piccolo frammento di una decisione condivisa, diretta a far crescere in America, insieme alle proprie fortune, anche quelle del paese d'origine, futuro rifugio proprio e/o dei propri figli. Certo anche se – sempre dai verbali sociali – appare diffusissimo il costume di andare e tornare spesso dalla terra madre, non si può, certo, dire che l'emigrazione filicudara avesse i caratteri della provvisorietà. C'era certamente nei soci la convinzione che il "sacrificio americano" sarebbe stato lungo ed era chiaramente contemplata l'eventualità che non necessariamente tutti avrebbero chiuso la propria esistenza nell'Arcipelago. Il paese restava tuttavia il teatro principale su cui rappresentare la propria esperienza migratoria e, attraverso le lettere spedite e ricevute, erano in molti ad aspettarsi il giudizio della Comunità d'origine sul proprio operato.

Il secondo elemento degno di nota nei sentimenti dei filicudari di Waltham, conseguenza diretta del primo, sembra essere l'assenza di quella corsa alla naturalizzazione diffusa nei salinari di New York e la tiepida indifferenza a trovare

---

[61] I documenti sono custoditi nel Museo dell'Emigrazione Eoliana di Salina.

gli strumenti politici per una piena integrazione nella società americana. Essi vivono la piccola sede sociale come un isolato lembo di terra che permette loro di assaporare il clima natale. Ed è probabilmente per il complesso di questi motivi che dal seno della Filicudi Society, più o meno negli stessi anni, scaturisce un altro sodalizio dove, invece, l'apertura alla società della terra d'accoglienza appare più marcata. Si tratta della *Santo Stefano di Filicudy Society* che si forma a Newton, poco distante da Waltham, intorno al 1908, ma viene incorporata nel 1913. Anche per questa Società, i filicudari tramandano una leggenda di fondazione, raccontando come il sodalizio ha origine dall'attività che alcuni filicudari svolgevano di alloggiare, in una grande casa bianca posta nella Langley Road di Newton, tutti i nuovi arrivati. Con il crescere della comunità, quasi naturalmente c'è qualcuno che decide di avviare la costituzione della società ed altrettanto naturalmente la *casa bianca* diventa la prima sede sociale. Lo statuto adottato scolpisce naturalmente la previsione di tutti i benefit mutualistici, ma non limita la membership ai soli isolani. Viene, invece, espressamente prevista la possibilità di accedere anche ai cittadini americani che contraevano matrimonio con una filicudara, ma anche per chi, parente o amico, mostrasse di condividere le finalità sociali. Lo statuto strutturava minutamente il mutuo soccorso, prevedendo – così come la Filicudi Society – il tetto massimo di 200 soci e distribuiva sussidi ed assistenza ai soli soci d'America. C'era, però, un attenzione più ampia verso i processi di americanizzazione che per le sorti dell'Isola madre. La sede sociale serviva anche per i corsi di lingua inglese e si affermava che la naturalizzazione restava un obbiettivo da conseguire al più presto possibile. Insomma, si ha l'impressione che questo secondo sodalizio raccogliesse uomini che si erano lasciati alle spalle il proprio passato e proiettavano nella terra d'accoglienza il proprio futuro. Questo non vuol dire naturalmente che i legami affettivi con la terra d'origine fossero assenti; ma c'era certamente una maggiore consapevolezza che prima d'ogni altra cosa bisognava star bene in America. Apparentemente, il contrasto interno, al momento della scissione, sembra vertere sulla necessità di prevedere nella ragione sociale anche l'intitolazione a Santo Stefano, protettore di Filicudi che, in effetti, darà il nome alla seconda società. I sentimenti di devozione che restavano comunque patrimonio di tutti i filicudari d'America erano ragioni piuttosto labili a motivare la separazione. E la circostanza che parecchi soci della prima società contribuiscono a formare la seconda, restando membri di entrambe, indica piuttosto che, forse, per decisione condivisa viene operata dalla stessa comunità una netta separazione sugli scopi da cogliere. Più tardi, dopo il 1935, quando i fini mutualistici vengono in gran parte assorbiti dalla legislazione federale e le associazioni accentuano i caratteri di social clubs e di assistenza agli studi per le nuove generazioni, la separazione diventa anacronistica e, dopo aver prodotto, entrambi i sodalizi, le società femminili, lentamente, finiscono per riaccorparsi dando origine a quella Filicudi Associates inc. che nel 2010 ha sontuosamente festeggiato il centenario dalla fondazione.

Delle altre isole siciliane abbiamo raccolto notizia della Congregazione e Fratellanza degli Italiani usticani che viene fondata a New Orleans nel 1878 ed incorporata nel 1879 con uno statuto diretto ad assicurare i classici benefici della mutualità ai contadini che giungono in Luisiana per trovare impiego nelle grandi piantagioni dopo l'abolizione della schia-

"Il Mutualismo dei Siciliani d'America"

vitù ed ai pescatori che trovano impiego sui pescherecci d'altura. Quella di Ustica è probabilmente la più antica società di mutuo soccorso siciliana in terra americana ed è tuttora attiva per la gestione di un piccolo cimitero costruito negli anni e di proprietà della comunità usticese. Vistosa ancora oggi è la festa di San Bartolomeo protettore dell'isola che si celebra, nelle strade di New Orleans, il 24 agosto di ogni anno[62].

Dei primi anni del Novecento è La *Società di Mutua Benevolenza dei pescatori di Marettimo*, la piccola isola delle Egadi, di fronte a Trapani. Sin dall'ultimo decennio dell'Ottocento affluiscono direttamente da qui a Monterey, San Francisco e San Pedro di California, abili uomini di mare che trovano impiego – nei pescherecci di altura e nelle locali fabbriche conserviere, ma anche, parecchi, precedentemente emigrati in altri luoghi del continente americano, che vengono poi attratti dalle possibilità d'impiego nel settore in cui vantano più consolidate professionalità. Con i ricongiungimenti familiari, sorge la necessità di un'organizzazione assistenziale che viene fondata nel 1907 con i classici scopi mutualistici. Con il passare degli anni, gli egadesi trovano l'energia per dare una veste cooperativistica al sodalizio, ed acquistano in proprio battelli e strumenti di pesca e di conservazione del prodotto. Negli anni 10 compiono le prime escursioni in Alaska per la pesca del salmone e col tempo quest'attività diventa l'occupazione principale che da la forza economica alla piccola comunità per diventare un impresa, ancora oggi, fiorentissima[63].

---

[62] M. Taranto, *Le Società Eoliane* in "NEOS..." cit., pp. 254 -255.
[63] La storia dei pescatori di Marettimo in California è sommariamente

5. Le società ragusane

Caratteristiche ben definite nelle origini e nelle finalità hanno anche i sodalizi creati dalle comunità provenienti dall'area Sud orientale dell'Isola. I ragusani portano anch'essi oltreoceano la cultura della terra d'origine e non è difficile cogliere nella loro esperienza migratoria quegli intensi tratti di mutua solidarietà che hanno caratterizzato la storia iblea sin dal secondo Ottocento. Per ben comprendere, tale vicenda, bisogna, però, prestare attenzione alla singolare esperienza maturata per secoli nella Contea di Modica (così era definita buona parte dell'attuale provincia di Ragusa), dove un deciso processo di frazionamento della proprietà terriera ha cancellato quasi completamente i latifondi, stratificando i ceti agricoli e creando ricchezza diffusa. Il modello economico emerso da questo processo, ancora in piedi per tutto l'Ottocento, ha registrato, quindi un'alta produttività che, pur distribuendo bassi salari ai braccianti, ha assicurato loro continuità di impiego e soprattutto speranza di poter diventare un giorno proprietari. Per tali ragioni, a fine Ottocento, quando si apre la stagione migratoria, i flussi in partenza dagli iblei appaiono molto lenti e soprattutto nettamente inferiori per quantità alla media siciliana. La frazionatissima proprietà garantisce maggiori possibilità e continuità d'impiego del latifondo, ancora vitale nel centro Sicilia e, in particolare, proprio

---

ricostruita da V. Vaccaro, *Pescatori nel mondo*, in "La Sicilia Ritrovata", Egadi, n. 1 2008, pp. 69 e segg. Vestigia e foto della Società sono custodite nel piccolo Museo del mare allestito a Marettimo nel 2007 e tuttora operante. Di recente, l'ANFE, (Associazione nazionale famiglie emigrate) ha ricostruito la storia dei pescatori di marettimo nel filmato *Il mare di Jo*, Palermo 2009.

"Il Mutualismo dei Siciliani d'America"

nella seconda metà dell'Ottocento, si assiste all'emersione dei ceti massarili che conducono in proprio le aziende con largo uso dei braccianti. In queste condizioni la decisione di partire e più ardua che altrove, anche perché, in tutti i paesi dell'area, sin dagli anni settanta dell'Ottocento operano più Società di Mutuo soccorso operaie e contadine, attivissime nella gestione di una rete assistenziale. Né la sconfitta dei fasci siciliani ha qui gli stessi esiti delle zone occidentali. Sono in parecchi a resistere, trovando rifugio nelle nascenti organizzazioni del movimento socialista che, proprio nel ragusano, trova uno sviluppo più ampio che altrove. La spinta all'esodo viene più tardi generata quando le Società di Navigazione riescono ad organizzare, anche in terra iblea, quella capillare rete di vendita dei passaggi transoceanici che produce la cultura del "sogno americano". E' soltanto allora che i flussi cominciano a crescere quantitativamente spingendo uomini e donne a cercare in America i mezzi di fortuna per abbreviare in patria il processo di acquisizione della proprietà. Chi parte, diversamente dagli uomini del latifondo, decisi a tagliare i ponti con la terra d'origine, è quasi sempre convinto di poter ritornare vittorioso per realizzare nel proprio paese l'ascesa sociale a lungo sperata. E' così che i santacrocesi si dirigono a Paterson e ad Hackensack nel New Jersey, trovando impiego nelle industrie della seta (le donne), nelle "farms" e nelle ferrovie (gli uomini); i modicani raggiungono New York e Bridgeport per fondare una fiorente comunità di piccoli artigiani e di muratori; i pozzallesi si dirigono verso Brooklyn, assecondando le loro prevalenti vocazioni marittime; ed i vittoriesi si distribuiscono per tutto il greater New York svolgendo varie attività agricole e commerciali. Da Ragusa, infine, c'è chi parte con un po' di soldi da investire ed, inevitabilmente, è il commercio di frutta e verdura che polarizza inizialmente l'attività di molti[64].

La consolidata vocazione a considerare l'espatrio come un fatto temporaneo e strumentale al proprio avanzamento sociale ed economico in patria è chiaramente visibile dal legame che si instaura tra la Società "Carlo Papa" di Modica e l'omonima americana fondata a New York nel 1916. Quest' ultima è diretta filiazione della prima ed anche se nello statuto adotta disposizioni dettate dalle necessità del contesto in cui nasce, è oltremodo significativo che il suo atto di incorporazione cita espressamente l'autorizzazione ad esistere spedita dalla Società d'origine. Dall'intensa corrispondenza tra i due sodalizi, pubblicata da Antonella Giardina[65], si rileva a chiare lettere la volontà degli espatriati di mantenere l'antica membership e le continue richieste di adesione, per coloro che membri non erano, spiega quanto sia importante per i modicani d'America l'appartenenza alla comunità d'origine. Alle tiepide risposte degli organi direttivi modicani che oppongono difficoltà statutarie ad accogliere gli emigrati e ad assicurare ai parenti in patria i benefici mutualistici, questi replicano chiedendo di modificare lo statuto. L'atteggiamento degli interlocutori resta comunque ambiguo e le risposte non presentano soluzioni risolutive. Le cose sembrano cambiare un po' quando il presidente della "Carlo Papa" di Modica, oppresso dalle vessazioni fasciste che gli impongono di lasciare i locali sociali, rivolge un accorato appello ai "Fratelli

---

[64] Per l'emigrazione ragusana e la nascita delle società iblee di mutuo soccorso si veda A. Giardina, *Dalle Società di Mutuo soccorso iblee negli USA ai Social Clubs*, in "NEOS, Rivista di Storia dell'Emigrazione siciliana", Anno II, n. 1 Dicembre 2008, pp. 119-204.
[65] Ibidem.

"Il Mutualismo dei Siciliani d'America"

d'America" per ottenere aiuti economici finalizzati all'acquisto della sede. Gli emigrati rispondono generosamente ed inviano i donativi, precisando, però, che questi sono da intendersi come quote sociali o, nel caso dei nuovi, come corrispettivi all'adesione. I modicani accolgono il denaro, ringraziando calorosamente, ma continuano a restare cauti specialmente sull'ammissione degli espatriati. Le ragioni del contrasto sono di natura squisitamente economica e riguardano l'impossibilità di concedere i contributi di assistenza e le spese funerarie in patria ai parenti, in considerazione della norma statutaria che sospendeva gli espatriati, per 10 anni, dall'erogazione dei contributi mensili. Così, l'unico parziale rimedio che viene adottato e quello di limitare ad un quinquennio la sospensione delle contribuzioni, riammettendo i benefici mutualistici, soltanto alla ripresa delle erogazioni. La voglia di restare soci del sodalizio d'origine o quella di essere lì ammessi, tuttavia, travalica la preoccupazione economica dell'assistenza e, nella corrispondenza, gli accenti sono sempre indirizzati alla insopprimibile voglia di essere considerati membri della comunità di nascita. In questo senso i modicani del Connecticut chiedono di essere autorizzati ad aprire una "Carlo Papa" a Bridgeport, ma la probabile opposizione dci newyorkesi, detentori del monopolio della rappresentanza, produce anche stavolta, una risposta ambigua che non si traduce mai in autorizzazione esplicita.

Più intensamente politica è la vicenda delle due società di Santa Croce Camerina che nascono, per scissione, a Paterson, in New Jersey, a distanza di 10 anni l'una dall'altra, rispecchiando contrapposizioni politiche già operanti in patria e aggravate, non in relazione a opzioni di politica americana, ma per le prosaiche dinamiche del divenire politico in Italia. Scrive Antonella Giardina:

> La prima, nata nel 1916 è d'ispirazione cattolica e si rifà alla Società Agricola San Giuseppe, attiva nel paese natio dal 1902. Raccoglie mezzadri, enfiteuti e persino piccoli proprietari terrieri giunti in America per guadagnare qualcosa che consentisse loro di non vendere le terre in Sicilia, ma di migliorarle; la seconda, invece, costituita nel 1925 da operai socialisti antifascisti, è espressione della Lega di Miglioramento fondata a Santa Croce nel 1912, anno in cui sono in molti ad emigrare dal paese. La Società più antica, nei primi anni del fascismo, aderisce alle idee del regime. La seconda, nata invece dopo la crisi del socialismo massimalista ibleo che genera anche un'emigrazione politica, è antifascista e anticlericale e non supporta l'eccessivo culto per San Giuseppe. Le due società si uniranno nel 1947, in un clima internazionale che accomuna tutti i santacrocesi d'America, animati dal desiderio di aiutare meglio i compaesani rimasti in patria, dove la seconda guerra mondiale ha causato molti danni, lasciando stralci di povertà. In piena guerra fredda, però, si dividono di nuovo sui due fronti politici contrapposti[66].

Di natura squisitamente politica sono le contrapposizioni iniziali tra i pozzallesi d'America che a Brooklyn fondano, nel 1918, la *Società di Mutuo Soccorso dei cittadini di Pozzallo*, di fede nazionalista, che viene incorporata nel 1919 con il nome *The Society of Citizens of Pozzallo* e la *Rinascente pozzallese* di orientamento radicale, che sorge nel 1924, con marcate no-

---

[66] Ivi, pp. 121-122.

"Il Mutualismo dei Siciliani d'America"

stalgie socialiste[67]. Anche in questo caso siamo di fronte alla gemmazione di sodalizi esistenti in patria ed operanti come *Società Operaia di Mutuo Soccorso V. Romeo*, sorta nel 1889 e la *Società Marinara di Mutuo Soccorso*, nata nel 1890. Gli scopi di entrambi i sodalizi sono rigidamente mutualistici e rispecchiano, anche loro, un'attenzione particolare alla comunità d'origine, perennemente in contatto per il tramite delle Società madri. Sanciscono negli statuti, insieme ai benefici assistenziali, il miglioramento del livello culturale e di istruzione dei soci, ma anche l'obbiettivo di riproporre in terra americana le feste e le tradizioni. Contrariamente a quanto avviene nella comunità dei santacrocesi di Paterson o dei santaninfesi di Williamsburg, nei marinai pozzallesi di Brooklyn, il retaggio delle lotte iblee non si salda con il radicalismo americano e quando le persecuzioni fasciste colpiscono in patria la *Società marinara*, gli omologhi della *Rinascente* americana, preferiscono attenuare la fiamma della contrapposizione politica rifugiandosi sotto l'ombrello protettivo della prima società, più gradita ai fascisti. Così, nel 1932, si celebra la fusione nell'unica società che mutua il nome della più vecchia. A prendere questa decisione sono le seconde generazioni che, disinteressate ad alimentare gli antichi conflitti dei padri, dismettono i propositi di ritorno in patria, dando vita, nel 1934, ad un Circolo Educativo con lo scopo precipuo di anglicizzare i membri e di favorire la naturalizzazione e la piena integrazione nella società d'accoglienza.

---

[67] Su la storia dei entrambe le società si veda R Sacarrozza, *Le Società di Mutuo Soccorso pozzallesi negli USA*, tesi di laurea, Università di Palermo, a.a. 2009-2010, relatore prof. M. Saija.

Marcello Saija

Di sicura derivazione dalla Società di Mutuo Soccorso "Senatore Rosario Cancellieri," attiva a Vittoria sin dal 1905, è l'omonima newyorchese che, con l'insegna di San Giovanni, nasce a New York probabilmente negli anni '10 del Novecento. Dai pochi e frammentari elementi raccolti da Antonella Giardina[68], sappiamo che la società era ancora attiva negli anni '20, con una forte carica di politicizzazione radicale ed antifascista, secondo le tradizioni del sodalizio di estrazione, ma, anche in questo caso, non assistiamo alla saldatura politica con il radicalismo americano e le labili tracce rinvenute ci indicano che ben presto, secondo il comune modo di sentire ibleo, l'emigrazione vittoriese si attesta come fatto temporaneo, e lo stesso sodalizio si spegne con il massiccio rientro in patria dei suoi fondatori.

Notizie più ampie ci fornisce la Giardina sul mutualismo dei marinai di Scoglitti, una frazione del comune di Vittoria, prospiciente il mar d'Africa[69]. Se, però, dobbiamo indicare una data di origine del fenomeno, ci troviamo in forte difficoltà perché, in realtà, per una curiosa singolarità la prima società non nasce in America come sarebbe logico supporre, ma, per iniziativa dei medesimi emigrati, al paese d'origine. E sono, probabilmente, gli inconvenienti che abbiamo visto operanti nel caso modicano che li inducono a costituire, nei primi anni Venti, la Società *Figli di Scoglitti d'America*, con il compito di amministrare in patria i contributi provenienti da oltre oceano a beneficio di mogli e figli dei soci espatriati. C'è insomma, nel caso in esame, una sorta di inversione nel

---

[68] A. Giardina, *Dalle Società di Mutuo soccorso iblee negli USA ai Social Clubs,...* cit, pp. 181-187.
[69] Ivi, pp. 193 e segg.

"Il Mutualismo dei Siciliani d'America"

modello di dipendenza che, diversamente dagli altri sodalizi iblei tutti in qualche modo dipendenti dalle matrici isolane, vede in questo caso il centro direzionale negli *States*. Non sappiamo se, e in quale misura, questa singolare esperienza incida sulla decisione, adottata dopo circa un decennio, nel 1930, di fondare ad Aburn, nello Stato di New York, la *Società di Mutuo Soccorso Maria Santissima di Porto Salvo*, incorporata, poi, a Paterson, nel New Jersey, nel 1934, dove intanto buona parte degli scoglittesi si era spostata. Rileviamo, però, che il nuovo sodalizio ha caratteristiche in gran parte differenti dal primo. Le preoccupazioni principali dei fondatori, infatti, al di là delle disposizioni riguardanti il mutualismo classico, che pure vengono previste, sono principalmente dirette a plasmare buoni cittadini americani, segno evidente del cambio di sensibilità, proiettata ormai sul percorso di americanizzazione, favorito anche dalla previsione statutaria di dedicare una parte degli introiti all'organizzazione di una scuola di lingua inglese per gli associati.

Nel 1935, il *Social Act* di Roosevelt rende anacronistica la mutualità privata e il sodalizio, ritoccando lo statuto, insieme con la previsione dei benefici funerari e cimiteriali, assicura ai soci soltanto un luogo di ritrovo che assume le tipiche caratteristiche dei social club che di lì a qualche anno si chiamerà *Scoglitti Society*, ma la terra natia appare molto più lontana.

Con finalità sostanzialmente diverse nasce, invece, a Brooklyn, nel 1935, la *Società Figli di Ragusa*[70] che già nel preambolo

---

[70] A. Giardina, *Dalle Società di Mutuo soccorso iblee negli USA ai Social Clubs*, cit, , pp. 196- 199

dello statuto manifesta l'aperta intenzione a proiettare nella società americana la comunità di riferimento:

> Lo scopo di questa Società — recita l'atto di incorporazione — è di promuovere una migliore conoscenza della Costituzione degli Stati Uniti d'America, di promuovere e sviluppare una migliore cooperazione tra i soci e di intraprendere missioni sociali civili ed educative tra i medesimi. La società è apolitica e si asterrà quindi da qualsiasi azione o manifestazione di carattere politico; rimanendo sempre fedele alla patria d'origine ed alla patria d'adozione[71].

Per comprendere meglio gli scopi sociali è necessario precisare che i membri fondatori sono quasi tutti affermati professionisti che contemporaneamente alla creazione del sodalizio, fondano anche il *Ragusan Credit Union*, un istituto bancario che ha il compito di sostenere le intraprese economiche dei ragusani in America. Se si eccettua, quindi, la previsione del "fondo unico mortuario" a beneficio dei soci, siamo lontani dal mutualismo classico che, del resto, all'epoca, era ormai superato dalle leggi federali. Colpisce invece l'esiguità della tassa d'ingresso ($1) e delle contribuzioni mensili (50c di $), che denotano come il sostegno finanziario alle attività sociali giungesse da altre corpose fonti. Il residuo legame con la terra natia viene, infine, testimoniato dalla previsione che in caso di scioglimento il patrimonio del sodalizio venisse devoluto ad un ospedale di Ragusa. Oggi il club è ancora attivo e vanta solidi legami politici ed economici con la società americana.

---

[71] Ivi, p. 197.

"Il Mutualismo dei Siciliani d'America"

6. Le società siracusane del Connecticut

Un attento esame della provenienza geografica degli emigrati siracusani in Connecticut ci permette di rilevare che i paesi d'esodo ricadono tutti in zona montana, lungo la dorsale orientale degli Iblei. Si tratta di Sortino, Solarino, Melilli, Palazzolo Acreide, Floridia Rosolini e Canicattini Bagni. Da qui, uomini e donne si dirigono in un'area molto circoscritta del territorio americano che ruota attorno ad Hartford, comprendendo insieme alla capitale, New Britain Winsted e Middletown. Si tratta, in prevalenza, di un'emigrazione povera, fatta di contadini, operai generici, barbieri, calzolai, sarti e carrettieri. I primi nuclei giungono da New York per lavorare nelle ferrovie e nelle imprese edili e quando la catena di richiamo rende consistente le comunità, l'impiego nelle fabbriche tessili per le donne e nelle industrie meccaniche e calzaturiere o nelle imprese edili per gli uomini diventa una meta obbligata. L'intenzione dichiarata per molti è quella di considerare l'espatrio come un fatto temporaneo, finalizzato ad accumulare una certa somma di denaro da investire in patria. Non c'è quindi una pulsione alla naturalizzazione ed all'integrazione politica come accade per altre comunità. Scarse aspettative di mobilità sociale caratterizzano la vicenda di questi primi migranti siracusani e gran parte dei denari guadagnati viene trasferita ai paesi d'origine in forma di rimessa. In tale contesto è più che naturale un approccio societario, almeno all'origine, circoscritto al mutualismo classico e alla solidarietà per i bisogni contingenti.

Nascono, così, a New Britain, nel 1913, la *Generale Ameglio Society*, per impulso di un militare della guerra di Libia che nel nome intende onorare il suo comandante; ad Hartford, nel 1919, la *Società di Mutuo Soccorso di Palazzolo Acreide*;

sempre ad Hartford, nel 1922, la *Cittadini Floridiani (Floridian men Society)*, e nel 1929, ancora ad Hartford, la *Figli di Canicattini Bagni*. Tra gli anni Trenta e Quaranta, nascono, poi, in tutte le comunità, i sodalizi femminili. Il fenomeno, non è circoscritto al solo Connecticut, anche nel Massachusetts e negli Stati di New York e del New Jersey assistiamo, in modo episodico, a simili iniziative. Qui, si ha, però, la sensazione che l'associazionismo femminile rappresenti, in modo più deciso, la crescita di un piccolo universo che a contatto con un mondo dove già da alcuni decenni le donne, contro il ritardato riconoscimento del suffragio elettorale, avevano affermato con forza i loro diritti, acquista una nuova coscienza civile che cancella imperiosamente la condizione psicologica femminile dei paesi d'origine. Nascono, così, a Middletown, la *Anita Garibaldi Society* (1931), a New Britain, la sezione femminile della *Generale Ameglio Society* (1933), ad Hartford, la *Figlie di Palazzolo Acreide* (1933), e, sempre ad Hartford, la *Floridian Ladies Society* (1934), e la *Daughters of Canicattini Bagni (1934)*[72].

Le società maschili, nate tutte prima del 1935, scolpiscono nello Statuto le previsioni mutualistiche, secondo il rituale consueto e qualcuna prevede anche un'indennità ai soci che, per incompatibilità di salute con l'ambiente, o per conclamate ragioni di necessità, intendono chiudere l'esperienza migratoria per far ritorno in patria. Fino a tutti gli anni Venti, raccolgono un discreto numero di soci e svolgono in modo egregio le finalità statutarie. Poi, qualcosa sembra cambiare nel comune modo di sentire dei più giovani che intendono

---

[72] Su le società di mutuo soccorso dei siracusani del Connecticut si veda M. Saija, (a cura di) *Il mutualismo dei siracusani nel Connecticut*, Trisform, Messina, 2014.

"Il Mutualismo dei Siciliani d'America"

costruirsi il proprio avvenire in America. Qualcuno, tra i vecchi, sembra comprendere le ragioni del cambiamento, ma difficilmente muta gli originari programmi. Scrive, per esempio il calzolaio canicattinese Corrado Uccello da Hartford, alla fine degli anni Venti:

> Ce una manera bellissima di tratare il lavoratore qui inamerica. Quando uno travagghia come travagghio io i soldi della semana ce li danno sempri e tutti, no come succedi a Canicattini che chiamano genti pi travagghiari ncampagna e ci dunanu pochi soldi o non ci ni dunano nenti. I soldi del travagghiu qua america sunu sempri sicuri anchi per li donni chi travagghianu comu all'omini. E per questo tanti non vonnu turnari e pensanu di stari sempri 'cca. Io no mogli mia, non voglio stare più inamerica (...) Ti fo sapere che io sono disfiziatto assai che non voglio stare più inamerica e spero che nella primavera venire sicuro, che non voglio stare più inamerica[73].

Non è, naturalmente, soltanto la filosofia americana del lavoro ad ingenerare nei giovani la voglia del nuovo. Le seconde generazioni, educate dalla scuola di Dewey, maturano relazioni e culture assai differenti da quelle trasmesse dai genitori e, mentre per questi ultimi, il rapporto *madre-nutrice* resta sempre oppositivo per l'affezione al paese natio, nei figli il binomio si scioglie coll'adozione dell'America come unica fonte del benessere da ricercare. E' questa la molla che trasforma anche le Società di mutuo soccorso in strutture pronte a veicolare i processi di americanizzazione, pur nel

---

[73] La lettera di Corrado Uccello è custodita in originale nella *Casa dell'Emigrante* di Canicattini Bagni.

rispetto di alcune tradizioni religiose e di cultura materiale. E' il caso, per esempio delle *Società Garibaldi* e *Sons of Italy* di Middletown, instancabili promotrici di sviluppo economico politico e sociale per i melillesi del Connecticut. In realtà, anche a Middletown si apre il conflitto tra chi vede nei sodalizi mutualistici solo uno strumento per conservare cultura e tradizioni della patria d'origine e chi, invece, pur non trascurando i fattori identitari, mira in modo più deciso all'integrazione sociale, politica ed economica nella Società d'accoglienza. La stessa nascita della *Società Garibaldi*, pochi anni dopo la fondazione della *Sons of Italy*, è il segno evidente di questi differenti modi di sentire. E', però, solo una dinamica delle origini. Negli anni Venti, entrambi i sodalizi si avviano con decisione alla conquista degli spazi politici ed economici della città, con il preciso scopo di affermare la Comunità come motore della trasformazione sociale e strumento per la conquista dell'egemonia. E' un progetto che va in porto nel breve volgere di un decennio. Nel 1926, i melillesi riescono ad eleggere il primo sindaco siciliano e, con la costruzione di un'imponente basilica dedicata al loro santo protettore, trasformano la cittadina americana che li ospita in una *Little Melilli*. Conquistata l'autonomia religiosa dagli irlandesi, i siciliani occupano poi, gradualmente, tutti gli spazi economici e culturali della città, promuovendo un contesto sociale che approda presto a valori e stili di vita di un universo fortemente americanizzato. Ed anche se c'è chi continua a coniugare America e Sicilia, in realtà, il teatro dove le seconde e terze generazioni intendono rappresentare la vicenda delle proprie esistenze è ormai soltanto l'America.

La penetrazione dell'ideologia fascista, molto diversamente da come è stato affermato, muove ben poco e soprattutto non contribuisce a far lievitare una identità italiana, perché figli e nipoti degli originari emigrati passano dalla cultura localistica direttamente all'identità americana. La seconda guerra mondiale è una eloquente cartina di tornasole del cambiamento radicale. I giovani partono per combattere nazismo e fascismo, ma non per salvare la patria dei padri e dei nonni, soltanto perché il proprio paese gli ha additato la bandiera per cui battersi. Ciò che resta, dopo la fine del conflitto, a Middletown, è questo strano mondo italoamericano nel quale le antiche società, diventate ormai social clubs, sventolano ancora taluni simboli della lontana patria italica non per sentimento di appartenenza, soltanto per ostentare un distinguo nella multietnica società nella quale ormai sono, a pieno titolo, inserite.

7. Alcune considerazioni conclusive

Abbiamo volutamente deciso di concentrare nel paragrafo conclusivo la valutazione sul piano storico di quello che appare il dato più marcato che emerge dall'analisi storica proposta: il campanilismo e con esso l'identità di partenza e l'identità di arrivo dei siciliani d'America.

E' difficile mettere in dubbio che gli emigranti della prima grande emigrazione dall'Isola possedessero un bagaglio identitario fortemente condizionato dalla loro appartenenza alla piccola terra d'origine che gli aveva fornito i natali. Molti di loro non avevano mai conosciuto nemmeno la città capoluogo di provincia ed avevano avuto un orizzonte geografico di mobilità e conoscenza limitato al piccolo comprensorio che registrava in modo deciso le piccole rivalità campanilistiche, soprattutto nei confronti dei paesi viciniori. I matrimoni, che pure intervenivano tra uomini e donne di terre contigue, ben lungi dal creare integrazione, avevano come effetto quello di rimarcare la propria identità sottolineando l'estraneità della scelta operata dai propri conterranei (*si maritau 'na barcellunisa*). Non era quindi pensabile, almeno all'inizio, che il travaso in terra americana colmasse distanze già marcate nelle culture di provenienza. Certo, il contatto con un contesto molto più ampio, rende sicuramente più labili le barriere identitarie, ma non a tal punto da prefigurare strutture associative capaci di valicare i confini della terra d'origine. Ed anche l'emergere dell'*Order of the Sons of Italy* scalfisce di poco il localismo e spesso capita, come nel caso dei liparesi a Norwich, nel 1912, o dei melillesi di Middletown nel 1914, che la loggia si costituisca di uomini provenienti da un solo paese. E' necessario pure annotare che anche i sodalizi corporativi che inevitabilmente sorgono sin dall'inizio, o le strutture sindacali che i siciliani trovano e scelgono nella terra d'accoglienza, generano spesso una doppia appartenenza, ma non cancellano le barriere geografiche[74].

Secondo una ben nota interpretazione, gli emigranti o i loro figli, con il passare degli anni, maturano in terra americana l'identità italiana che non avevano fatto a tempo ad acquisire in patria[75]. E questa coscienza sarebbe stata mediata,

---

[74] Ed è il caso dei santaninfesi, dei santacrocesi, dei ripostesi e di tutti i sodalizi politicamente attivi in senso radicale di cui abbiamo parlato.
[75] E' questo il filo conduttore, da ultimo adottato anche dal citato saggio di Sergio Bugiardini che documenta l'impegno di consoli, prominenti italoamericani, e Chiesa cattolica, tendente a far superare il localismo agli italiani d'America in favore di una coscienza nazionale. Leggendo con molta attenzione l'accurato saggio di Bugiardini, si ha però l'impressione che tutti gli sforzi naufragano in limiti temporali assai esigui e che la matrice localistica resista piuttosto a lungo, cedendo soltanto agli inevitabili

"Il Mutualismo dei Siciliani d'America"

in particolare, dall'attiva propaganda fascista che, soprattutto nel decennio delle conquiste imperiali, avrebbe dato agli italiani d'America un comune modo di sentire ed un movente psicologico per reagire alle discriminazioni xenofobe[76]. Senza voler negare del tutto questo modo di vedere le cose, è, però, necessario addentrarci un po' più a fondo nell'analisi storica distinguendo con maggiore precisione le aree in cui questi fenomeni hanno corso. E' nostra impressione, infatti, che il nazionalfascismo americano sia concentrato nelle aree metropolitane, soprattutto del Nordest, là dove taluni quotidiani di lingua italiana come *Il Progresso Italoamericano* di Generoso Pope, tentano di coniugare Mussolini e Roosevelt, alla ricerca di un ruolo riconoscibile dalle autorità, sulle due sponde[77]. La stragrande maggioranza degli emigrati resta però fuori da quest'area di propaganda. Ma è proprio la retorica dei giornali, il clamore sulle donazioni dell'oro alla Patria e le cartoline di rame coniate in occasione delle guerre coloniali che hanno portato alcuni storici contemporanei ad attribuire all'intera comunità (6 milioni, negli anni Trenta), quello che era il comune modo di sentire di poche centinaia

---

processi di americanizzazione, inesorabili a partire dalle seconde generazioni. S Bugiardini, *L'associazionismo negli USA*, in P. Bevilaqua, A. De Clementi, E. Franzina (a cura di) *Storia dell'Emigrazione italiana...* cit., vol II (arrivi), pp. 551-577.

[76] J. Diggins, *L'America Mussolini e il fascismo*, Laterza, Roma, Bari, 1982; S. Luconi, *L'ombra lunga del fascio. Canali di propaganda fascista per gli italiani d'America*, M&B edizioni, Milano, 2004, pp. 146-147.

[77] S. Luconi", La diplomazia parallela" in *Il regime fascista e la mobilitazione degli italo-americani*, Franco Angeli, Milano, 2000; S. Vaccara, *Al servizio di due padroni: Generoso Pope, Mussolini, Roosevelt and the Coming of WWII*, in "NEOS Rivista di storia dell'emigrazione siciliana", anno 1, N.1, dicembre 2006, pp.97-106.

di migliaia[78]. Ed è un fatto di non trascurabile entità la frattura che interviene, anche nelle grandi aree metropolitane americane, dopo l'emanazione delle leggi razziali da parte di Mussolini e soprattutto quando la conclamata alleanza tra il duce ed il furher getta gli italiani nel più grande sconcerto. In quel momento, la conclamata identità italiana si dilegua come neve al sole ed anche nei giornali e nelle enclave che avevano inneggiato al fascismo, si manifestano chiari segni di distacco.

Per tornare al nostro campo privilegiato d'indagine, tuttavia, negli anni Trenta, anche dopo il *Social Security Act* di Roosevelt, non assistiamo alla trasformazione in senso nazionale delle strutture associative esistenti e sono ben pochi (concentrati soprattutto in alcune città) i sodalizi che hanno per bandiera l'Italia *tout court*[79]. E' invece evidente, dall'analisi svolta, che il processo di americanizzazione, nelle seconde generazioni, si innesti direttamente, senza alcun passaggio nazionale, sulla originaria cultura localistica che si snatura, pur conservando taluni elementi, soprattutto materiali, della cultura d'origine. Gli studi sul comportamento elettorale degli italiani d'America, d'altronde, che registrano una concentrazione etnica su candidati di origine italiana, trovano ragioni che vanno molto al di là della formazione di una inesistente coscienza nazionale. Ed appare convincente Anna Maria Martellone che spiega il fenomeno con la sopravveniente

---

[78] M. Saija, *Italy and America over a Span of Three Italian American Generations: First Results of a Research Project*, in A. Bove, G. Massara (a cura di), *'Merica*, in Forum Italicum, Stony Brook, N.Y. 2006, pp. 39-50.

[79] S. Bugiardini, *L'associazionismo negli USA*, in P. Bevilaqua, A. De Clementi, E. Franzina (a cura di) *Storia dell'Emigrazione italiana...* cit., vol II (arrivi), pp. 551-577.

"Il Mutualismo dei Siciliani d'America"

necessità di formare un gruppo di pressione omogenea a favore della comunità italoamericana, in nome di bisogni concreti avvertiti in terra americana, piuttosto che per improbabili processi di acquisizione di un appartenenza mai nata e comunque lontanissima[80]. E sotto il medesimo profilo, di grande interesse per trovare il punto d'arrivo identitario degli italiani d'America, appaiono, infine, altre considerazioni della Martellone che mostrano come l'originario localismo della cultura italoamericana determina una sorta di sbigottimento nelle terze e quarte generazioni che visitando l'Italia, trovano oggi un Paese assai diverso da quello tramandato loro dalla cultura familiare[81].

Dal nostro angolo visuale, è possibile affermare, quindi, che grazie alle Società di mutuo soccorso, molte comunità siciliane hanno avuto brillanti percorsi d'inserimento individuali e /o collettivi nella società americana. Questo non significa che le *mutual aid societies* siano state le uniche strutture di mediazione. In parecchi casi i siciliani si sono serviti di strutture associative più vaste o si sono fatti la strada da soli tra mille difficoltà. Le Società, però, sono state un punto di riferimento importantissimo e attraverso esse, le comunità, soprattutto fino agli anni Venti del Novecento, hanno mantenuto un legame sostanziale con la cultura della terra natia. Era difficile, per esempio, con la Società alle spalle, cedere alla tentazione di cambiare cognome per sfuggire alla sempre più diffusa xenofobia; così come era più difficile non sen-

---

[80] A. M. Martellone, *Generazioni e identità*, in P. Bevilaqua, A. De Clementi, E. Franzina (a cura di) *Storia dell'Emigrazione italiana* ...cit., vol II (arrivi), pp. 739 e segg.
[81] *Ibidem*, pp. 249-250.

tire la necessità di trasmettere ai figli la lingua e le tradizioni di famiglia. Poi, però, a partire dagli anni Trenta, e, soprattutto, quando, nel 1935, con il *Social Security Act* di Roosevelt, i fini mutualistici ed assistenziali vengono assorbiti dallo Stato e dai datori di lavoro, le Società perdono molte delle loro funzioni e scompaiono o finiscono per diventare soltanto social club, più inclini ad assorbire riti e tradizioni americane che a riproporre la cultura delle origini. Certo, a partire dal secondo dopoguerra, con l'ultima ondata di emigrazione, i nuovi siciliani, nelle strutture sopravvissute, trovano ancora rifugio e talvolta contribuiscono a creare nuovi sodalizi per mantenere legami con la terra di partenza, ma, nella grande maggioranza dei casi e salve le dovute eccezioni, le nuove strutture associative assolvono anch'esse più al compito di agevolare il processo di americanizzazione dei nuovi arrivati che non a quello di recuperare i legami con le antiche comunità di riferimento.

Nel complesso, la storia dell'associazionismo mutualistico dei siciliani d'America rappresenta una pagina luminosa dell'emigrazione siciliana e ad essa va ascritto il merito di poter offrire agli studiosi una chiave di lettura ben più ampia e complessiva di quanto non facciano gli studi settoriali sugli emigrati di successo, sul ruolo della Chiesa cattolica, sul radicalismo politico e, meno che mai, sul fenomeno mafioso e sulla criminalità organizzata di siciliana origine. Il quadro che abbiamo presentato non ha naturalmente la pretesa esaustiva delle grandi ricerche. Intende, però, offrire alcuni parametri interpretativi che sottoponiamo al giudizio storico ed al confronto per chi intende percorrere la strada qui abbozzata.

You are an Italian American Writer, Like it or Not

Richard Vetere
CUNY Queens College

In the talk that I am about to give, you might find me contradicting myself and at the same time, making some points with confidence and self-assurance. This will happen because I am Italian by ancestry and Italians like to make contradictions just to get attention, while the American part of me prefers to focus on a point and examine it as coolly as possible and in the process ignore all other points of view.

When I was hired to write a movie in Rome, a gangster movie to be exact, I was hired because of the popularity of my first film, *Vigilante*. When in Rome, I was told by my director, Giacomo Battiato, that he saw in me that rare combination of writer who was a dreamer and doer all in one. This happened, he said, because I was American and Italian. The Italian part of me was artistic and visionary and the American part of me was practical and knew how to "get things done."

So starting my talk, if I had to define myself as a person and an artist, concerning my interests and focus, I would have to say that I am a New Yorker first. I live ten miles from where I was born and whatever that means has informed a lot of my work. Secondly, I would define myself as a heterosexual male without children and never married. I have been

From: *Theater of the Mind, Stage of History*. Bordighera Press, 2015

told that I write women characters very well, however, I consider a lot of my work very male. Thirdly, I would define myself as Catholic. The underlying images and the spiritual world are all very Catholic. Then I would describe my work as American not only because of the location and interest of my work but also its point of view. Lastly, I would describe myself as an Italian American writer whose grandparents were born in New York City.

However, if others were to define me as an artist I would hope that they would answer, with the same objectivity that I work hard to bring to my craft, and say that I am a New York writer who writes about *whatever* he wants to write about. Yet, I have been told many times by non-Italian Americans that my work is very Italian American. Why? Well, to them it is operatic, comedic, sometimes bloody, sometimes sexy, and usually intense.

To me, unfortunately, most Italian American writers are driven by several subjects — the old rehashing of gangster stories, food, sex, and family. After that, it seems we have not any other subjects to write about. My contributions to these topics include the following. I have written about gangsters in one of my most produced plays, *Gangster Apparel*, which is a "funny and wild parody of gangster movies" according to the New York Times. I have written about obsession with family in my play *Johnny on the Pony*. I have written recently about food in my play, *Meatball Hero*, called one of the best of 2010, and also about sex in my comedy *An Epic Story of Love and Sex Told in Ten Minutes: Chapter One*, which chronicles my sex life from ten years old to the age of seventeen growing up Italian American in Queens and Brooklyn in the 1970s.

So, I have tackled these subjects, but did so in a way of making fun of their importance. Ironically, when I started writing poetry and plays when I was barely a teenager, I had no Italian or Italian American role models. My literary heroes in poetry were John Keats, Lord Byron, Yeats, and T.S. Eliot and eventually other Europeans including Rilke and Baudelaire. In fiction, it was Dickens and Graham Greene, and in theater, Becket, Pinter, and Williams. Not one of them could be considered operatic, sexy, comedic, or bloody but some are intense and at least one is Catholic.

I started out as a poet and over the years published two volumes of poetry where most reviewers stated that my early poetry had a strong sense of technique and was well-polished and objective, making the work powerful and contemporary. My one poem about a historical figure was in the form of a letter written by Alexander the Great's mother to her son on her visit to a temple where she was told that he was a god. No one would have thought I was Italian American by my subject matter.

Interestingly enough, however, my first plays were a trilogy that compared the fall of New York City to ancient Rome. They were *Nero, Hadrian's Hill,* and *Night over the Tiber* — all three in my archives housed here.[1] This is a stunning notion to me that my first plays were about ancient Rome. It was followed by a realistic play about Italian Americans living in Queens. *Rockaway Boulevard* was about Johnny Montinelli and his wife Helen and how they had to care for his invalid father who Johnny demanded live at home with them. *Rockaway Boulevard* was produced many times in the 1980s and

---

[1] Ed. Note: The Vetere Archives are at Stony Brook's Melville Library.

1990s and Michiko Kakutani stated in her review of the play in the New York Times that, "Vetere demonstrates the ability to mix the poetic with the colloquial." The play was produced widely in New York City including a production with an African American cast, another with a Latino cast, and eventually with the playwright, me, playing Johnny.

That was followed by a satire about an Italian American family influenced by Pinter's *The Homecoming* called *Johnny on the Pony*. The play is about Sando Fiscarelli who demands from his sons that they live for the family construction business and that they sacrifice everything, including their lives, wives, and children as homage to their Italian grandfathers and great grandfathers who sacrificed everything to get them to America. Actor Paul Sorvino will be performing in the play this year as Sando.

Though as I stated earlier, I did write several more times during the 1980s and 1990s about Italian Americans, including *The Engagement*, a comedy about male friendship versus romantic love; the autobiographical *The Classic* about an Italian American writer who does not want to have children; *The Vows of Penelope Corelli* about a wife whose husband walks out on her and then she hits the lottery for sixty-three million dollars; *Painting X's on the Moon* about an art loving gangster who is sexually obsessed with a movie star; and *Gangster Apparel*, a story about friendship. However, I learned quickly that if I wanted to get my work into the mainstream, it was better that I stopped giving my characters Italian American surnames.

So even though my novel *The Third Miracle* published by Simon & Schuster, as well as *The Marriage Fool*, *Vigilante*, and *How to Go Out on A Date in Queens* are all extremely personal and somewhat autobiographical and Italian American in feel and tone and point of view, all have characters with ambiguous ethnic backgrounds.

My original screenplay for *Vigilante* could have been easily titled *Vendetta*. It is about the revenge a small group of working class men in Queens take on the criminals in their neighborhood. The lead character, played by actor Robert Forester, is called Nicky Marino but he is the only character with an Italian surname.

The Marriage Fool, first a stage play then the most successful television movie ever produced on CBS with over 25 million viewers and 18 million on its rerun, is the story of my father and me, starring Walter Matthau playing my father and John Stamos playing me. Carol Burnett played Florence. The family surname in this piece is Walsh. I did not make the characters Italian American because I knew that if I had, I would have to interject the mafia or food, violence, shouting and yelling in the script as we all experienced when HBO presented an Italian American family in *The Sopranos*.

I stop here and make a personal point. My parents were Italian-American and though working class, they were elegant. They did not allow cursing in the house and education was valued above everything. The home was quiet and though they loved to have parties with their friends on Saturday nights in the basement and backyard while dancing to Sinatra and Dean Martin, it was always cocktails, the cha cha, and laughs. Even my grandmother dressed in the latest fashionable style and she was also one of the first women shop stewards in the electrician's union in Brooklyn Navy Yard. My mother attended high school but my father did not graduate grammar school, and yet he dressed in a suit and tie every day for work, never spoke like a gummba, and nowhere did you see women with buns in their hair in my family. Nor did my mother hang holy pictures in every room. We went to church and I was an altar boy but religion with all of its clichés did not even make an appearance in our house.

The hero of my novel, *The Third Miracle,* published by Simon & Schuster, is an Irish-American priest. I could have easily made him Italian American but I did not. I was afraid that my story of a priest assigned by the Vatican to investigate a statue crying tears of blood in a small parish in Queens to see if a woman long dead is a saint, would never be cast by an Italian American star. I doubted the studios would accept an Italian American actor as an intellectual. Oddly, at one point, Sylvester Stallone wanted to play Father Moore. Ed Harris eventually was cast as my subdued and haunted priest, Frank Moore, who has written a book about Christian theology. I did imagine Al Pacino while creating the character in the novel.

I could have set the story in an Italian American neighborhood but decided to put it in a Polish one instead for the same reasons. I did not want to deal with the clichés of Italian American neighborhood life. Although Francis Ford Coppola produced the movie, famed Polish director, Angieszka Holland directed it. It was recently shown at MOMA and is considered a classic about faith by many film critics.

What is an Italian American writer? That really is not the right question. The right question is what is a *good* Italian American writer? The answer to that question is that they are people who can write about anything they want. Shakespeare is not defined by writing only about the English. His most popular plays include a story about a Danish Prince; a love story set in Italy; a haunting story of jealousy about a Moor, and of course, the Scottish Play.

My first network writing job was when CBS hired me to write for *Dellaventura*. I got the job thanks to its star, Danny Aiello, who liked my plays. The second time I was asked to write for the networks was when ABC hired me to write an action drama about Homeland Security called *Threat Matrix* because the head writer saw my play about a marine sniper titled *One Shot, One Kill*. No one in *One Shot, One Kill* is Italian American. In fact, the lead character is a white Anglo Saxon Protestant.

This leads me to two plays and one novel I have written that contradicts everything I have just stated. They are my stage plays *Caravaggio* and *Machiavelli* and my new novel *Baroque*. I wrote them because I am Italian American. In the former play I focused on the artists' need to explain God, love, and art. In the latter, I created Machiavelli's worst nightmare, his daughter falling in love with his own greatest enemy.

In *Baroque*, I was able to explore art, sensuality, love, and greatness from the point of view of a second rate painter. Mario Minniti has the misfortune of having a great painter as his friend and roommate, Caravaggio, while falling in love with the most sought after prostitute in seventeenth century Rome.

Baroque, Caravaggio, and *Machiavelli* freed me to write geniuses who had Italian surnames without having to deal with clichéd stereotypes. I did not even realize this until I wrote this and said to myself, "Wow, that makes a lot of sense."

So, in conclusion, I leave it to *you* to decide if I am an Italian American writer. I feel I *am* one, like it or not.

CONTRIBUTORS

LUIGI BONAFFINI is professor of Italian language and literature at Brooklyn College. He has translated into English numerous books by Italian poets, written both in Italian and dialect. He has edited five trilingual anthologies of dialect poetry and has co-edited the anthology *Poets of the Italian Diaspora* (2014). He is the editor of *Journal of Italian Translation*.

PETER CARRAVETTA is the Alfonse M. D'Amato Professor of Italian and Italian American Studies at Stony Brook University. He is the author of four books of criticism and the editor of several anthologies. His book *The Elusive Hermes* appeared in 2013 with Davies Group Publishers.

JEROME KRASE, professor of sociology at Brooklyn College from 1970-2003 and chair of the sociology department twice, taught classes in urban sociology, inter-ethnic group relations and introductory courses. For three decades, he worked as a community activist-scholar and was a student of "ordinary" urban neighborhood life by lecturing, giving photographic exhibitions, and writing for alternative newspapers. He lectured and did research at Universities of Perugia, Pisa, Trento, and Trieste. Dr Krase was a visiting professor at the Jagiellonian University in Krakow and University of Rome, "La Sapienza."

STEFANO LUCONI teaches US history at the universities of Padua, Pisa, and Rome "Tor Vergata" and specializes in Italian immigration to the United States. His publications include *From Paesani to White Ethnics: The Italian Experience in Philadelphia* (Albany: State University of New York Press, 2001); *The Italian-American Vote in Providence, Rhode Island, 1916-1948* (Madison, NJ: Fairleigh Dickinson University Press, 2004); *La questione razziale negli Stati Uniti dalla Ricostruzione a Barack Obama* (Padova: Cleup, 2008). He also edited, with Dennis Barone, *Small Towns, Big Cities: The Urban Experience of Italian Americans* (New York: American Italian Historical Association, 2010).

SANTE MATTEO is Professor and Coordinator of Italian Studies at Miami University, in Oxford, Ohio. His publications include the books: *Radici sporadiche: letteratura, viaggi, migrazioni* (2007), *ItaliAfrica: Bridging Conti-*

nents and Cultures (2001), *Africa Italia: Due continenti si avvicinano (1999), The Reasonable Romantic: Essays on Alessandro Manzoni* (1986); *Textual Exile: The Reader in Sterne and Foscolo* (1985); and numerous articles on topics ranging from the 13th century's *Le Roman de la rose* and Marco Polo, to Machiavelli, Vico, and "Ossian," to Giose Rimanelli, Fellini, Scola, and Bertolucci.

MARIO MIGNONE, SUNY Distinguished Service Professor, is the founder and Director of the Center for Italian Studies. He is also the Director of the Summer Program in Rome and the student exchange programs with both the University of Rome "La Sapienza" and the University of Messina. He served as Chairman of the Department of French and Italian at Stony Brook for nine years, co-founded the Association of Italian American Educators and served as its first president, is a former president of the Long Island Chapter of the American Association of Teachers of Italian and has taken an active role in many professional, civic, and fraternal organizations. He has given numerous lectures and presentations at international, national and regional forums. Mignone is the author of several monographs, including *Italy Today* (1998, rev. ed. 2008).

VINCENZO PASCALE has taught in the Department of Italian at Rutgers University and is the author of *Lo sguardo e la storia*. His research focuses on transatlantic relations, Italian literature, and Italian American cultural productions. He is working on a book about Naples in the 20th century.

JOSEPH PERRICONE teaches and writes about modern Italian poetry, narrative, theater and film at Fordham University. He is the author of *Vittorio Bodini: saggio critico* (Schena, 1986). Most recently, he has edited Maria Cirignano's poetry collection, *Schegge di vita* (Tracce, 2008). His publications also include a translation of Grazia Deledda's novel *La danza della collana (The Pearl Necklace*, Epos International, 2007), book chapters on Ardengo Soffici and Vittorio Bodini for the *Dictionary of Literary Biography* (Bruccoli Clark Layman, 1993), and several articles which have appeared in *Forum Italicum, Literature/Film Quarterly* and *Italian Poetry Review*, among other journals. A member of the American Literary Translators Association, he is also Associate Editor of *Journal of Italian Translation* and a member of the Advisory Board of *Italian Poetry Review*.

ANITA PINZI holds the Ph.D. in Comparative Literature and Italian Studies at the Graduate Center of the City University of New York (CUNY). Her academic interests and publications include Migration Literature, Bilingualism, Postcolonialism, Mediterranean Studies, and Theory of the Body. She teaches Italian Language and Literature at Hunter College and Queens College in NYC. She is writing her doctoral dissertation on Contemporary Albanian-Italian Literature.

ALESSANDRO RAVEGGI received his BA/MA from Università degli Studi di Firenze in 2004 and his Ph.D. at Università degli Studidi Bologna in 2008. He held a post-doctoral fellowship in Italian Studies at Universidad Nacional Autónoma de México for two years. He has also taught at The International Studies Institute at Palazzo Rucellai and Universidad Anahuac. He has published essays on Italo Calvino, Pier Paolo Pasolini, Carlo Levi, Carlo Collodi, literary theory, postmodern fiction and the Latin-American novel. He monograph, *Calvino Americano. Identità e viaggio nel Nuovo Mondo*, appeared in 2012 with Le Lettere. Two forthcoming books will explore the figure of David Foster Wallace and a theory of the literary travelogue form in Modern Italian writers journeying through America, The East and Africa. Professor Raveggi is also a novelist and a poet.

MARCELLO SAIJA, professor of political science at the University of Messina, is chair of the Dipartimento di Studi Politici Internazionali, Comunitari, Inglesi ed Angloamericani, director of the Rete dei Musei Siciliani, and editor of *Neos*, a journal of the history of Sicilian emigration.

RICHARD VETERE is a playwright, novelist, film and TV writer, producer, director actor and poet. He is an elected Council member of the Writers Guild of America East and was made a Lifetime Member in 2010. The Richard Vetere Collection is at the Frank Melville Library at Stony Brook University. The archives were created in 2005. He wrote *The Third Miracle* (published by Simon & Schuster) and co-wrote the screenplay adaptation produced by Francis Ford Coppola starring Ed Harris and directed by Agnieszka Holland released by Sony Picture Classics. His plays are published by Dramatic Publishing and they include *Caravaggio*, *Machiavelli*, and *Gangster Apparel*. His novel *The Writers Afterlife* was published by Three Rooms Press in early 2014. His most recent novel before that is *Baroque* published by Bordighera Press and *The Other Colors in a Snow Storm* (poetry). He has a master's degree in English and Comparative

Literature from Columbia University and has taught in the Master's Program at NYU and teaches film writing at Queens College. His other stage play adaptations into film are *The Marriage Fool* (starring Walter Mathau and Carol Brunet) and *How to Go Out on a Date in Queens* (starring Jason Alexander). He also wrote the cult classic *Vigilante*. He was born and still lives in NYC.

Index of Names

Adams, John, 51
Aiello, Danny, 282
Alba, Richard D., 34
Albert, King Charles, 62
Alberto of Savoy, King Carlo, 96
Alexander the Great, 278
Alfieri, Vittorio, 164-166, 171-172, 176
Alighieri, Dante, 54, 63, 65, 150-151, 153, 161-162, 164
Allemann-Ghionda, Cristina, 28
Amelio, Gianni, 186
Amfitheatrof, Eric, 1
Anderson, Leon, 18
Anderson, Sherwood, 12, 16, 202
Antonini, Luigi, 224
Aprile, Pino, 160
Argenti, Felice, 49n1
Attinelli, Giuseppe, 54

Bachi, Pietro, 53-54, 73
Balzac, Honoré de, 4
Bargnani, Alessandro, 58
Barolini, Antonio, 208
Barsotti, Carlo, 149
Barth, Frederik, 20-21
Batolo, Ignazio, 53
Battiato, Giacomo, 276
Baudelaire, Charles, 278
Beckett, Samuel, 278
Bellini, Carlo, 50
Benigni, Roberto, 101
Bernardi, Ulderico, 143
Bettinelli, Padre, 158

Bhabha, Homi K., 196
Billanca, Augusto, 220
Blue Fairy, 81-82, 90, 91n19, 92
Bonaffini, Luigi, 18
Bordonaro, Tommaso, 178-190
Borsieri, Pietro, 53, 55, 60
Botta, Vincenzo, 73, 75
Bouchane, Mohamed, 185
Brooks, Cleanth, 14
Brumidi, Constantino, 114
Bugiardini, Sergio, 271n75
Burnett, Carol, 280
Burnier, DyLysa, 19
Byron, Lord, 4, 278

Cairoli, Benedetto, 153
Calvino, Italo, 193-213
Cambon, Glauco, 170
Cannavo, Leonardo, 28
Cardella, Peter, 222
Carli, Gian Rinaldo, 158
Carlyle, Thomas 4
Carnevali, Emaneule, 10
Carocci, Giampiero, 160
Carravetta, Peter, 181
Castellucci, Paola, 212
Cattaneo, Carlo, 169-170, 177
Charles of Anjou, 67
Christ, Jesus, 6, 188
Ciongoli, A. Kenneth, 181
Cipriani, Amilcare, 111
Clifford, James, 194, 196, 207
Collodi, Carlo, 80, 83-84, 89, 92
Columbus, Christopher, 150
Confalonieri, Federico, 60, 68

Coppola, Francis Ford, 281
Costa, Andrea, 108, 111
Crane, Harte, 9
Cricket, Jiminy, 87
Crispi, Legge, 152

D'Alessandro, Pietro, 60
D'Annunzio, Gabriele, 11
D'Azeglio, Massimo, 78n3, 85, 87
Da Ponte, Lorenzo, 50-52, 57, 59-60
Dawkins, Richard, 98n26
De Albuquerque, Fernanda Farías, 185
De Attellis, Orazio, 53, 59, 63
De Casali, Giovanni Francesco Secchi, 53
De Gasperi, Alcide, 116, 136
De Sanctis, Francesco, 152-155, 158
DeAmici, Edmondo, 94
Dell, Floyd, 7
Denaro, Salvatore, 224
Depretis, Agostino, 108
Deville, Michel, 12
Di Cavour, Camillo Benso, 97, 99n27
Di Donato, Pietro, 185
Di Fiore, Gigi, 160
Dickens, Charles, 278
Disney, Walt, 103
Donizetti, Gaetano, 159
Douglas, Stephen, 71
Duce, Il, 112
Durante, Francesco, 182
Eastman, Max, 7

Eliot, T.S., 8-9, 14-15, 278
Emanuel II, King Victor, 87, 97, 99n27
Enrico, 94-95
Ettor, Joseph, 2, 4, 6

Fabbri, E.P., 75
Fante, John, 185
Femminella, Frank, 22
Ferraro, Antonio, 246
Fiscarelli, Sando, 279
Fisichella, Domenico, 159
Fiva, Anthony, 50
Fontanella, Luigi, 18, 181
Forester, Robert, 280
Foresti, Eleuterio Felice, 52-53, 55-56, 59, 70-72
Fortunato, Giustino, 125
Foscolo, Ugo, 159, 165-172, 175-177
Fox and the Cat, 88-89
Franchetti, Leopoldo, 124-125
Franklin, Benjamin, 51
Frost, Robert, 9
Fuller, Margaret, 56
Furey, Hester, 2, 7, 13

Gabaccia, Donna R., 30, 49
Galileo, 200
Gallenga, Antonio, 62-63, 69
Gans, Herbert, 33
Gardaphè, Fred, 181, 185
Garibaldi, Giuseppe, 56-57, 71, 73, 77-78, 80, 83, 87, 94-96, 98-99, 99n27, 101-103, 150, 153
Gavitti, Nino, 2

288

Geertz, Clifford, 20
Giannone, Pietro, 159
Giardina, Antonella, 259, 261, 263
Ginzburg, Natalia, 178-180, 187
Gioberti, Vincenzo, 67
Giolitti, Giovanni, 127, 130
Giovannitti, Arturo, 1-16
Giovannitti, Len, 11
Gold, Mike, 7
Goldman, Emma 7
Green, Rose Basile, 181-183, 185
Greenblatt, Stephen, 199
Greene, Graham, 278
Guerrazzi, Francesco Domenico, 67
Guglielmo Oberdan, 109-110, 112

Habermas, Jürgen, 196
Haller, Herman, 188-189
Handlin, Oscar, 36
Harrington, Joseph, 14
Harris, Ed, 281
Hawthorne, Nathaniel, 202
Headley, Joel Tyler, 69
Hegel, G.W.F., 203
Hemingway, Ernest, 202
Holland, Angieszka, 281
Howe, Julia Ward, 71

Il Corsaro, 2

Jefferson, Thomas, 51
Joseph II, 61
Joseph, Emperor Franz, 110
Juarez, Benito, 111

Kakutani, Michiko, 279
Kant, Immanuel, 3-4
Keats, John, 278
Keller, Helen, 7
Kennedy, John F., 243
Khouma, Pap, 185
King Jr., Martin Luther, 206-207
King of France, 67
Klopp, Charles, 65
Kramer, Aaron, 10-11
Krase, Jerry, 27-28, 37-39, 42-46
Kreymborg, Alfred, 10

Lejeune, Philippe, 184
Leopardi, 162
Lévi-Strauss, Claude, 197, 202, 212
Libasi, Jerome L., 40-41
Lincoln, Abraham, 57
Longfellow, Fanny Appleton, 73
Longfellow, Henry Wadsworth, 54, 63, 73
Lorenzini, Carlo, 80, 83
Lowell, Amy, 10
Lowell, James Russell, 54, 73
Luconi, Stefano, 28

Machiavelli, Niccolò, 63, 65, 282
Maffi, Antonio, 108
Magaro, Gaudence, 171
Manfred of Sicily, 67
Mangione, Jerry, 185
Manzoni, Alessandro, 151, 159
Marie-Louise, Piacenza, 53
Maroncelli, Piero, 55, 57-68
Martin, Dean, 280
Matthau, Walter, 280

Mattoni, Rosa, 111
Mazzei, Filippo, 51
Mazzini, Giuseppe, 52, 56, 67, 74, 87, 97, 150, 153, 177
McKinley, William, 238
Mecchio, Salvatore, 54
Merkel, Angela, 119
Micalizzi, Alberto, 224
Mignone, Mario, ix, 17-18, 20
Monroe, Harold, 8
Monti, Luigi, 54, 66-68
Moore, Clement Clarke, 51
Morgan, John Pierpont, 75
Mozart, Wolfgang Amadeus, 50
Muratori, Ludovico Antonio, 164, 167
Mussolini, Benito Amilcare Andrea, 111, 272-273

Napoleon, 160, 166, 170
Natali, Giulio, 66
Natoli, John and Frank, 244-245
Nelson, Cary, 13
Newcomb, John Timberman, 15
Nievo, Ippolito, 177
Norton, Catherine E., 68, 70
Norton, Charles Eliot, 54, 57, 68

Oberdank, Wilhelm, 109-110
Oppenheimer, James, 5

Pacino, Al, 281
Paino, Angelo, 239
Parini, Giuseppe, 164-168, 172
Parini, Jay, 181
Parsons, Thomas William, 54
Pasolini, Pier Paolo, 196

Patch, Jason, 19
Pécout, Gilles, 157
Pellico, Silvio, 65-66, 68-70
Peragallo, Olga, 10
Petrarch, 162-164, 173-174
Petrosino, Joe, 238
Pinter, Harold, 278-279
Poe, Edgar Allan, 202
Polk, James K., 72
Polo, Marco, 200
Pope, Generoso, 272
Pound, Ezra, 8-9, 14
Pozzetta, George E., 236

Ransom, John Crowe, 14
Re, Edward, 231-233, 235, 238n39, 240n41, 243
Reed, John, 7
Rilke, Ranier Maira, 278
Roosevelt, Franklin Delano, 239, 241-242, 272
Roosevelt, Theodore, 237, 240, 245
Roscoe, Thomas, 68
Rossini, Gioacchino, 159
Rousseau, Jean Jacques, 165
Rubattino, Raffaele, 106
Russo, Gaetano, 150

Said, Edward, 193
Saija, Marcello, 18
Salem, Salwa, 185
Sandburg, Carl, 9, 12, 16
Sarrazin, Thilo, 119
Scalabrini, Giovanni Battista, 120

Schiavo, Giovanni Ermenegildo, 60
Schlictman, John Joe, 19
Sedgwick, Catherine Maria, 70
Sedgwick, Theodore, 71
Serra, Ilaria, 179-180, 190
Serretta, Carlo, 54
Shakespeare, William, 3-4
Shelley, Percy, 4-5
Sinatra, Frank, 280
Sismondi, 167
Smith, Adam, 126
Sorvino, Paul, 279
Sottile, Pietro, 224
Spivak, Gayatri, 180
Stallone, Sylvester, 281
Stamos, John, 280
Stella, Gian Antonio, 77n1, 185
Stendhal, 204
Stevens, Wallace, 9, 14
Strong, Anna, 14
Struriale, Salvatore, 224-226

Taine, Hippolyte, 4
Taranto, Maria, 244
Tasso, Torquato, 63, 65
Tate, Allen, 14
Taylor, Zachary, 72
Ticknor, George, 69, 71
Tinelli, Luigi, 58-59
Tirabassi, Maddalena, 28
Tiraboschi, Girolamo, 167
Tuckerman, Henry Theodore, 71

Uccello, Corrado, 268
Ulysses, 201
Untermeyer, Louis, 9-10, 15

Valesio, Paolo, 18, 181
Veccaria, Gianluigi, 164
Vecoli, Rudolph, 36
Verdi, Giuseppe, 151, 153, 159
Verri, Pietro, 164
Vetere, Richard, 279
Vianello, Mino, 27
Viscusi, Robert, 18
Vittorini, Elio, 146

Wasser, Henry, 22
Waters, Mary, 34
Weber, Max, 20-21
Whitman, Walt, 5, 11
Whittier, John Greenleaf, 69
Wilde, Oscar, 5, 10
Williams, William Carlos, 8-9, 278

Yeats, W.B., 278
Young, Art, 7

Zanolini, Frank, 236

CENTER FOR ITALIAN STUDIES

THE ALFONSE M. D'AMATO CHAIR
IN ITALIAN AND ITALIAN AMERICAN STUDIES

PROGRAM

THE THIRD
Forum on Italian American Criticism (FIAC)

ON

Theatre of the Mind, Stage of History

Italian Legacies Between Europe, the Mediterranean, and North America on the 150th Anniversary of Unification

A *Festschrift* in honor of Professor Mario Mignone on his 70th birthday

STONY BROOK UNIVERSITY

Friday, March 18, 2011
Center for Italian Studies, E-4340 Frank Melville Jr. Memorial Library

Saturday, March 19, 2011
Charles B. Wang Center, Lecture Hall 2

FREE AND OPEN TO THE PUBLIC

This conference has been made possible in part thanks to the generous support of
The Office of the Provost
and by
International Academic Programs and Services

Additional support from Fordham University, Department of Romance Languages; John D. Calandra Italian American Institute, New York; Bordighera Press, New York; Humanities Institute at Stony Brook University; Department of European Languages, Literatures, and Cultures; Department of History; *and* Gradiva International Poetry Society Inc.

PROGRAM OF THE DAY

FRIDAY, MARCH 18, 2011
Center for Italian Studies • E-4340 Frank Melville Jr. Memorial Library

Opening Remarks • 9:30 am
William Arens, Dean, International Academic Programs and Services
Nicholas Rzhevsky, Chair, Department of European Languages, Literatures, and Cultures
Peter Carravetta, Alfonse M. D'Amato Professor in Italian and Italian American Studies

Morning Session • 10:00 am to 12:15 pm
Chair: Giuseppe Gazzola, Stony Brook University

Paolo Valesio, Columbia University
"Antonio Barolini, a Writer Among Several Worlds"

Luigi Bonaffini, CUNY/Brooklyn College
"Arturo Giovannitti and the American Literary Establishment"

Luigi Fontanella, Stony Brook University
"Cultural Bridges and Reciprocal Influences Between Italian and American Poetry"

Vincenzo Pascale, Rutgers University
"Intellectuals and Migrants: Bridging the Gap"

Lunch Break • 12:15 pm to 1:30 pm

Afternoon Session • 1:30 pm to 5:00 pm
Chair: Irene Marchegiani, Stony Brook University

Antonio Morena, Stony Brook University
"The Origins of Italian Studies in the United States"

Anthony Julian Tamburri, The John D. Calandra Italian American Institute, NY
"The Fortunate Pilgrim: The Italians' American Dream of Staying Alive"

Jerome Krase, CUNY/Brooklyn College
"Discovering My Sicilian Roots"

Richard Vetere, playwright
"You Are an Italian American Writer Like It or Not"

(Coffee Break • 3:30 pm to 3:45 pm)

Gallya Lahav, Stony Brook University
"Italy as an Immigration Country"

Lucia Grillo, filmmaker
Screening of short documentary *Terra sogna terra* (with subtitles)

General Discussion • 5:00 pm to 5:30 pm

PROGRAM OF THE DAY

SATURDAY, MARCH 19, 2011
Charles B. Wang Center · Lecture Hall 2

Morning Session · 9:30 am to 12:30 pm
Chair: Robert Viscusi, CUNY/Brooklyn College
Sante Matteo, Miami University
"Garibaldi, Pinocchio, Emigration: 'There Are No Strings on Me!' Or: Are There?"

Alessandro Raveggi, Universidad Nacional Autónoma de México
"American Otherness and Italian Traveling Culture in Italo Calvino"

Anita Pinzi, CUNY/Graduate Center
"Bordonaro's *La Spartenza:* Between Tradition and Singularity"

Respondent: Joseph Perricone, Fordham University

Lunch Break · 12:30 pm to 2:00 pm

Afternoon Session · 2:00 pm to 3:30 pm
Chair: Frank Myers, Stony Brook University
Claudio Rossi, Università di Roma
"Institutional Mediation Between Dominant Culture and Imported Culture"

Marcello Saija, Università of Messina
"Sicilian Mutualism in USA During the Great Migration"

Peter Carravetta, Stony Brook University
"Migration, Nationalism, and the Challenge of Historical Relativism"

Concluding Remarks · 3:30 pm
Mario Mignone, Stony Brook University
"Our Historical Role in Creating the Image of Italy"

Reception · 4:30 pm to 6:30 pm
Charles B. Wang Center Chapel

This conference is dedicated to Mario Mignone, distinguished service professor of Italian, founder and director of the Center for Italian Studies at Stony Brook University, and for a quarter of a century editor of the journal *Forum Italicum*. Since he first arrived at Stony Brook in 1970, Professor Mignone has brought well over 3,000 students to study Italian language and culture at the Stony Brook Rome Center, which he also started. He is a committed intellectual and author of authoritative critical works on fiction and theater and on Italian migration, editor of several anthologies, and author of the most accessible general Introduction to Modern Italy. It is therefore fitting that on his 70th birthday, the community of friends, colleagues, and scholars from several fields dedicate this scholarly gathering to him as a token of appreciation for his lifetime dedication and achievement in higher education and in bridging cultures across time and space.

PARTICIPANTS

LUIGI BONAFFINI is professor and chair of the Modern Languages and Literatures Department at CUNY/Brooklyn College. He has translated numerous books by Italian and dialect poets, edited five trilingual anthologies of dialect poetry, and is the editor of *Journal of Italian Translation*.

PETER CARRAVETTA is Alfonse M. D'Amato Professor of Italian and Italian American Studies at Stony Brook University. He is the author of four books of criticism and the editor of several anthologies. His book *The Elusive Hermes* is forthcoming from Davies Group Publishers in 2011.

LUIGI FONTANELLA is professor of Italian at Stony Brook University. Poet, novelist, and literary critic, he is the author of more than 20 books, among them *La parola transfuga* (2003) and *Land of Time: Selected Poems 1972-2003* (2006). He is the editor of *Gradiva*.

LUCIA GRILLO received her B.F.A. in acting from New York University. She is associate producer and editor of *Italics* (Calandra & CUNY TV) and producer/director of the yearly music special "Jukebox." Actress and filmmaker, she has been awarded the "Premio Nazionale Ambasciatori di Calabria."

JEROME KRASE, Emeritus and Murray Koppelman Professor of Sociology at CUNY/ Brooklyn College, is the author of *Race and Ethnicity in New York City* and *Ethnicity and Machine Politics*. He has written widely on European migration, urban anthropology, and the politics of integration.

GALLYA LAHAV is associate professor of political science at Stony Brook University and the recipient of a MacArthur Fellowship. She is the author of *Immigration and Politics in the New Europe: Reinventing Borders* and co-editor of *The Migration Reader* and *Immigration Policy in Europe*.

SANTE MATTEO is professor and coordinator of Italian studies at Miami University, Oxford, Ohio. Author of six books and numerous articles on literature and cinema, he served as editor of *Italian Culture*. His latest book is *Radici sporadiche: letteratura, viaggi, migrazioni*.

ANTONIO MORENA, lecturer at Stony Brook University, received his Ph.D. from Harvard University. His interests range from Italian American film and political literature to modern Italian culture. He is currently writing a book on Italian American radical Carl Marzani.

VINCENZO PASCALE is a faculty member in the Department of Italian at Rutgers University and the author of *Lo sguardo e la storia*. His research focuses on transatlantic relations, Italian literature, and Italian American cultural productions. He is working on a book about Naples in the 20th Century.

JOSEPH PERRICONE is professor of Italian and literary studies at Fordham University. Author of books on Vittorio Bodini and Dario Fo, he has translated Grazia Deledda and Giuseppe Berto and is co-editor of the forthcoming *Poetry of the Italian Diaspora* (Fordham UP 2011).

ANITA PINZI is a doctoral candidate in the Comparative Literature Program/Italian specialization at the CUNY/Graduate Center. She has published articles dealing with migration literature, bilingualism, translation, identity, and borderlands.

ALESSANDRO RAVEGGI holds a postdoctoral fellowship in modern literature at the Universidad Nacional Autónoma de México. He has written on postmodernism for his Italian doctorate at the University of Bologna, and is currently doing research on literature and identity.

CLAUDIO ROSSI is professor of the sociology of immigration at the University "La Sapienza" in Rome. Since 1993 he has also worked for the Ufficio Speciale Immigrazione of the City of Rome. He has written widely on mobility and cultural and institutional interfaces.

MARCELLO SAIJA, professor of political science at the University of Messina, is chair of the Dipartimento di Studi Politici Internazionali, Comunitari, Inglesi ed Angloamericani, director of the Rete dei Musei Siciliani, and editor of *Neos*, a journal of the history of Sicilian emigration.

ANTHONY JULIAN TAMBURRI is professor and dean of the John D. Calandra Italian American Institute at CUNY/Queens College. Co-founder of *VIA Voices in Italian Americana* and of Bordighera Press, he is the author of *Semiotics of Ethnicity* and co-editor of *From the Margin*.

PAOLO VALESIO is the Giuseppe Ungaretti Professor in Italian Literature and chair of the Department of Italian at Columbia University. He is the author of five books of literary criticism, two novels, a collection of short stories, a novella, a one-act play in verse, and 16 volumes of poetry.

RICHARD VETERE, lecturer on film writing at CUNY/Queens College, is the author of *The Third Miracle*. He has worked with Francis Ford Coppola and Agnieszka Holland, and his plays include the Off-Broadway productions of *Caravaggio*, *Machiavelli*, and *One Shot, One Kill*.

www.ingramcontent.com/pod-product-compliance
Lightning Source LLC
Chambersburg PA
CBHW022105150426
43195CB00008B/274